Softwa

C000214666

About the Authors

Andreas Spillner is professor of computer science at the Faculty of Electrical Engineering and Computer Science at Bremen University of Applied Sciences. For more than 10 years he was president of the German Special Interest Group in Software Testing, Analysis, and Verification of the German Informatics Society (GI). He is also a member of the German Testing Board. His work emphasis is on software engineering, quality assurance, testing, and object-oriented system development.

Thomas Rossner is cofounder of imbus AG. As a member of the board of directors, he is responsible for research and technology projects. In this function he has, in recent years, led several international research projects on, among others, software reliability and model-based testing. In addition, he is actively involved in test management projects and in consultancy projects on the subject of test process improvement.

Mario Winter is professor at the Faculty of Computer Science and Engineering Science of Cologne University of Applied Sciences and a member of the Software Quality Group. From 1983 to 1987, he was engaged in the execution and management of industrial and scientific engineering projects, and between 1994 and 2002, he was research fellow at the FernUniversität Hagen. Currently he is spokesman of the German Special Interest Group in Software Testing, Analysis, and Verification of the German Informatics Society (GI) and a member of the German Testing Board. His teaching and research focus is on software development and project management, especially on the development and quality assurance of object-oriented software.

Tilo Linz is CEO of imbus AG, a leading service company for software testing in Germany. He is president of the German Testing Board and was, from 2002 to 2005, president of the ISTQB. His work emphasis is on consulting and coaching projects on software quality management, optimizing software development, and testing processes.

Andreas Spillner · Thomas Rossner · Mario Winter · Tilo Linz

Software Testing Practice:

Test Management

A Study Guide for the Certified Tester Exam
- **Advanced Level**
- **ISTQB compliant**

Andreas Spillner
spillner@informatik.hs-bremen.de

Thomas Rossner
thomas.rossner@imbus.de

Mario Winter
winter@gm.fh-koeln.de

Tilo Linz
tilo.linz@imbus.de

Editor: Jimi DeRouen
Translator: Dieter Wachendorf, Stuttgart, Germany
Copyeditor: Judy Flynn, Santa Barbara, USA
Layout and Type: Josef Hegele, Heiligkreuzsteinach, Germany
Cover Design: Helmut Kraus, www.exclam.de
Printed in the United States of America

ISBN-13: 978-1-933952-13-0

1st Edition
© 2007 by Rocky Nook Inc.
26 West Mission Street Ste 3
Santa Barbara, CA 93101-2432

www.rockynook.com

This 1st English book edition conforms to the 1st German edition
Praxiswissen Softwaretest: Testmanagement (dpunkt.verlag GmbH,
ISBN 978-3-89864-275-0), which was published in August 2006.

Library of Congress catalog application submitted

Distributed by O'Reilly Media
1005 Gravenstein Highway North
Sebastopol, CA 95472-2811

Foreword by Stephan Goericke

Errors that are missed when testing software may result in an incalculable explosion of costs for a company. In other words, software testing is not only a vital part of the quality assurance process within a software development company, it is also a way for the company to be a responsible partner for its customers, both in terms of the services rendered and the products provided.

The complexity of software projects has risen sharply, and continues to be on the rise. Today, the software in a cell phone has an average of 2.6 million lines of code. This means that any functioning software test management that takes a holistic approach to its task will be facing ever greater challenges. Software testing management comprises tasks such as planning, monitoring, and controlling software tests. The test phases of a project must be accurately planned and documented, and support tools must be carefully selected. Last but not least, the test project must continually be monitored in order to reduce risks, while having an early error detection system in place. Good test management considerably abbreviates the time required before a project is ready to be accepted by the client, and helps keep the maintenance costs and subsequent costs within budget.

In an effort to assess and optimize the skills and abilities of software testers, it must be ensured that the testers are qualified, and reliably so, in the field of test management, and they must have a certificate to prove it. That is why the economic sector is demanding standards that fully satisfy the criteria of independence, transparency, and international acceptance. The International Software Quality Institute (iSQI), headquartered in Erlangen, Germany and Potsdam, Germany, is the coordinating body for software quality standards of this type worldwide. Due to the excellent reputation of the iSQI, the certifications earned from us are recognized and respected all over the world. We are proud to say that by now, certifications according to the Standard ISTQB Certified Tester are being implemented in 34 countries and on 6 continents. This universal certification offers many advantages for the companies concerned, some of which are:

1. *Professionalism:* Software must be synonymous with dependability. This means software developers must be well trained, and we must be able to rely on that, since otherwise, the reputation of the entire sector will suffer. By giving software developers standardized and proven training that takes into account the practical aspects of programming, we can trust that a minimum qualification for this particular profession is ensured.

2. *Lifelong learning:* Software is becoming increasingly more complex, and the demands that must be met are growing daily. Lifelong learning is indispensable, since often, the initial training undergone by programmers may become out-dated and may have been too general in nature.

3. *Standardization:* Standardization that is independent from manufacturers and products creates transparency, and as a result, ensures acceptance and validity of the software across national boundaries and language barriers. Furthermore, employers and employees alike appreciate the ability to compare professional qualifications on a national and international level, which in today's global market ensures the ability to cooperate and compete internationally.

This book addresses the need to establish such standards in the field of software testing. With its focus on test management, it is excellent reading for those already active in the profession, since it supplements the know-how they have gained in a compact and competent manner. Between 90 and 100 percent of the examination candidates who consulted the first book in this series, *Software Testing Foundations*, prior to taking the ISTQB Certified Tester – Foundation Level exam, met the requirements and received the certificate. We hope that similar results can be achieved at the Advanced Level with the aid of this book. The authors have, once again, earned high merits in the further development of the Certified Tester scheme. To all of this book's interested readers: enjoy working through it, good luck in the certification exam you will take later, and, last but not least, the best of success in all your projects!

Stephan Goericke
Director, International Software Quality Institute

Foreword by Tim Koomen

Certification is big. For some years, the number of certified testers has been rising rapidly. And this is great! To make testing into a truly accepted profession, certification is an essential instrument. Although other test certification programs exist, the International Software Testing Qualifications Board (ISTQB) has, without a doubt, the most important and popular program. Supported widely in many countries by many organizations, its success contributes considerably to the worldwide, and still badly needed professionalization of testing.

The thing I like very much about the ISTQB certification is its independence of particular test methods (and yes, I say this even though I'm closely associated to a particular test method) and suppliers; it's a source of knowledge that is commonly agreed on, but detailed enough to satisfy the often demanding and critical testers of this world.

To certify yourself for the ISTQB Advanced Level, you have to pass a nontrivial exam. How can you increase your chances of passing this ultimate "test of the tester"? Combining your practical experience with detailed knowledge of the ISTQB syllabus is easier said than done. Training is an important method to gain the required knowledge, but in my opinion, which is shared by the authors of this book, at least as important is the ability to read, learn, and understand the subject matter in your own time, at your own pace, as preparation for the exam. The syllabus itself is too concise for this purpose, which is the very reason for this book.

However, to call this book only a good preparation for the ISTQB Advanced exam wouldn't do justice to the completeness of this work. I'm very glad, therefore, that the authors have decided to publish their book in English and not restrict their work for the German reading audience alone.

I found it easy to summarize what I like about this book:

- *Easy to learn*
  Its alignment to the test management topics of the Advanced Level, plus the side column with key points and the summaries at the end of each chapter, greatly facilitate learning. My expectation is that this book will also be popular at universities and colleges. This book would be a very good development tool, as we testers definitely need to raise the far-too-low awareness of testing in most educational organizations where IT is taught.
- *Complete and thorough in its scope of test management*
  Virtually every important aspect of test management is dealt with, including test process improvement practices (which has my particular interest) and (many) available standards. This book clearly demonstrates how extensive the test management profession has become. "Another book" is, therefore, not a problem; the profession evolves, and in order to keep up, a test manager must continually extend his or her knowledge and skills. This book supports that further education.
- *Good combination of practice and theory*
  Just looking at the background of the four authors will convince you that this book is really a result of "theory meets practice". From my own experience in writing, I know how hard it is to find the right balance between these two, but the authors have, without a doubt, succeeded in finding this right balance.

All in all, I congratulate the authors on writing this highly inspiring book that you will find very useful, not only for preparing for your ISTQB exam, but also for grasping what modern test management is about and for finding (new or alternative) ideas and solutions for managing your tests.

Tim Koomen
Independent consultant, coauthor of the books
TMap Next and *Test Process Improvement* (TPI®),
and co-editor of *TMap Test Topics*.

Foreword by Hans Schaefer

Another book about test management, do we need this?

If you have read many testing books before, then maybe not. But, if you want to learn about test management, and have *not* read so much yet, then the answer is definitely *yes*. This should be the first book to read for a new test manager.

Why do I like this book?

This book is short and to the point. It contains the things a test manager needs to know, without all the extra ballast. It helps people to plan and control the testing effort in many projects, with no restriction as to what kind of software is developed. It does not make a science out of the practical skills to manage a testing effort. It greatly helps to prepare for the ISTQB Advanced Level – Test Manager exam, and people do not waste time reading a lot of unnecessary other stuff. The book covers the current ISTQB Advanced Level syllabus, as well as most areas of the draft 2007 version of the advanced syllabus. It should be possible to pass the ISTQB exam based on studying the book.

The application example used throughout the text is the same as in the earlier *Software Testing Foundations* book, thus making reading a lot easier for the continuing reader.

Chapter 9 about risk-based testing is probably the most important chapter. The language of test managers should revolve around risk. Risk is what stakeholders understand. Testing should measure the residual risk in an application.

But there is a lot more to this:

- As test execution comes last in any project, the testing phase will always be under pressure. Often, the option to delay delivery is not open, thus the test manager must know how to prioritize and manage all the problems inherited from other people's work. Doing this proactively helps a lot. But, not only must test execution get differing priorities; there are also risks to the test project itself. Many of these risks are shown in the book, together with examples of how they can be overcome or dealt with. However, I would have liked to see more details about how to prepare for project risks to materialize. This might, however, be too special for this book.

- Chapter 7 deals with process improvement. Several industry standard models are described. With this book and just a few more references, the reader should be able to execute an initial process assessment and find some important improvement ideas. However, one method is described in less detail: Examples for root cause analysis of defects, especially defects found too late, i.e., surviving the testing effort. However, this is a flaw in the ISTQB syllabus and thus outside the scope of this book.

- The other chapters in the book contain the more conventional tools for a test manager, such as a description of differing application development models and the place of testing within them; issue tracking and handling; use of metrics; configuration management etc.

- The trouble in other literature is that one often needs several books, not just one. Thus, this single book is effective for its readers.

Get it, read it, think through it, and pass the ISTQB advanced test manager exam!

Best regards,

Hans Schaefer
Leader, ISTQB Norway
Software Test Consulting

Foreword

The success of our book *Software Testing Foundations* greatly encouraged us to write a second book, this time building on the foundation level to address the advanced courses and still provide the same mix of theory and practice the first book contained. We, Tilo Linz and Andreas Spillner, were glad to win Thomas Rossner of imbus AG and Mario Winter of the Cologne University of Applied Sciences as coauthors for this book. All four of us hope that we have yet again succeeded in covering the present topics, from both the theoretical and the practical perspective.

The content of this book on test management conforms to the syllabus of the Certification Course "Advanced Level: Test Manager" (Version 1.2, [URL: ISTQB] -Syllabi). In some places, however, we found it expedient to go beyond the scope of that syllabus and provide the reader with additional advice and information. As a result, this book has become rather more comprehensive than the ISTQB syllabus.

Current syllabus

The training scheme based on the ISTQB Certified Tester Standard [URL: ISTQB] has been well received in many countries. So far, approximately 50,000 Foundation Level examinations and approximately 1,500 examinations on the Advanced Level syllabus (April 2007) have been held.

ISTQB-Standard

Currently, more than 25 nations are represented in the International Software Testing Qualifications Board (ISTQB, [URL: ISTQB]).

Worldwide recognition

Thus, the number of participating countries has almost doubled in the past two years. Representatives from the following countries or national testing boards cooperate in the ISTQB: Austria, Bangladesh, Brazil, Canada, China, Denmark, England, Finland, France, Germany, India, Israel, Japan, Korea, Latin America, Netherlands/Belgium, Norway, Poland, Portugal, Russia, South Eastern Europe, Spain, Sweden, Switzerland, Turkey, Ukraine, the United States, and Australia/New Zealand.

The ISTQB has become truly international, with syllabi and certificates that are recognized worldwide. See chapter 1 for further details on the structure of the ISTQB.

Higher education   The contents of the Foundation Level syllabus have been adopted by many universities and colleges in Germany. It appears that in higher education, we are seeing the emergence of a common syllabus in the field of software testing. The number of college and university students interested in this field has been increasing steadily over the past years.

In software testing, we have now covered a good distance toward our goal, which was formulated by David Parnas in his foreword to the first edition of the German book *Basiswissen Softwaretest* as being the standardization and regulation of the educational content in the field of informatics.

Thank you notes   We want to thank our readers of the German version of this book for their helpful comments and our colleagues in the GTB (German Testing Board) and ISTQB, without whose great work there would be no Certified Tester scheme. We want to cordially thank Stephan Goericke, Tim Koomen, and Hans Schaefer for their forwards.

Andreas Spillner, Thomas Rossner, Mario Winter, Tilo Linz
Bremen, Möhrendorf, and Wuppertal
April 2007

Table of Contents

1 Introduction

Like never before, everyday life has become dependent on software and software-based systems. Most of today's appliances, machines, and devices are completely or at least partly controlled by software. Administrative proceedings in state agencies and industry, too, rely to a large extent on highly complex IT systems. Examples are the management of insurance policies, inventory control systems, biometric characteristics in passports and ID cards, and the electronic health chip card.

High dependency on software

This strong dependency on software requires ever higher investments in quality assurance activities to enable IT systems to perform reliably. Software testing is developing toward a specialized, independent field of study and professional discipline within the computer sciences.

Software testing – a professional discipline in its own right

Within the discipline of software testing, "test management" is of particular importance. Test management comprises classical methods of project and risk management as well as knowledge of the appropriate use of well-defined test methods. With this stock-in-trade, the test manager[1] can select and purposefully implement appropriate measures to ensure that a defined basic product quality will be achieved. In doing so, the test manager adopts an engineering approach.

Test management

Whereas today's project management training is well established, and while there are a tremendous number of study courses, training programs, and specialist literature to choose from, there has, until recently, been hardly any attempt at defining or standardizing the contents of training programs for the "software test manager". In view of the increasing responsibility assumed by test managers in the execution of their job, this has been an unsatisfactory situation.

Training for test managers

With the ISTQB Certified Tester – Advanced Level – Test Manager we have, for the first time, developed an internationally recognized training and qualification scheme that defines training contents and qualification

ISTQB Certified Tester – Advanced Level – Test Manager

---

1. Note: For ease of reading, we use the male pronoun throughout this book where general references are made to persons. By no means is there any intention of gender bias or discrimination against women.

modules for the tasks of the test manager. This book sets out to convey the associated teaching contents and may be read as a textbook in preparation for the exams.

Foundation Level

The "ISTQB Certified Tester" qualification scheme consists of three levels. The basics of software testing are described in the syllabus for the Foundation Level ([URL: ISTQB] -Syllabi), whereas the corresponding subject matter is explained in detail in *Software Testing Foundations* [Spillner 07].

Advanced Level

The Advanced Level curriculum ([URL: ISTQB] -Syllabi) defines advanced proficiency skills in software review and testing and shows possible opportunities for specialization:

- Exhaustive treatment of different black box and white box test methods in the Advanced Level, Technical Tester, and Functional Tester modules
- Extensive, in-depth presentation of test management methods and techniques in the Test Manager module[2]

Since the "Advanced Level" syllabus is very comprehensive, it will not be treated in its entirety in this book; instead, we shall concentrate exclusively on the "Advanced Level – Test Manager module". The topic of "reviews"[3], however, will be excluded.

Expert Level

The third level, the "Expert Level", is in the process of being defined by expert groups and comprises topics such as the specific characteristics of object-oriented software testing, advanced knowledge in Testing & Test Control Notation (TTCN-3, [URL: TTCN-3]), advanced knowledge in test process improvement methodology, and various other areas of expertise associated with software testing.

International Software Testing Qualifications Board (ISTQB)

The "ISTQB" [URL: ISTQB] provides for the homogeneity and comparability of the teaching and examination contents of all participating countries.

Today, the ISTQB has become an affiliation of more than 25 national initiatives and associations worldwide (see figure 1-1). More national boards will follow.

---

2. The new version of the ISTQB Advanced Level syllabus is currently under development and will presumably adopt and advance this module structure.
3. Regarding reviews see, for example, [Gilb 96].

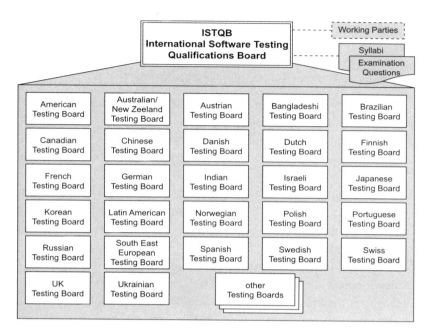

Figure 1–1

Structure of the ISTQB

As independent expert bodies, the national testing boards are responsible for the provision of training (accreditation of providers of proficiency testing schemes) and examinations (certification by an independent institution) in their respective countries and native languages and for ensuring compliance with ISTQB standards.

National Testing Boards

The three levels of the ISTQB qualification scheme build on one another. This book, *Software Testing Practice: Test Management*, presumes that the reader is familiar with the subject matters dealt with in the Foundation Level.

Knowledge of software testing foundations required

Readers new to software testing are advised to first acquire knowledge of the content of the Foundation Level, either by attending an accredited provider's seminar or by working through the book *Software Testing Foundations* [Spiller 07]. The present book contains only a brief recapitulation of the most important basic principles.

1.1   Software Testing Foundations – Condensed

This section provides a brief summary of the Foundation Level syllabus and of the book *Software Testing Foundations*.

Measures to improve
software quality

There is a multitude of approaches and proposals available on how to improve software quality through preventive (constructive) actions and the use of verifying (analytical) methods. The following measures are among the most important to improve software quality:

- Defined software development processes that contribute to a structured and traceable development of software systems
- A well-defined test process and controlled change and incident management as a requirement for the efficient and effective execution of test activities
- The application of metrics and quality data to objectively evaluate software products and development processes, to detect improvement potentials, and to verify the effectiveness of correction and improvement activities
- The use of formal methods that allow for the precise formulation of development documents and their verification or evaluation by tools
- Methods for the systematic identification and execution of test cases that allow efficient detection of defects and anomalies in the developed programs
- Methods for static testing, primarily reviews through which defects and anomalies are detected in design documents at an early stage

Quality goals
and quality attributes

Test managers must master or at least be familiar with these methods, techniques, and processes in order to be able to select and apply appropriate measures during the course of the project.

The suitability of quality assurance measures, however, also depends on the defined quality goals. The required quality level can thereby be defined based on different quality attributes. A catalogue of such quality attributes (e.g., functionality, reliability, and usability) is defined by the [ISO 9126] standard.

When do we speak of a defect or an error and what do we actually mean when we use these terms? A situation or result can only be classified as faulty, defective, or erroneous if we have previously defined what the expected, correct situation or result is supposed to look like. If the actual software behavior deviates from the expected behavior, we use words such as defect, fault, bug, and anomaly.

Test oracle

In order to establish expected values or expected behavior, a so-called test oracle is required that serves the tester as a source of information. Requirements documents, formal specifications, and the user guide are examples of such information sources.

The term "error" is actually rather imprecise. We do in fact need to distinguish between *error*, *fault*, and *failure* (including their synonyms). For example, a developer's error while programming leads to a fault in the software that may (but not necessarily) result in a visible failure. In most cases, the impact of a fault or defect only shows itself in uncommon situations; for instance, the erroneous calculation of the leap year becomes effective only on February 29.

Error terminology

Figure 1–2 illustrates the relationship between error, fault, and failure and shows which countermeasures or methods may be used for their detection.

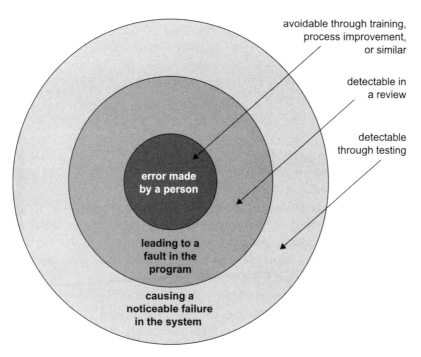

avoidable through training,
process improvement,
or similar

detectable in
a review

detectable
through testing

error made
by a person

leading to a
fault in the
program

causing a
noticeable failure
in the system

Figure 1–2

Relationship between the different terms used to denote errors

Similar to the term error, the word "test" has different meanings.

Test terminology

Testing frequently denotes the entire process of systematically checking a program to gain confidence in the correct implementation of the requirements[4] and to detect failures. It is also a generic term for all the activities and (test) levels in the test process. Each individual execution of

---

4.   Testing cannot prove that requirements are met 100% because it conducts only spot-check-like verifications.

a test object under specified conditions to verify the correctness of the expected results is also called testing.

Fundamental test process

Testing includes many individual activities. The following basic test process is defined in the Foundation Level syllabus, comprising the following activities:

- Test planning and control
- Test analysis and test design
- Test implementation and test execution
- Test evaluation of the test exit criteria
- Post testing activities

Test levels

During testing, the product under test (the test object) can be considered at different levels of abstraction or on the basis of different documents and development products. The corresponding term is test level. We distinguish between the different levels of component test, integration test, system test, and acceptance test.

Each test level has is own characteristic test objectives, test methods, and test tools.

Test types

Furthermore, we distinguish between different →test types: functional test, nonfunctional test, structural test, change-related test, and regression testing. [Spillner 07, section 3.7]

During testing, we distinguish whether testing is performed by execution of the test object or whether it is done "only" on the associated program text or underlying specification or documentation.

Static and dynamic testing

In the first case, we have the so-called dynamic tests, represented by black box and white box test methods [Spillner 07, chapter 5], and in the second case, we talk about static tests, represented, among other things, by different types of reviews [Spillner 07, chapter 4].

Independence between test and development

Regardless of which method is used for testing, it is essential that in terms of organization, development/programming and testing are kept separate and that they are performed independently from each other. A developer testing his own code will be blind toward his own mistakes and not very keen on detecting them himself.

Test tools

There are many supporting tools in use for software testing. Depending on their intended use, we distinguish between different tool classes, such as, for instance, tools for test management and control, tools for test specification, and tools for static, dynamic and nonfunctional testing [Spillner 07, chapter 7].

In our discussion of the Foundation Level syllabus, we reviewed the *Test management*
test management fundamentals. In addition to test planning, test control,
and test reporting, test management includes topics such as change and
configuration management as well as the economy of testing [Spillner 07,
chapter 6]. This book will cover these test management tasks in more
detail.

For illustration purposes, we shall continue the case study example
introduced in the book *Software Testing Foundations*:

A car manufacturer develops a new electronic sales support system called   ***Case study***
VirtualShowRoom (VSR). The final version of this software system will be   ***"VirtualShowRoom" (VSR)***
installed at every car dealership worldwide. Customer interested in buying a new
car will be able to configure their favorite model (model, type, color, extras, etc.)
at the terminal with or without the guidance of a salesperson.

The system shows all possible models and combinations of extra equipment
and instantly calculates the accurate price of the configured car.

This functionality will be implemented by a subsystem called *DreamCar*.

When customers make up their mind, they will be able to calculate the most
suitable payment method (*EasyFinance*) as well as place an order online
(*JustInTime*). Of course, they will have the opportunity to sign up for the
appropriate insurance (*NoRisk*).

Personal information and contract data about the customer is managed by the
ContractBase subsystem.

Figure 1-3 shows the general architecture of this software system.

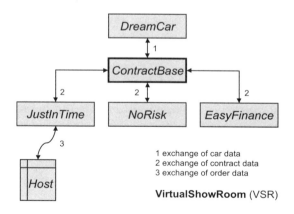

Figure 1–3

Architecture of the VSR-System

Each subsystem will be designed and developed by separate developer teams.

Altogether, about 50 developers and additional employees from the respective
user departments are involved in working on this project. External software
companies are also involved.

In *Software Testing Foundations*, we described the different →test design techniques used for in-depth testing of the VSR system before putting it into operation.

VSR-2 development follows an iterative development process. Based on the current *VSR-1* system, *VSR-2* is supposed to be developed in four successive iterations. The planned schedule is one year, with approximately one increment per quarter. Each new increment is expected to provide the full functionality of the previous version; it may, however, be based on a better or more efficient implementation. In addition, each increment introduces a set of new functionalities.

The product manager expects two things from the test manager:

- First, the test team must ensure that the old functionality is correctly retained in each intermediary VSR-2 version.
- Second, the test team should fairly quickly be able to judge objectively if, and how well, a new feature has been implemented.

The tasks that the test manager has to perform regarding such issues will be discussed and illustrated in the following chapters.

1.2 Software Testing Practice: Test Management – Overview

Software testing practice – overview

The topics of the book and the contents of each chapter are briefly described here.

- Chapter 2 discusses the fundamental test process and the types of tools that can be used to support it. Both topics were covered in *Software Testing Foundations*.
- Chapter 3 explains how testing is related to the software life cycle. It discusses different life cycle models used in software development and evaluates the particular importance given to testing in each model.
- The significance given to testing in an organization is of great importance to the test manager. The organization's quality and test policy must be defined by management. Chapter 4 deals with these issues.
- Chapter 5 takes a closer look at test planning, one of the important, if not most important, tasks of the test manager.
- Planning must be adjusted during the project's life cycle. Control of the test process based on test progress reports is an essential task for the test manager in order to perform successful testing. This aspect is addressed in chapter 6.

- The development and test processes themselves can be evaluated and improved. Chapter 7 describes which techniques and processes are to be applied to accomplish this improvement.
- How do we deal with deviations and failures detected during testing? Chapter 8 provides some answers.
- Risk evaluation and risk-based tests are important instruments for the test manager to allocate limited test resources. They are used to control the test project with minimized risk. Chapter 9 contains advice on how to proceed.
- Without qualified and skilled staff – that is, without consideration of the human factor – the test manager will not be able to succeed. Chapter 10 describes what needs to be considered when selecting a test team.
- Test metrics help in defining test exit criteria and in finding evidence on the quality of the test object. Chapter 11 will provide some examples.
- In most cases, the test process can be performed more efficiently with adequate tool support. Chapter 12 describes how the test manager selects and introduces such tools.
- The last chapter, chapter 13, presents relevant standards.

The glossary contains all the terms that are newly mentioned in this book, the first occurence of which will be preceded by an arrow "→". All glossary terms used in *Software Testing Foundations* [Spillner 07] can also be found at [URL: ISTQB] -download.

2 Test Process and Test Tools

This chapter introduces the fundamental test process, its associated activities, and appropriate tool support[1].

2.1 Test Process Fundamentals

In order to perform structured tests, a general description of the task as found in most development models (see chapter 3) is not sufficient. Besides integrating testing into the development process it is also necessary to provide a detailed test procedure (see figure 2-1). The development task consists of the process phases test planning and control, analysis and design, implementation and execution, evaluation of the test exit criteria and reporting, as well as test completion activities. Although the presentation and description of the individual tasks suggest a sequential procedure they may of course overlap or be performed in parallel.

2.1.1 Test Planning and Control

Planning a comprehensive task such as testing ought to start as soon as possible in the initial stages of software development.

Resource planning

The role and purpose of testing must be defined as well as all the necessary resources, including staff for task execution, estimated time, facilities, and tools.

The associated specifications are to be documented in the test plan. An organizational structure including test management needs to be in place and ought to be adapted, if necessary.

---

1. A more detailed introduction to the fundamental test process is given in [Spillner 07, section 2.2 and chapter 7] Readers familiar with its content may skip this chapter.

Figure 2–1

Fundamental test process

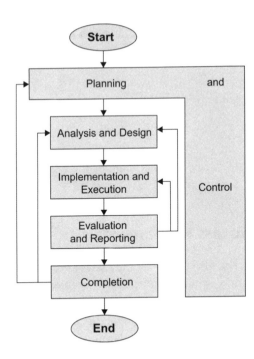

Test management is responsible for the administration of the test process, the test infrastructure, and testware. Regular control is necessary to see if planning and project progress are in line. This may result in the need for updates and adjustments to plans to keep the test process under control. The basis for controlling the test process is either staff reporting or relevant data and its evaluation by appropriate tools.

Determining the test strategy

Since exhaustive testing is impossible, priorities must be set. Depending on the risks involved, different test techniques and test exit criteria must be specified when establishing a test strategy. Critical system components must be intensively tested. However, in the case of less critical components a less comprehensive test may suffice or testing may even be waived. The decision must be very well-founded to achieve the best possible allocation of the tests to the "important" parts of the software system.

Determining test exit criteria

→Test intensity is determined by the test methods employed and by the intended degree of coverage when executing the test cases. The degree of coverage is one of several criteria for deciding when a test is completed.

Prioritizing tests

Software projects are often under pressure of time, a fact which must be anticipated during planning. Prioritizing tests causes the most critical software components to be tested first in case not all planned tests can be performed due to time or resource constraints.

Without adequate tools the test process cannot be sufficiently per- *Tool support* formed. If tools are missing, their selection and procurement must be initiated early in the process.

Moreover, parts of the test infrastructure themselves often need to be established, for instance the test environment, in which system components can be executed. They need to be put in place early so that they are available when coding of the test objects is completed.

2.1.2   TestAnalysis and Design

The test strategy developed during planning defines the test design tech- *Verification of the test basis* niques to be used. As a first step of test analysis, the test basis needs to be checked to see if all required documents are detailed and accurate enough to be able to derive the test techniques in agreement with the test strategy[2]. The specification of the test object determines its expected behavior. The test designer uses it to derive the prerequisites and requirements of the test cases.

Depending on the analysis results it may be necessary to rework the test basis so that it can serve as a starting point for the test design techniques techniques defined in the test strategy. For example, if a specification is not accurate enough it may need to be improved. Sometimes it is the test strategy itself which may need to be changed, for instance, if it turns out that the selected test design techniques cannot be applied to the test basis.

During test design, test techniques are applied to identify the respective test cases, which are then documented in the test specification. Ultimately, the →test project or test schedule determines the timing of the test execution sequence and the assignment of the test cases to the individual testers.

When specifying test cases, logical test cases must be defined first. *Logical and concrete* Once this is done, concrete, i.e., actual input and expected output, values *test cases* may be defined.

However, this is done during implementation, which is the next step of the fundamental test process.

---

2.   This check can already be done while developing the test strategy and may influence it if the documentation is already available at that time.

Black box and white box techniques

Logical test cases can be identified based on the specification of the test objects (black box techniques) or based on program text (white box techniques). Thus, the specification of the test cases may take place at quite different times during the software development process (before or after or parallel to coding, depending on the test techniques selected in the test strategy). In this connection, many of the life cycle models described in the next chapter show only test execution phases (e.g., the general V-model). Test planning and specification activities can and should take place concurrently with earlier development activities, as explicitly pointed out in the W-model or in extreme programming.

Test cases comprise more than just test data

During test case specification the particular starting situation (precondition) must be described for each test case. Test constraints to be observed must be clearly defined. Prior to test execution it needs to be defined in the post-condition which results or which behavior is expected.

Test oracle

In order to determine the expected results a test oracle is queried which predicts the expected outcomes for every test case. In most cases the specification or the requirements are used as the test oracle to derive the expected results from individual test cases.

Positive and negative test cases

Test cases can be distinguished according to two criteria:

■ Test cases for testing specified results and reactions to be delivered by the test object (including treatment of specified exceptional and failure situations)

■ Test cases for testing the reaction of the test objects to invalid or unexpected inputs or other conditions for which "exception handling" has not been specified and which test the test object for robustness

Setting up the infrastructure

The required test infrastructure to run the test object with the specified test cases is to be established in parallel to the other activities so as to prevent delays in the execution of the test cases. At that point the test infrastructure should be set up, integrated, and also tested intensively.

2.1.3   Test Implementation and Execution

In this step of the test process, concrete test cases must be derived from the logical test cases, and executed. In order to run the tests, test infrastructure and test environment must both be implemented and in place. The individual test runs are to be performed and logged.

Timing and test case sequence

The actual tests are to be run observing the priorities that we defined earlier. It is best to group individual test cases into test sequences or test scenarios in order to allow for the tests to be run efficiently and to gain a clear structure of the test cases.

The required test harness must be installed in the test environment before the test cases can be executed.

At the lower test levels, component and integration testing, it makes sense to run automated rather than manual tests (e.g., using JUnit [URL: JUnit])

During test execution an initial check is done to see if the test object is, in principal, able to start up and run. This is followed by a check of the main functions ("smoke test" or acceptance test during entry check of the individual test levels).

Checking main function completeness

If failures occur already at this stage further testing makes little sense.

Test execution must be logged accurately and completely. Based on test protocols, test execution must be traceable and evidence must be provided that the planned test strategy has actually been implemented. The test protocol also contains details concerning which parts were tested when, by whom, to what extent, and with what result.

Tests without a test protocol are useless

With each failure recorded in the test log a decision needs to be made whether its origin is thought to lie inside or outside the test object. For instance, the test framework may have been defective or the test case may have been erroneously specified.

Evaluating the test protocols

If a failure exists it needs to be adequately documented and assigned to a incident class.

Based on the incident class the priority for defect removal is to be determined. Successful defect correction needs to be ascertained: has the defect been removed and are we sure that no further failures have occurred?

Correction successful?

The earlier made prioritization has the effect that the most important test cases are executed first and that serious failures can be detected and corrected early.

Most important tests come first!

The principle of equal distribution of limited test resources over all test objects of a project is of little use since such an approach leads to equally intensive testing of critical and non-critical program parts.

2.1.4 Test Evaluation and Test Report

It needs to be checked if the test exit criteria defined in the plan have been met. This check may lead to the conclusion that test activities may be considered completed but may also show that test cases were blocked and that

Test completion reached?

not all planned test cases could be executed. It may also mean that additional test cases are required to meet the criteria.

Closer analysis, however, may reveal that the necessary effort to meet all exit criteria is unreasonably high and that further test cases or test runs had best be eliminated. The associated risk needs to be evaluated and taken into account for the decision.

If further tests are necessary, the test process must be resumed and the step has to be identified from where test activities are to be resumed. If necessary, planning must be revised as additional resources are required.

Besides test coverage criteria, additional criteria may be used to determine the end of the test activities (see chapter 11).

Allow for several test cycles   Test cycles develop as a result of observed failures, their correction, and necessary retesting. Test management must take such correction and test cycles into account in their planning (see also the W-model in section 3.4). Otherwise, project delays are the rule. It is rather difficult to calculate the effort needed for the test cycles in advance. Comparative data from earlier, similar projects or from already completed test cycles may help.

Exit criteria in practice: In practice, time and cost often determine the end of testing and lead
time and cost   to the termination of test activities.

Even if during testing there is more budget spent than planned, testing as a whole does cause savings through the detection of failures and subsequent correction of software defects. Defects not detected here usually cause considerably higher cost when found during operation.

Test report   At the end of this activity of the test process, a summary report must be prepared for the decision makers (project manager, test manager, and customer, if necessary) (see also [IEEE 829]).

2.1.5 Completing the Test Activities

Learning from experience   Unfortunately, in practice, the closing phase of the test processes is mostly neglected. At this stage, the experiences gained during the test process should be analyzed and made available to other projects. In this connection, the presumed causes of differences between planning and implementation are of particular interest.

A critical evaluation of the activities performed in the test process, taking into account effort spent and the achieved results, will definitely reveal improvement potential. If these findings are documented and applied to subsequent projects in an understandable manner, continuous process improvement has been achieved. Chapter 7 will take a closer look at the models for analysis, evaluation, and test process improvement.

A further finishing activity is the "conservation" of the testware for future use. During the operational use of software systems, hitherto unde-tected failures will occur despite all previous testing, or customers will require changes. In both cases this will lead to revised versions of the pro-gram and require renewed testing. If testware (test cases, test protocols, test infrastructure, tools, etc.) from development is still available, test effort will be reduced during the maintenance or operational phases of the software.

Testware "conservation"

2.2   Test Tools

The following section provides an overview over different types of test tools[3]. Tool types are comprehensively described in *Software Testing Foun-dations* ([Spillner 07, chapter 7]). A closer look is taken at tools that sup-port test management. It is particularly important for the test manager to learn how to select and use such tools (see chapter 12).

Short overview

There are many tools supporting or automating test activities, all of which are known as CAST tools (Computer Aided Software Testing), analgous to CASE tools (Computer Aided Software Engineering).

CAST tools

Depending on which activities or phases in the test process are sup-ported, we may distinguish between different tool types.

As a rule, not all available test tools are applied in a project. However, the test manager should know available tool types in order to be able to decide if and when to use a tool efficiently in a project.

The following sections describe the various functions provided by the different tool types.

2.2.1   Tools for Management and Test Control

Planning and control are the first activities in the test process. The respec-tive test management tools offer mechanisms for easy capturing, prioritiz-ing, cataloguing, and administration of test cases. They allow test case sta-tus tracking, i.e., they document and evaluate if, when, how often, and with which result a test case has been executed. Moreover, they may be used to

Test management tool

---

3.   [URL: Tool-List] provides a list of useful links regarding tool information.

support resource and schedule planning for the tests. The test manager can plan the tests and remain informed at all times about the status of hundreds or thousands of test cases.

Support for advanced management tasks

In addition to these core tasks, test management tools offer support for tasks and activities such as:

- Requirements-based testing: system requirements are linked with those tests that check the corresponding requirement. Different consistency checks can be performed, for instance to see if for each requirement at least one test case has been planned.
- Defect management: tool support is indispensable for the management of problem or incident reports. Capturing, administration, and statistical evaluation of incident reports should not be done manually, since this is simply too error-prone. Tools help the test manager to be kept informed about the actual project at all times.
- Preparing test reports and test documents: both test management and incident management tools provide extensive analysis and reporting features, including the possibility to generate complete test documentation (test plan, test specification, test report) from their data repository.

2.2.2   Tools for Test Data and Test Script Specification

Test data and test script generators

So-called test (data) generators can support the test designer in generating test data. There are several approaches, depending on the test basis used:

- Database-based test data generators create test data on the basis of database schemas or database content.
- Code-based test data generators analyze the source code to derive the test data. Target or expected values, however, cannot be derived.
- Interface-based test data generators derive test data through identification of interface parameter domains (for example, using equivalence class partitioning and boundary value analysis). Here, too, the problem exists that target values cannot be generated.
- Specification-based test data generators derive test data and associated target values from a formal specification.
- Model-based test generators derive test scripts from formal models, starting, for instance, from a UML sequence diagram specifying the call sequences of methods.

2.2.3   Tools for Static Testing

Static checks can be carried out on design documents, given the availability of a formal notation, and on (also only partially available) source code, i.e., even before executable program (parts) are available. Tools supporting the static test help to detect defects and discrepancies already in the early phases of the development process. Therefore a test manager should consider using these tools.

Static analysis

- Static analyzers provide measures of miscellaneous characteristics of the program code which can be used to identify complex and hence defect-prone or risky code sections. Violations of programming guidelines, broken or invalid links in website contents and many other anomalies or discrepancies can be analyzed statically.
- Model checkers analyze specifications if they are available in a formal notation or as a formal model. For example, they can find missing states, missing state transitions, and other inconsistencies in the state model to be checked.
- Furthermore, there are tools to support reviewing and which help in the planning, execution, and evaluation of review results.

2.2.4   Tools for Dynamic Testing

Test tools for automating test execution relieve the tester from carrying out unnecessary mechanical tasks. The tools supply the test object with test data, record the test object's reactions, perform a comparison with the expected reactions, and log the test execution.

Tool support for functional tests

- In the narrow sense, a debugger is not a test tool but is very useful for root cause analysis and for enforcing exception handling in the program code.
- Test drivers and test bed generators offer a mechanism to address test objects via their application programming interface (API), or via another interface not directly accessible to the end user, such as, for example, the Ethernet, serial interface, and so on.
- Simulators can be used to emulate an operating environment. They are particularly used for testing embedded software if the target system is not yet available, or if testing in the target system is very expensive or if it requires a disproportionally high effort.

- Test robots (capture and replay tools) record all input that is manually performed inputs (keyboard inputs, mouse clicks) during a test session and save them in a test script. The recorded test can be automatically repeated by replaying the test script as often as one likes.
- Comparators are used to identify differences between expected and actual results. They are typically included in other tools.
- Dynamic analyzers acquire additional information during program execution, for instance on allocation, usage, and release of memory (memory leaks, pointer allocation, pointer arithmetic problems, and so on).
- Coverage analyzers provide structural test coverage values measured at code level during test execution (see also chapter 11).

Tool support for non-functional tests

Besides tools that support functional testing there are also tools for testing non-functional features of the test objects:

- Load and performance test tools generate a synthetic load, e.g., database queries, user transactions, or network traffic, for the execution of volume, stress, and performance tests.
- Monitors are used to support tests and analysis in that they identify and evaluate necessary data. They are typically integrated in load and performance test tools.
- Tools for checking access and data security analyze possible security gaps in the test object.

2.2.5 Constraints to be Considered

Tool use and test process

Creative test activities can be supported by tools. The mechanical test execution can be automated, reducing the test effort or allowing the execution of more test cases without spending any additional effort. More test cases, however, do not necessarily mean better tests.

Without a well-established test process and adequate test methods, tools cannot achieve the desired cost reduction. The introduction and efficient use of tools requires a thorough evaluation of the test processes and accompanying process improvement activities (see also chapters 7 and 12).

On the other hand, the economic execution of the test processes can only be achieved with appropriate tool support; for instance, to be able to execute and evaluate many test cases within an adequate time frame.

The test manager must be aware of all these constraints and must act accordingly.

2.3 Summary

Testing must be divided into individual process steps. A fundamental test process is divided into the following steps:

- Test planning and control: Define required resources (staffing, schedule, tools), define the test strategy together with the selection of the test methods to be used, the respective coverage criteria, and prioritization of the tests. Also, determine the sequence of test execution in the test schedule. Intervene to control during the whole test processes if there are any deviations from the plan.
- Test analysis and design: Check the test basis for completeness and sufficient accuracy. Design logical test cases using the test methods of the test oracle. Begin creating the test infrastructure.
- Test implementation and execution: Draw up test cases and group them to test sequences or scenarios, and complete the test infrastructure. The first step in the execution is to check that the test object is executable and that calling up main functions does not cause any serious failures. All test runs are to be recorded and evaluated in detail.
- Test evaluation and report: Show that the test exit criteria have been satisfactorily fulfilled. If not, decide if further tests are to follow or if the test process may be finished nonetheless. Draw up a summary test report.
- Completion of the test activities: The main task of this last activity of the test process is to learn from experience and to provide the testware needed for maintenance.
- For each phase of the test process tools are available that help the test manager and the tester to qualitatively improve their test activities.
- The use of test tools is only of advantage if the test process is a controlled and defined process.

3 Testing in the Software Life Cycle

This chapter illustrates the relationship between the test process and the software development process. It provides a classification of process models, introduces some current software development process models, and explains the role that testing plays within these models.

3.1 Test and Development Process

During the development of software systems, software development models, or development processes[1], are applied to ensure a controlled organizational structure and workflow management.

Goal: systematic organizational structure and workflow management

In recent years, a whole range of new process models have been introduced and applied. The objective of all these models is to provide a systematic and structured approach in the development and maintenance of software systems.

Each model has several important components:

Model components

- Individual activities
- Technical and schedule-related criteria for the transition into the next activity phase (milestones, quality gates)
- Definition of roles and responsibilities
- Documents to be created during the different phases, and the methods, guidelines, standards and tools to be applied.

Depending on the development process, model components have varying characteristics and are described or defined in different degrees of detail. Given the widely varying importance of testing in the different models, this chapter will take a closer look at some of them.

The list of models we'll look at is neither representative nor complete since there is a multitude of models used in the development of software

---

1. Life cycle model and process model are also commonly used terms.

systems. The reader can use Wikipedia and search for software development process to find a survey and links to the individual processes described in detail.

Strong interaction with the development processes

The way in which the fundamental test process is applied in all software development, independent of the model being used, was described in some detail in the previous chapter. The test process is closely related to the development and maintenance activities of software systems, some examples of which will be given below.

Requirements change

To assume that we can completely identify all software requirements at the beginning of a project is highly unrealistic. Requirements do change during development. This, of course, has an influence on the test process. We must always keep in mind that whenever requirements change, all the necessary adaptations in associated test documents[2] must also be made. Divergence of documents must be avoided because this would mean that for changed or new requirements, we would be without relevant test cases or we would test on requirements that are no longer relevant. It is a prerequisite that requirements can be traced to the corresponding sections in the test documents. Hence, not only development but also test documents are subject to change management.

Configuration management

During the development and maintenance of software systems, different versions and configurations evolve together with the associated testware. It is obvious that configuration management must also be applied to testware, that is, to all test documents and test tools.

Project management

One of the objectives of testing is the detection of failure. The tester writes an incident report that is passed on to the development or maintenance department. There the cause of the failure is identified and corrected accordingly. Subsequently, we need to ascertain whether the failure has been removed or not and that the correction has not caused any new failures. After that, another test cycle is performed.

Project management needs to coordinate the development (i.e., the change and test process) well enough to ensure smooth interaction between them.

The same is true for changes during the operational application of the system. Changes are to be tested before the system can go into production, and the associated technical and user documentation needs to be adapted. Here, too, an interface exists between development and test.

---

2.   [IEEE 829] calls these documents "test documents." [ISO 12207.1] defines the term more broadly as "life cycle data" (information item).

The strong interconnection between the test process and the develop-   *Generic test process*
ment and maintenance processes means that appropriate adjustments
must be made to achieve optimum collaboration. In this connection, we
talk of the generic test process, which can be adjusted in a relatively flexible way to the specific activities of the applied development and maintenance processes.

3.2   Classification of Development Processes

Software can be developed according to different development or life cycle
models. The difference is in whether they presume a single sequence of
individual activities, as is the case with the general V-model[3] ([Boehm 79],
see section 3.3) or whether they describe system development as a
sequence of several iterations (see figure 3-1).

The waterfall model (see [Spillner 07, section 2.2]) and the general   *Sequential models*
V-model are sequential models. They share the linear sequencing of constructive activities that are usually performed for the entire system.

The iterative models can be broken down further into evolutionary
and incremental models.

In evolutionary models, a customer's core requirements are the starting   *Evolutionary models*
point of development. Once the first version has been released, the customer can articulate his wishes and requirements for the next release
based on his experience with the first release. This approach also applies
to future product versions. It is expedient in this context that the customer
obtains useable products within relatively short time frames, although the
functional scope increases slowly and cannot really be planned.

Incremental models capture and model system requirements as com-   *Incremental models*
prehensively as possible. However, in the first increment, only a fraction of
the requirements is included and implemented so that the customer can
have an operational system at an early stage, though with limited functionality. The next incremental step takes into account the experiences that the
customer had with the previous increment.

---

3.   The "V-model" is tagged "general" to distinguish it from the "Lifecycle Process
     Model of the Federal Republic of Germany" (version 92 and 97), which in German
     publications is often also referred to as the "V-model".

Figure 3–1

Sequential and iterative
system development

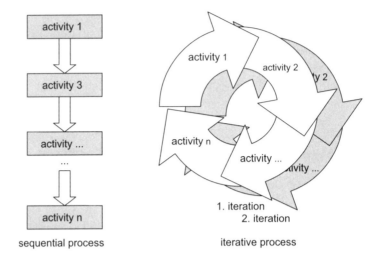

sequential process   iterative process

Agile processes   Rapid application development (RAD, see section 3.8) and Extreme Programming (XP, see section 3.7) are examples of incremental and evolutionary models. The boundaries between the models are somewhat vague, and precise assignment to the different kinds is not always possible.

XP, for instance, is a lightweight process that gives developers a lot of freedom. It is also difficult to classify the Rational Unified Process (RUP, see section 3.5) clearly, since it defines both, phases (inception, elaboration, construction, transition) and iterations, in individual phases of software development.

Selecting the development   The following section introduces some process models; our main focus
process   will be put on the interfaces to the test process. The applied development model plays a decisive role for the test manager because it defines, if only indirectly, the importance or status that the test process has within the development process. In most cases, the test manager has no or only very little influence on the selection of the development process.

3.3   The General V- Model

Requirements definition   The starting point for the development of software systems is the requirements definition, documenting the wishes and requirements of the customer and later users.

Purpose, features, and quality requirements of the system under development must be documented in the requirements definition.

This document serves as a basis for all further development activities, in particular for the functional system design. Moreover, the requirements document forms the basis for the specification of the acceptance test. Requirements must be formulated accurately enough to be able to derive test cases from them.

During functional system design, the requirements are mapped onto functions and dialogues of the new system. The evolving documentation is required by the testers so that they can write the functional system test cases and test the user interfaces before the system undergoes customer acceptance testing.

Functional system design

During technical system design, the interfaces to the system environment are defined and the system is decomposed into manageable system components and interfaces, taking into account the way the different parts interact with each other.

Technical system design

Integration testing uses this information to simulate the system environment and to sufficiently test the interfaces between the different system components.

Component specification defines the behavior and inner structure or sequence within the component. This information is later used in coding and component testing.

Component specification

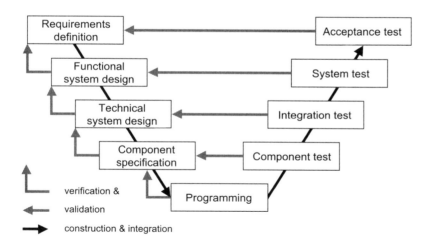

Figure 3–2

General V-model

The relationship between the different test levels (component, integration, system, and acceptance test) and the corresponding development phases (requirements definition, functional and technical system design, components specification) is illustrated by the general V-model (see figure 3-2).

The model emphasizes quality assurance. Besides its graphical layout, the model derives its name from the initial letters of the terms verification and validation [Boehm 79].

3.4   The W-Model

In the general V-model, testing is explicitly presented in individual test levels, and test cases are developed based on the corresponding development activities and associated documents. Test cases must be specified once the corresponding requirements and design specifications are available. Unfortunately, this is not made clear in the graphical presentation of the V-model (see figure 3-2).

W-model

However, a model that illustrates the concurrency of the test and development processes and explains the approach taken by the general V-model is called the W-model (see figure 3-3). It shows that test preparation activities are carried out in parallel to the definition and specification activities performed in development ([Spillner 02]).

Figure 3–3
W-model

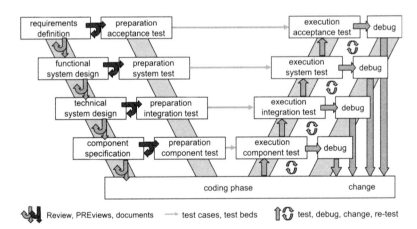

Preparatory activities are those activities of the test processes that are to be performed prior to execution of the test cases, i.e., planning, analysis, design, and test implementation (see chapter 2). The right-hand branch of the V-model is also broken up into different activities, i.e., into test execution and debugging.

Testing and debugging

Debugging is often equated with testing, although they are very different tasks performed by different people. In the strict sense, testers are responsible for test execution, test logging, and test evaluation.

Detected failures are to be reported to the developers, whose task it is to identify their causes by debugging and to ensure their removal. Subsequent retesting must then verify that the failure does not reoccur and that changes made by the developers have not caused any new failures. This often leads to cycles that are also explicitly reflected in the W-model.

Cycles occur

What is also becoming clear is that changes imply a "fall back" to the coding level. Once the changes have been made, a "renewed loop" is necessary, which takes up time and resources.

Test managers know this, and the chosen representation of the W-model may help project leaders to become aware of the fact that testing is not a once-only activity in software development, as some of the process models may suggest, but rather one that is repeated in cycles.

It is very likely that during test execution, we also find defects from design or specification. A "jump" from the right to the left branch is then necessary to correct the errors in the respective documents, followed by a "renewed cycle" through the W accompanied by corresponding adaptation of all impacted documents. However, for the sake of better clarity, this is not graphically shown in the model.

In the W-model, testers are involved in development activities right from the start of a project, becoming, for instance, acquainted with the requirements to be able to specify adequate acceptance test cases. According to the W-model, questions relating to acceptance testing should already be asked during the requirements review. Requirements are not only analyzed with regard to whether documents are available in sufficient quality to start the next development step (in this case, functional specification), but also with regard to whether or not the requirements are precise enough to be able to specify appropriate acceptance test cases. Since this is a look into the future—the feasibility of the acceptance test—this check may also be called "PREview".

PREviews

PREviews, too, are to be performed at subsequent development levels. With testers participating in PREviews, documents are analyzed using the testers' expert knowledge. Negative effects on testing, such as a high test effort for a complex interface between two system components, can be recognized early and, if possible, trigger any necessary changes.

A further advantage of the PREviews is that the test case specifications are developed early and in conjunction with the development documents. Test case specifications may serve as additional documents for further development. Test cases are very precise and can be used to obtain information about the required functionality of the system.

Test cases as additional development specifications

Thus, in addition to the actual development documents, we have additional documentation relating to the same subject matter. This helps to specify inaccuracies and to resolve ambiguities, which in turn helps to avoid defects.

Test manager   The W-model lends itself to a division of test management tasks. In large projects, several test managers should be assigned; one responsible for the entire process and one for each individual test level. Overall management is responsible for the coordination of the specific test activities, whereas individual test-level managers are responsible for coordination within their respective levels. Depending on level, test managers must select different checks and test methods and control their application and intensity of use.

3.5   Rational Unified Process (RUP)

As its name suggests, this process was created by the Rational Software Corporation.[4] RUP is intended to be applied in the development of object-oriented systems using UML (Unified Modeling Language, see figure 3-4).

Figure 3–4
RUP—
Rational Unified Process[5]

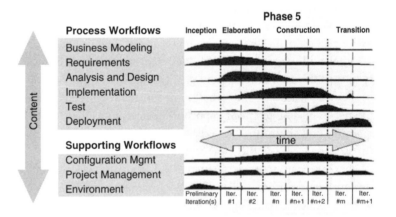

Activities   RUP is divided into a horizontal dimension showing the dynamic aspect of a project in terms of four phases (inception, elaboration, construction, transition) that are again subdivided into several iterations. As a rule, each

---

4.   Now IBM.
5.   The RUP chart is from [Kruchten 04].

iteration produces one executable, tested prototype or version and adds an increment to the functionality of the previous version.

The nine "workflows"[6] are divided into engineering process activities (business modeling, requirements, analysis and design, implementation, test, and deployment) and support activities (configuration and change management, project management, and development environment). Figure 3-4 illustrates the relationship between the different phases and iterations and the different workflows together with their associated efforts in different phases. Almost all activities range across all phases, although with varying intensity.

In RUP, test activities begin early in the project, starting with test planning in the inception phase. Test activities are structured in such a way that testing is never done all at once. The model distinguishes between component, integration, system, and acceptance testing, reflecting the test levels found in the V-model.

Test activity

Besides test levels, RUP distinguishes between the following test types: benchmark test, configuration test, function test, installation test, integration test, load test, performance test, stress test, and regression test. The test model describes what needs to be tested and contains a list of all the test cases, test procedures, test scripts, and expected test results.

Different test types

The model lists the following "workers" involved in the test activities: test designer, tester, system tester, performance tester, and integration tester. Essential artifacts (documents) are the test schedule, the test model, a load model for performance testing, and the documentation of the defects.

The list illustrates the importance given to testing in RUP. Unfortunately, it does not show the strong interaction between the development and test activities.

Testing in the RUP

The tasks of a test manager are comparable to those of a test engineer and extend across the entire development process. He is responsible for the following artifacts: test model, test case, test procedure, test evaluation, and test plan.

Test manager

IBM Corporation offers a whole range of tools to support development and test process activities.

----

6.   A term also frequently used is "disciplines".

3.6   V-Model XT

The "Lifecycle Process Model of the Federal Republic of Germany" (known as V-model) was first published in 1992 and revised in 1997. The current model, called "V-model XT", has been available since 2005. XT stands for "eXtreme Tailoring" and points out the model's adaptability to a given project type ([Kuhrmann 06], [URL: V-Model XT], [URL: V-Model XT Browser], sorry, some in German).

Who, when, what?   The model defines "who must do when and what" in a project. It defines the activities that need to be performed and the products (results) that need to be created during system development and the responsibilities of each person participating in the project. As with all other models, the objective is again the minimization of project risks, improvement and guarantee of the quality of the (interim) products, reduction of total cost, and improved communication between all stakeholders.

Two elements of the V-model XT need to be particularly emphasized:

- Tailoring, i.e., the project-specific adaptation of the model to a concrete project
- Explicit involvement of the customer in project planning and execution

Tailoring   Tailoring provides the opportunity to adapt the model to suit different project constellations. Thus, the V-model XT represents a generic standard that can be tailored to suit the specific requirements of a project. A tool called V-model XT Project Assistant to support tailoring is available free of charge. The project is first characterized by a list specifying project characteristics (e.g., safety and security). Important characteristics are the subject matter of the project and the project role.

Subject of the project   The subject matter of a project is either the development of a system or an organization-wide process that needs to be improved. Here the V-model XT differs from the previous models, which refer only to the development of systems. Models for process evaluation and improvement are described in chapter 7.

Project role   The project role is assumed either by the customer or the supplier and designates the position of the project as compared to other projects. Each role implies specific points of views with regard to the development project and includes a range of defined project tasks.

Model components   For every possible project type resulting from the subject of the project and the role, the model provides at least one execution strategy as well as mandatory and optional process modules. This makes the model tailorable in a very flexible way because it provides the opportunity to take individual modules and "assemble" the model from components best suited for the project.

Three project types are specified in the V-model XT: *Project types*

▪ System development project of a customer: It includes the preparation of a request for proposal and the selection of a supplier. The supplier develops the system and delivers it, and the customer accepts it.
▪ System development project of a supplier: After preparation of an offer to the customer and after acceptance, the contract will be concluded and the system developed.
▪ Introduction and maintenance of an organization-specific life cycle model: The V-model XT provides a framework for organization-wide quality management. It distinguishes between the first-time introduction of a process description and the repeated execution of process improvement programs.

The first two V-model project types are found in each system development project. They cannot be considered separately because they are closely connected via the so-called Customer/Supplier interface. The V-model XT provides specifically adapted project execution strategies and standardized interface products that are exchanged between the customer and supplier's V-model projects.

The model provides a wide range of information on tailoring, roles,   *Thirty roles,*
products (including standards), and activities. For instance, it defines 30   *but no test manager*
different roles but none explicitly related to the test manager. Roles relevant to the test process are tester, quality assurance engineer, and quality manager. Since the tasks of the test manager are shared among several roles, there is no separately recognizable test process. However, looking at the individual activities, it does become clear that test activities start early and that they occupy an appropriate position in the overall process. Moreover, the V-model XT lists all the necessary documents required for the execution of a smooth test process.

3.7   Extreme Programming (XP)

For some time now, so-called lightweight processes have moved into the focus of interest and discussion. The goal of all lightweight processes is the reduction of software bureaucracy; i.e., documents are rated less important. One representative of lightweight processes is Extreme Programming [Beck 00].

The following section provides a brief description of XP (see figure 3-5).

Figure 3–5

XP project overview[7]

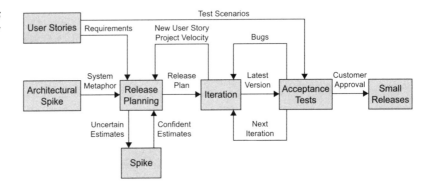

Stories   The so-called "user stories" are the starting point for every project. They are comparable to the use cases in the UML and are used to describe requirements from the user's point of view. But even all stories taken together do not make up a complete requirements definition; it is rather that a single story contains the description of one customer requirement that may serve as a unit for the planning, implementation, and control of one small release or a part thereof. During the life of a project, new stories are added and existing ones are refined. Effort estimation and planning for the implementation of a story are jointly conducted by the developer and customer, and the decision as to which story is to be contained in which release is made based on priorities and risk estimation.

Acceptance test   Stories also drive the development of so-called "test scenarios", which are executed during acceptance testing. The user or customer is responsible for acceptance testing, and it is he who must decide whether or not the tests failed. However, to perform acceptance testing for each release, these tests need to be automated.

Prior to acceptance testing, unit tests are performed (see figure 3-6). During Extreme Programming, test cases are created or coded before the individual module or increments are coded. Frameworks are used to create and automate execution of unit tests (e.g., JUnit; see [URL: JUnit]).

---

7.   See [URL: EP].

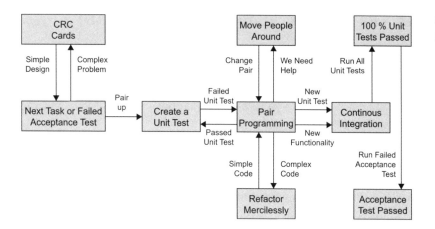

Figure 3–6
XP-test activities[8]

Test cases serve as a specification of the requested functionality of the indi-   *Unit test*
vidual stories or system increments. Automating test execution allows new
or changed modules to be checked very quickly. All unit tests must run
"bug free" before development may be continued.

In XP, testing is of paramount importance and is the focus of attention
right from the start of the project. Other lightweight processes have taken
up this approach (Test Driven Development or Test First Development,
see [URL: XUnit]).

One problem is that during development, focus is put entirely on unit   *No systematic test case*
tests, i.e., on testing the individual unit. The customer is responsible for   *creation*
system and acceptance testing. Integration testing[9] to detect interface
defects is not addressed at all in XP[10]. An additional problem is that XP
offers or prescribes no systematic approach for the creation of test cases.
Thus, success always depends on how well test cases have been selected.

XP does not put much emphasis on management tasks. XP projects are
more or less "self-governed" and of limited scope so that there are hardly
any "real" management tasks left to perform. The role of the tester does
actually exist in the model; however, contrary to customary understanding, his role is rather seen as merely supporting the customer in his execution of acceptance testing because unit tests are developed and executed by
the developers themselves prior to and during coding.

---

8. See [URL: EP].
9. Continuous integration (see figure 3-6) is performed, but there are no specific test
    cases to check on interfaces; instead, unit test cases are repeated.
10. However, there is a series of publications providing suggestions related to systematic
    test execution (e.g., [Crispin 02]).

3.8 Rapid Application Development (RAD)

Shortening development cycles and enhancing the quality of software systems is the goal of "rapid application development" (see also [Martin 91]). This is to be achieved through increased use of tools across the entire development process. In connection with this, Computer Aided Software Engineering (CASE), should also be mentioned.

Besides the use of intensive tool support, a reduction of development cycles is achieved through iterative development (evolutionary prototyping). Only parts of the requirements are implemented and then presented to the customer, who then expresses his requirements for the next iteration. Figure 3-7 provides a possible view of the RAD processes.

Figure 3–7

RAD—rapid application development

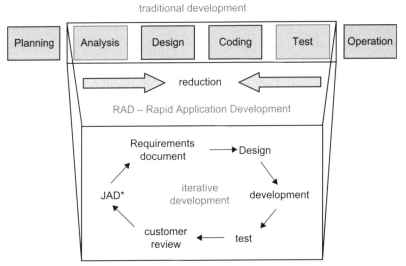

*Joint Application Development

Today, RAD serves as a generic term for a whole range of tool-supported development approaches, such as the development of user interfaces by means of user interface development environments (GUI-builder), the use of Visual Basic (VB) or Delphi, and the application of authoring systems for the creation of multimedia applications. All of them use tools for creating systems or parts of them, often without prior completion of a detailed analysis and design phase.

Roles   Explicit roles for testing or test management are not defined. The University of California RAD web page [URL: RAD] does not list the roles of the tester or test manager among the RAD Key Players. A "SWAT Team" (Skilled Workers with Advanced Tools) exists and is composed of two to six well-trained developers.

3.9   Dynamic Systems Development Method (DSDM)

In the mid-1990s, a consortium of international companies got together to find out why RAD could be successfully applied in some projects while failing in others. DSDM refines RAD by adding a defined process largely resembling "Scrum" [URL: Scrum] but defining more precise process steps and roles.

DSDM has nine fundamental principles, which can be summarized as fol-   *DSDM principles*
lows:

- Software development takes place in a team. A product can be successful only if the customer's application know-how is combined with the development know-how of the IT experts. The customer is actively involved in the teamwork.
- As a rule, decisions are made by the team and not by individual team members.
- The objective is to have regular product or product increment releases.
- These (incremental) releases must have an added business value for customers or users compared to previous releases (relevant acceptance criterion, business-value driven).
- Iterative and incremental development are applied to achieve adequate solutions.
- It must be easy to revoke already implemented changes.
- Requirements are defined at a high level.
- Testing is taken into consideration throughout the entire development process.
- Collaboration and cooperation of all stakeholders involved in the project is important.

Time-boxing & MoSCoW   There are many obvious parallels to XP (section 3.7). In DSDM, a number of techniques are to be applied, two of which are listed here:

- Time-boxing
  Time-boxing is a technique or approach used to carry out all activities in a number of separate time intervals specified in advance. This implies that the time frame is fixed and that all performed activities must be accomplished "in accordance" with the time budget. The only remaining variables are the requirements. Delays are not accepted.
- The "MoSCoW" principle
  Requirements are categorized based on the following rules:

  - **M**ust have—fundamental for the project's success
    or
  - **S**hould have—important requirement, but project success does not directly depend on it
  - **C**ould have—can be left out without adversely affecting the project
    or
  - **W**ould have—at a later date if there is some time left (or in the future, next version)

Five stages   DSDM projects (phase project life cycles) are realized in five stages, whereby for each product increment stages 3 to 5 are iteratively repeated:

1. Feasibility Study, which may lead to the decision not to implement
2. Business Study, to specify essential requirements
3. Functional Model Iteration, system architecture definition, specification of product increments, and prototype development.
4. Design and Build Iteration, implementation and test of the product increments
5. Implementation, release of the finished product increment to the user

The tester's role   DSDM defines 12 roles. The role of the test managers is not on the list. The only role mentioned with regard to testing is that of the tester who is responsible for the execution of the "non-user" tests.

3.10 Summary

Besides illustrating that there is close interaction between the development and test processes, this chapter introduced a whole range of different software process models. In doing so, it particularly emphasized the degree of priority the test process and its activities are given in each of the models.

- A distinction is made between sequential and iterative system development models. In sequential models, individual activities are performed consecutively, whereas in iterative development models, we have product increments whose functionality will be enhanced with each further increment until the end product is completed.
- The general V-model emphasizes test levels and how they are related to the corresponding analysis, design, and specification phases. Preparatory test activities (e.g., test planning, test specification) are not made explicit in the model.
- Preparatory test activities for individual test levels are clearly distinguished in the W-model as activities performed concurrently to the analysis, design, and specification phases. The model distinguishes between test execution/test evaluation, and debugging. The test process and development process are closely connected.
- The Rational Unified Process (RUP) represents a link between the sequential and iterative processes. In RUP, test activities begin early and accompany other processes spanning across all iterations. However, which test activities are to be performed when is not made clear enough in the model.
- The V-model XT life cycle process model of the Federal Republic of Germany in its 2005 version allows tailoring of a development model from predefined modules to match the individual requirements of a project. Particular attention is given to customer and supplier communication. The model provides support during system development and a process to establish and continuously improve a corporate-wide quality management.
- In eXtreme Programming, testing is at the center of the development effort right from the start (test first). Test cases serve as specifications and iterations take place at short intervals. The customer is responsible for acceptance testing during each release. However, the main emphasis is put on unit testing of individual modules.

■ During Rapid Application Development (RAD), too, the system is developed in short iterations and with customer involvement. In addition, the model advocates extensive use of tools.

■ Another agile process model, the Dynamic System Development Method (DSDM), puts its focus on development through teamwork, close cooperation with the customer, and iterative system development. Following the MoSCoW principle, increments important to the customer are to be produced first. Imperative is schedule adherence of individual activities (time-boxing).

In most cases, test managers have little say in the selection of the development processes and must try to come to terms with the processes used. Processes, however, may be adapted to suit particular circumstances; thus, the test process may gain greater presence than was first intended.

It is not possible to recommend one particular process that best supports the test process because the choice or adaptation of the model depends on many different factors. A model may have become established in one organization for many years and changes may not be desired, or the development model was prescribed by the customer.

Whatever model is chosen as a basis, though, the test manager must ensure that documents must be subject to reviews (also in the early phases). In addition, he must ensure that documents are made available to the test team early enough to allow for proper test preparation.

4   Test Policy and Test Handbook

The purpose of the test policy and test handbook is to provide a test definition that can be applied to all projects in an organization. Their purpose is to standardize and simplify the creation of test plans and test schedules, gather best practices, and provide them to future projects.

4.1   Quality Policy and Test Policy

Usually, an organization producing (software) systems puts certain demands on the quality of its products. These demands are based on the desire to capture market share, win customers, and push sales—ideally, in order to increase profit. Often the quality demands that a company expects of itself are molded into a publicly available, documented quality policy.

The →quality policy expresses the particular importance that an organization attaches to "quality" and the demands it makes on the quality of its products, services, and processes. It forms the basis from which it derives its guidelines, specifications, and instructions for the implementation of these demands and the practices for the verification of quality actually achieved. Furthermore, the quality policy is expected to contain the organization's commitment to continuous improvement.

Quality policy

Consequently, the quality policy constitutes the basis for the work of the quality management (QM) staff or department and of all the quality assuring bodies within the company. It goes without saying that an organization's senior management must bear full responsibility for its corporate quality policy as it is the only authority that can ensure the policy's appropriateness to the organization's business objectives and its proper dissemination, comprehension, and compliance within the entire organization.

Senior management must also ensure that the policy is reviewed to confirm its continuing appropriateness [ISO 9001].

Excerpt from the quality policy of ARM [URL: ARM]

ARM Quality Policy:

Customer Focused

- Satisfy our customers' needs and expectations
- Make commitments we fully understand and believe we can meet
- Meet all commitments to customers on time
- Performance Driven
- Verify that our products and services meet agreed requirements
- Monitor, benchmark and continuously improve our business, products and services, organization and employees' performance

Achieve ARM's Mission and Goals

- Sustain and develop business growth and Intellectual Property

Consequently, the testing of software-based products or processes as a quality assurance method must likewise be performed based on the organization's quality policy. With regard to the test process, this corporate philosophy is called →test policy.

Contents of a test policy   The test policy comprises the following components:

- The definition of the term "test" in the organization: Which problems are supposed to be solved by testing? What relative importance is given to test in the overall development process? How is the process delimited against other quality assurance measures?
- A description of the test processes: Which phases and subtasks does the test process consist of? Which roles are involved, which entry and exit documents are associated with which subtasks, and which test levels need to be considered?
- Specifications for test evaluation: Which metrics are to be used to ensure test effectiveness in the project?
- The quality level to be achieved: Which quality criteria are to be tested and which quality level is the system required to achieve prior to its release with regard to these criteria?
- An approach to test process improvement: At what times and by which means is the quality of the test process to be evaluated and what are the techniques to recognize improvement potentials and derive improvement actions? Which objectives are being pursued?

Like the quality policy, the test policy is to have validity across the entire organization. It is typically drawn up and maintained by a central authority with test competence, such as the quality management staff, →test center, or IT department. It comprises requirements concerning testing of new systems as well as requirements concerning testing within the context of system maintenance. Moreover, in addition to being a corporate directive, the test policy has a second, equally important role:

Testing is a spot-check-oriented technique supposed to create confidence in the quality of the tested systems. Such confidence is increased if the basis and objectives of testing are known, documented, easy to understand, and consistent with corporate quality goals.

Since the test policy is often part of the quality policy, it may be difficult to maintain it as a separate entity, and keeping both together makes the relationship between the two easier to see. In practice, though, rather than keeping quality and test policy as one single document, they are often found under different names or spread over several other, "regulative" corporate documents such as the quality manual according to ISO 9001:2000, process definitions, procedures, and guidelines.

Quality and test policy as documents

The following excerpts from a genuine test policy lead us to ask what is it that makes a "good" test policy:

Excerpts from a test policy

- On the significance of testing: "Testing is performed in the organization to verify and validate developed systems. Test activities in the area of validation (testing the system's usability for the purpose it was designed for) are usability tests and alpha and beta tests. For verification, testable system requirements are defined whose correct implementation can be tested through system tests. Besides testing, the QM manual describes additional quality assurance activities used for validation and verification purposes."
- On the targeted quality level: "For each system requirement we define explicit acceptance criteria … The task of verification is to ensure that a released system satisfies each functional acceptance criterion fully and all nonfunctional acceptance criteria at least 95% with regard to efficiency (compare with the definition in ISO 9126)."
- On the approach to test process improvement: "Test processes are audited as part of our regular project and process audits under ISO 9000:2000 and the following pages to monitor test effectiveness and continuous process improvement. Identified improvement potentials are included in our regular improvement projects based on the TMM.

The long-term process improvement objective is to cut down on follow-up defect and quality assurance costs spent on software systems developed in the organization."

4.2   Bring the Test Policy to Life

The basic structure of the test policy as we have just discussed forms a skeleton to be fleshed out according to the organization's specific needs. Useful extensions are, for instance, a general statement of corporate attitude toward qualification and further training of testers and the latter's share in the responsibility for achieving the quality goals.

An essential aspect is the acceptance of the policy by those affected and the feasibility to put the principles defined in it into practice. Thus, a viable test policy is a critical factor for the success of testing. To ensure that this happens, the test policy must, in addition to those components mentioned above, meet the requirements outlined in the following paragraphs.

Relevance to Business Objectives

Features of a "good" test policy

Implementation of the test policy is largely a matter of motivation. If the requirements defined in the test policy are directly related to the organization's business objectives, it is much easier for those implementing the policy to fend off the inevitable arguments and discussions about cost and necessity.

Be Realistic

Unrealistic requirements or expectations may crop into a test policy if they are not defined by testers. The following is an example of a definition raising exaggerated expectations as to the importance of testing in an organization:

Avoid exaggerated expectations

"In our company, testing serves as proof that our products are free from defects at market launch."

First of all, testing is no method of proof, and second, testing is based on samples and can therefore never prove the absence of defects. But even technically justified requirements such as "the test must achieve 100% branch coverage" may turn out to be unrealistic in the organizational context and should not be used as a yardstick in the test policy.

Adequate Maturity

No matter how ambitious a test policy may be, it is bound to be ineffective and will fail if chances for its implementation in the organization are slim. A common cardinal error is an overprecise definition of the test processes—for instance, by defining phases and roles that cannot be enforced or efficiently organized. Many organizations introduce into their test policy a test process that relies on test automation as a means of cost reduction without taking into account that the test process is predominantly resting in the hands of testers who aren't technically trained.

Measurability

During the definition stage, when evaluation criteria are set up and the quality level is determined, the same care must be taken, as with the definition of any other metric, to define criteria (ideally with little effort) that can actually be measured.

The following serves as a negative example of the definition of a quality target: "At the time of its release to the market, a system must not contain any functional defects."

It is impossible to algorithmically calculate the number of defects in a system; they can at best be statistically estimated. A suitable, because it's measurable, definition of the targeted quality level would be as follows: "For a newly released system, no more than 100 high priority defects shall be found by customers." Based on this target, we can estimate how many defects must be found by system test or other test levels before the product can be released.

Liveliness

A test policy is not carved in stone but lives from "feedback" reflecting the success or failure of its implementation. A good test policy incorporates in its test process all necessary feedback mechanisms whose constant application ensures—for instance, in its approach to test process improvement—that the test policy is regularly reviewed and improved in a goal-oriented fashion.

4.3   Test Policy and Test Handbook

Test handbook: a concretization of the test policy

The test policy has corporate validity across all departments, projects, test levels, and test phases. As such, it needs to be kept at a relatively abstract level. However, in order to be able to support the implementation of the test policy in concrete cases, a further level of detail is useful: the test handbook.

The →test handbook takes up the demands set up in the quality policy and addresses those quality risks that may be, and should be, reduced through testing. When a test manager plans his tests in a new project, he can, ideally, draw upon the test handbook as a catalogue for the test activities to be performed.

The concrete realization of these activities is then documented in the project's test plan (see chapter 5).

Contents of a test handbook

First, the test handbook describes all possible test levels and outlines the test activities for each applicable test level. For each test level, the following aspects are considered:

- The entry criteria for the start of the test level (may be identical to the exit criteria of the previous test level; see below)
- The test procedure (e.g., top-down, bottom-up, priority driven)
- The test specification techniques used to derive the test cases, specifying the system's quality characteristics to be verified as described, for example, in [ISO 9126]
- Test completion criteria and their specifications (i.e., suitable metrics and threshold values)
- Exit conditions for process phases (for instance, process documentation to be created and criteria for its release)
- Degree of independence of the testing (i.e., whether testing is performed by developers or an independent team)
- Standards to be complied with; can be standards pertaining to the area of software testing itself or and more general standards (see chapter 13)
- The environment in which software tests are performed; descriptions of reference hardware and software as well as setup procedures in preparation for the tests
- The approach toward test automation (e.g., suitable tools and automation methods and decision criteria regarding test automation, such as feasibility and benefit)
- The approach to reusability of testware at successive test levels

- The approach to retesting and regression test planning (criteria, scope, selection of tests, etc.)
- The detailed definition of the test process (outlined in the test policy, including documents and test results such as, for example, test reports)
- The measures and metrics to be recorded
- The approach for incident management (incident status model, involved roles, incident report format, tools to be used)

The art of preparing a test handbook is in keeping it concrete enough to be of benefit to the user (for instance, by making it easier for him to structure tasks or make decisions) and at the same time not letting it become project specific.

Balance between reusability and concreteness

A pragmatic approach would be to generalize from a test plan that has already proved its worth in a project and make it available to other projects in a first version. Applying the handbook in other projects will then quickly reveal content matter that cannot be applied generally so that it can be deleted.

Another possibility to succeed in this balancing act is to draw up several test handbooks with decreasing scope of application and increasing degree of detail.

For instance, it is possible to write a generic corporate test handbook and then tailor it into further test handbooks for different product ranges with greatly differing requirements regarding test intensity. The motivation factor for this kind of split could be differences in the criticality of the systems developed in the different units.

Like the test policy, a test handbook must regularly be aligned with the evolving test plans and adapted to changing circumstances.

Updating the test handbook

One well-proven approach is to plan regular project audits at the end of test projects during which the effectiveness and implementability of test policy and test handbook in the test plan are systematically evaluated. If necessary, improvement actions are initiated. It is best to define this feedback loop as a fixed component in the test policy and to integrate it in the test handbook as part of the process improvement program.

4.4 Summary

▨ To establish software testing in a company strategically, test policy and test handbook can be used to regulate common aspects of the software testing process.

▨ The strategic approach to testing begins with the definition of an implementable test policy. It is a component of the general corporate quality policy.

▨ The test handbook is derived from the test policy, which contains the generic test requirements of an organization. It addresses the risks, shows the relationship between testing and risk reduction, and describes a process that addresses these risks in compliance with the test policy.

▨ The test handbook serves as a starting point for each test plan and consequently for the implementation of all test activities. It contains descriptions of all applicable test levels.

▨ A mature test handbook also incorporates the approach toward test process improvement in the organization.

▨ The test policy and test handbook are translated into practice by the users, i.e., all those involved in testing. Both documents therefore require feedback and regularly derived improvements. With time, they evolve into valuable means of interproject knowledge transfer.

▨ The test handbook does not necessarily exist as a single document but may be integrated in the QM system and process documentation, or it may be distributed over several documents like a corporate test handbook and some additional test handbooks for specific product ranges.

▨ The latter makes sense if different application areas in the organization require very different test regulations, such as, for instance in sections of the organization that develop safety critical applications.

5 The Test Plan

This chapter describes the relationship between the strategic concepts of the quality and test policies and their concrete implementation in test planning.

A core element of test planning is creating a set of test plan[1] documents. This chapter provides a detailed account of the typical contents of these planning documents and the activities that lead to them.

5.1 General Test Plan Structure

5.1.1 From Strategy to Implementation

Chapter 4 described the relationship between a quality policy, test policy, and test handbook. Whereas quality and test policy can be considered strategic corporate guidelines, a test handbook ideally represents a collection of "best practices," supporting and facilitating the implementation of strategic guidelines in concrete applications.

In most cases, these applications—that is, the planning and execution of concrete test activities—take place within a software or system development project. Test activities performed in the development project are subsumed under the term test project.

According to [PMBOK 04], "a project is a temporary endeavor undertaken to create a unique product, service, or result."

Central features of a project are its plannability and controllability of activities.

---

1. According to [URL:ISTQB], *test plan* is a synonym for *test concept.*

Test plan: planning basis
for the test project

In the test project, planning of activities that are geared toward achieving the test objectives is done in the test plan, whose function, among others, is as follows:

- To describe, in brief, all activities of the test project, determining project costs and test execution times and putting them in relation to the project results to be tested, thus forming the basis upon which budget and resources can be approved
- To identify project results (e.g., documents) to be created
- To identify conditions and services to be provided by persons or departments external to the test team

In chapter 2, we explained that the test project is composed of several phases; in a project, these phases are usually repeated in test cycles performed at the various development levels of the test object.

- The test plan must also identify test cycles and major test cycle content, assign activities to the cycles, and align them with the software release plan.

The test plan is the central planning basis of the test project, translating corporate quality goals, test policy principles, and generic test handbook measures into project reality.

The project plan of a development project usually refers to the test plan in its section on test activity planning.

Figure 5-1 illustrates the relationship between the basic components from which test project activities are derived and shows their different life cycles. The figure lists the individual items according to their strategic importance and in the sequence of their "average life expectancy":

- Usually, quality and test policy are changed rarely and are only adapted to incorporate changing corporate goals and long-term project experience.
- Test manuals, whose validity generally encompasses all projects, are also revised at regular intervals, incorporating experiences gained in test projects.
- The test plan is created at the beginning of the test project as the central planning document and is valid throughout the entire project life cycle. However, some of its planning directives are of a dynamic nature and must be revised and adjusted to reality several times during the test project's lifetime (details are discussed in chapter 6). These are as follows:

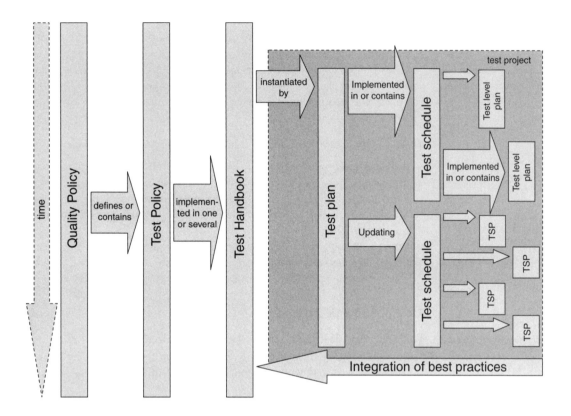

■ The test schedule, linking all executable test activities in the project to concrete resources and dates. Changes in the availability of resources, but also changes in planning requirements (e.g., delivery dates of test objects), regularly lead to changes in the test schedule. In larger test projects with several comprehensive test levels, the test schedule will often be divided further into test level plans.

■ Test level plans[2] break down the test schedule to the test procedures for each of the planned test levels such as component or system test. They are revised at each test cycle or even more frequently and may even be created anew or derived from the overall test schedule.

Figure 5–1

From quality policy to test level plan

_____

2. According to [URL:ISTQB], *test level plan* is a synonym for *test step plan*.

*Monolithic document or
granular document structure*

As you saw in chapter 4, the quality policy, test policy, and test handbook need not necessarily be separated into three documents.

The hierarchical contents of the (project-wide) test plan, the test schedule, and the test level plans can be contained in one document or may be split in several ones. The recommended contents of a test plan should then be covered by the whole set of documents.

There are good reasons to split the contents into several documents:

- If divided as proposed, strategic, or rather static, content is separated from parts that become more and more dynamic and that may need to be revised several times during the test project, making repeated changes and releases a lot easier.
- The single documents can be distributed separately to stakeholders of different parts of the contents.
- Whereas strategic components are usually written down in a text document, a test management tool is best used to manage the dynamic content.

5.1.2   Strategic Parts of the Test Plan

*A test handbook simplifies the
creation of the test plan.*

The test plan describes how testing is organized and performed in a project. At best, we have a mature test handbook filled with easily applied specifications, in which case the test plan can in many parts simply refer to the test handbook and only document and explain necessary deviations. Here are some examples of test plan components (see also section 4.3):

- Test entry/exit and completion criteria for the respective test levels
- Applicable test specification techniques
- Standards and document templates to be complied with
- Test automation approach
- Measurements and metrics
- Incident management

*The test plan adds project
specifics to the test handbook.*

In addition, the test plan describes the project-specific organizational constraints within which testing may operate.

Although general specifications provided in the test handbook may be used to describe these constraints, every project needs to document facts above and beyond those stated in the test handbook.

These include the following:

- Project-related test objectives
- Planned resources (time, staffing, test environment, tester work places, test tools, and so on)
- Estimated test costs
- "Deliverables" to be created, such as test case specification, test reports, and so on
- Requirements for test execution, such as necessary provisions
- Contact persons internal and external to the test team with required communication interfaces
- identification of components making up the test basis, test objects, and interfaces for testing

The test plan documents the test objectives and appropriate test strategy. Test objectives and test strategy are used to derive the mandatory and the optional test topics, building an initial test design specification. They are, initially, listed by key words and roughly prioritized, resulting in a first draft that will be further elaborated into test case specifications during the course of the project.

The test plan provides the skeleton for the test specification.

All test plan components listed here are of a "static" nature in the sense that they are defined at the beginning of the test project with usually little or no changes at all later on. This does not apply to the components covered in the following sections.

5.1.3   The Test Schedule

Keeping the test strategy in mind during testing, concrete technical resources, responsible staff and target dates must be assigned to test cases listed in the test case catalog. The test manager determines who is to specify, implement, and, if necessary, automate test cases and at what times. The definition and execution of test cases are thus brought into a chronological order, and the initial (created by the ideal assumption of having unlimited resources available) test specification and prioritization is brought into line with available resources. Adding these time and resource specifications, the initial test design specification will eventually grow into the test schedule that needs to be maintained at regular intervals.

The test schedule maps the general planning to concrete dates and resources.

A test schedule may, for example, be structured as follows:

Time and resource planning
in the test schedule

1. Organizational Planning
   - Scheduling of start and end dates of test cycles depending on delivery dates for the builds of the test objects
   - Resource planning consisting of
     - task assignment to the test team
     - layout for the test infrastructure (hard- and software, testware)
   - Scheduling for acceptance testing[3] and release testing during transition to subsequent test levels, for the execution of all high-priority tests and any anticipated retests, and so on.

Planning test schedule content

2. Content Planning
   - Scoping of test cycle content depending on the anticipated functionality of each of the test objects. Generally, the aim is a mixture of initial, new functionality testing, retesting of areas containing defects from previous cycles, and regression testing of all other areas.
   - Step-by-step refinement of the assigned scope per test cycle to build up a list of all planned tests, starting with the test objectives specified in the test plan. In longer, cyclic test projects, this refinement process will not be restricted to test execution but extend to simultaneous specification and, where applicable, test automation for test cases to be executed in subsequent test cycles.
   - Effort estimation for each planned cycle as a basis for scheduling. Distribution of effort to specification, automation, and execution depends on the functional scope of the test objects, on test strategy and test objectives, and on resources available for each respective test cycle.
   - Planning of an efficient test sequence to minimize redundant actions; for instance, through executing test cases that create data objects before executing those that manipulate or delete them. This way some test cases are a precondition for subsequent ones.
   - Additional test cases, defined ad hoc or by explorative testing if resources are available.

---

3. This refers to tests of a test level that were defined as an entry criterion for delivery of the test objects from development or a previous test level, but not customer acceptance tests.

- Resource assignment to specific test topics:
    - Test personnel with application or test task specific know-how, such as, for instance, for explorative or ad-hoc tests, load tests, and so on.
    - Definition of the specific test infrastructure for the selected test tasks (e.g., load generators, usability lab infrastructure ...).
    - Provision of test data (-bases)

Chapter 6 describes all the tasks involved in test scheduling, maintenance, and control.

5.1.4   The Level Test Plan

The test plan defines the test procedure for an entire test project, passing through several test levels such as component testing, integration testing, and system test. In large or complex test projects in which different teams may be in charge of different test levels, it may make sense to set up different test plans for different test levels. One test level plan details the planning for a particular test level and represents the application and substantiation of the test plan specifications for that level. It covers the same topics, but it's constrained to a particular test level. When using a test management tool, such test level plans may not exist at all in document form but only in the form of planning data.

From test plan to level test plan

5.1.5   IEEE 829 – Standard for Test Documentation

The [IEEE 829] standard defines the structure and content of some of the standard documents required in testing; among others for the test plan. Using the standard as the basis for the creation of a test plan guarantees coverage of all relevant aspects of test planning for the project.

Standard for test plan structure and content

Besides the test plan definition, IEEE 829 also provides templates for three levels of test specifications, test item transmittal reports, test logs, test incident reports, and test summary reports. A project's test plan defines which of those documents are to be created by whom and whether or not to use the IEEE 829 or other templates.

The new IEEE 829 (2005) draft currently out for ballot provides appreciably improved specifications for the planning of complex test projects in the form of "master" and "level" documents outlining, for instance, the structures of a "master test plan" and a "test level plan".[4]

According to the standard, the structure of the test plan comprises the items listed in the following table (the table also states where the required items are discussed in more detail in this chapter). If you compare this list with what was said about static and dynamic test plan components, you'll see that IEEE 829 covers both. The relevant sections for dynamic content are sections 10 (testing tasks) and 14 (schedule).

Chapter according to IEEE 829	Refer to section
Test plan identifier	5.2.1
Introduction	5.2.2
Test items	5.2.3
Features to be tested	5.2.4
Features not to be tested	5.2.5
Approach	5.2.6
Item pass/fail criteria	5.2.7
Suspension criteria and resumption requirements	5.2.8
Test deliverables	5.2.9
Testing tasks	5.2.10
Environmental needs	5.2.11
Responsibilities	5.2.12
Staffing and training needs	5.2.13
Schedule	5.2.14
Risks and contingencies	5.2.15
Approvals	5.2.16

5.2   Test Plan Contents

The following section addresses the content of the test plan in more detail; sequence and subchapter names correspond to the structure of the IEEE 829 standard. In this book, we concentrate on those aspects that, according

---

4.   For test strategy planning in more complex projects, [IEEE 1012] offers an alternative structure for a "verification and validation plan".

to the ISTQB Advanced Level Syllabus, need to be described in detail and that were not exhaustively treated in [Spillner 07].

5.2.1   Test Plan Identifier

The name, or identifier, of the test plan ensures that the document can be clearly and uniquely referenced in all other project documents. Depending on the organization's general document naming conventions, a number of different name components can be defined by means of which storage and retrieval of the test plan is managed. Minimum requirements are the name of the test plan, its version, and its status.

The identifier ensures that the test plan can be uniquely referenced.

5.2.2   Introduction

The purpose of the introduction is to familiarize potential test plan readers with the project and to provide guidance as to where information relevant to their particular role can be found.

The purpose of the introduction is to get the reader acquainted with his role in the test plan.

Typical readers of the test plan (besides the test team itself) are the project manager, developers, and even the end customer.

All external information sources necessary for the understanding of the test plan must also be listed, such as, for instance, the following:

- Project documents (project plan, quality management plan, configuration management plan, etc.)
- Standards (see chapter 13)
- Underlying quality policy, test policy, and test handbook
- Customer documents

Ensure that relevant versions of these sources are referenced. In addition, the introduction is intended to provide an overview of the test objects and test objectives.

5.2.3   Test Items

This section provides a detailed description of the test basis and of the objects under test:

Identifying the test objects

- Documents that form the basis for testing and which is input information for test analysis and design. Among them are requirements and design specifications for the test objects but also all system manuals.

■ Components that constitute the test object itself; that is, all components that need to be present for the associated tests to be executed. This includes providing reference to the versions of the test objects.

■ This section also deals with the way in which test objects are passed from development to the test department—is it, for instance, delivered via download, CD/DVD, or any other medium?

Particular system components that are not test objects but are required for testing are also mentioned here. Some system components, for example, are supplied by subcontractors and are already tested, so they do not need to be tested again by the project.

5.2.4   Features to Be Tested

Identifying the test objectives

During the development of a system, project objectives contain objectives for the implementation of the project, such as the intended release date and overall budget, but also, and in particular, the targets for the quality level; i.e., the nature and implementation of the system's quality attributes.

With respect to the quality attributes, the test plan constitutes a kind of contract between project management and test management. The test plan determines which of the quality attributes are to be verified in which way during testing; in other words, it defines what the test objectives of the project are.

In order to achieve a traceable and consistent attribution of quality attributes to test objectives and test techniques required for their verification across all test levels, it is best to use a well-defined quality model, such as [ISO 9126], shown in figure 5-2.

This standard divides the features of software systems into 6 main quality attributes and 21 subattributes (see also [Spillner 07, section 2.1.3]).

This model allows you to describe the (functional as well as nonfunctional) software features well and particularly supports the description of suitable verification techniques and the quantification of acceptance criteria (see also section 5.3).

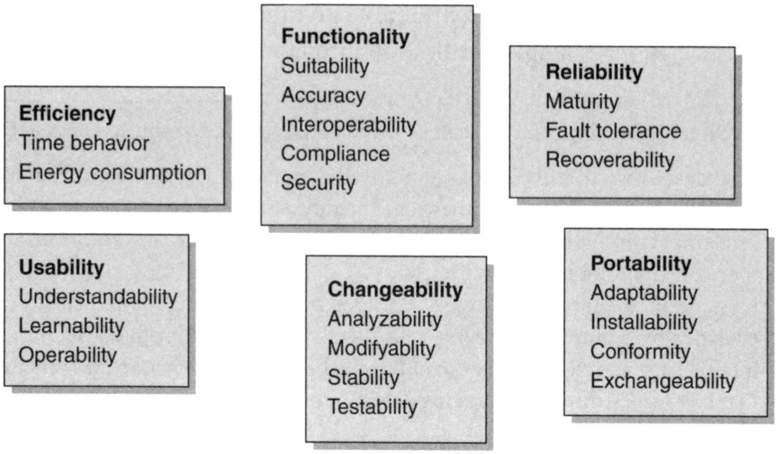

Figure 5–2
ISO 9126 software quality attributes

For instance, the VSR test plan contains the following statements relating to the *DreamCar* subsystem

Example:
Test goals
of the VSR test plan

- The quality attribute "functionality" will be tested extensively at the different test levels using all the available test methods. It represents the focus of test activities since accuracy of the calculated vehicle price is the most important feature. The test objective is to test as many functional use cases as possible with all the available data on vehicles, special editions, and car accessories.
- Since *DreamCar* is supposed to be used by car dealers and prospective buyers alike without any previous experience, special attention is given to the quality attribute "usability." This quality attribute will be addressed later in the context of system testing,[5] where a usability test is to be carried out by at least five car dealer representatives and five arbitrarily chosen people.

5.2.5 Features Not to Be Tested

This section describes which project objectives are not a constituent part of the test plan, i.e., which quality attributes are not subject to testing. In particular, stating explicitly which objectives will not be pursued and providing reasons why particular quality attributes and/or system components will not be tested are important parts because they provide for a clear

Identification of the non-objectives of test projects

---

5. Since an operational prototype has already been developed, later users are already familiar with the user interface. Otherwise, an initial usability test at system test level would be very risky because the results of the test may cause considerable system changes.

division of responsibilities between test and other forms of quality assurance, such as, for example, verification through reviews.

Example:
Non-objectives for VSR
DreamCar testing

The VSR test plan, for example, states the following for the *DreamCar* subsystem:

- Changeability and portability are non-testable quality attributes but must be verified through reviews or other static quality assurance measures.
- Implementation efficiency does not play an essential role in *DreamCar* and therefore does not need to be tested.
- In addition, the test plan states that the database containing the vehicle data is provided by a subcontractor that sells them as a standard product. Because of mutual trust and the distribution of the database in the market, we may assume that it is sufficiently tested and the defects are minimized.

 Hint

It helps readability if besides non-tested quality attributes, "not-to-be-tested" system components are listed or referenced too (see section 5.2.3). This way, everything not covered by the test plan is listed in one section.

5.2.6   Approach

The test strategy is the "heart" of the test plan, and its elaboration is closely connected with topics such as the estimation of the test effort attributable to the strategy, organization, and coordination of the different test levels. This is why a major section in this chapter is devoted to this topic (see section 5.3).

5.2.7   Item Pass/Fail Criteria

Test exit criteria and metrics
belong together.

There must be clear rules for each test level and for the entire test project as to when a test object will be tested and when respective test activities may be stopped.

This question is, in principle, closely connected with the definition and application of suitable metrics. Chapter 11 lists corresponding metrics and chapter 6 explains their application in test control and reporting. On the other hand, the definition of entry and exit criteria also depends on the organization of the test levels. Section 5.5 provides further information on this issue and lists examples for entry and exit criteria.

Like the test strategy, test completion and acceptance criteria should be oriented toward the project and product risk of the system under test, not only with regard to the stringency of the criteria to be applied (i.e., the necessary accuracy of the metrics) but also with regard to the definition of release criteria based on these metrics (that is, the measurement values that need to be reached for test completion or acceptance).

Often it is useful to distinguish between test exit criteria and acceptance criteria. Test exit criteria are applied in each test cycle to determine the end of a test cycle. Generally speaking, they solely relate to test progress and not to test results. In contrast, acceptance criteria are used to determine the ability to deliver the test objects to the next test level or the customer.

(Hint)

There may be a considerably wider spectrum of acceptance criteria—for instance, test results, the availability of release documents, official release signatures, etc.

5.2.8   Suspension Criteria and Resumption Requirements

If a test object is not ready to complete a test level (i.e., to meet the test exit criteria), there is the risk of wasteful testing on that test level while executing the test level plan. In that situation, it makes much more sense to return the test object for repair to development and earlier test levels.

One partial solution for this problem is the definition and application of suspension criteria; another lies in defining entry criteria used for each test level (their application will prevent such a situation or at least reduce its probability).

Test suspension criteria and test entry criteria compliment each other.

Such entry criteria can also be used as resumption criteria for resuming an interrupted test level. Again, section 5.5 will provide more detailed information.

5.2.9   Test Deliverables

The test plan must state the following very clearly:

- Which documents are to be created in the project?
- What the formal standards and content-related specifications (release criteria) are for these documents?

As mentioned in section 5.1.5, IEEE 829 provides a good baseline for necessary or urgently required documents in the test project; others, such as test automations, may be project-specific additions. Auxiliary testing tools and test automation must be treated as documents, too; if applicable, this also applies to test reference databases.

Test documents under configuration management

Like any other software development document, test documents must be subject to projectwide or locally maintained configuration and version management.

In smaller test projects, the author himself will be mostly responsible for this (likewise for the their distribution to the recipients as defined in the test plan). Larger projects sometimes have their own testware configuration manager who is also usually responsible for versioning the deliveries of test objects within the test environment and for assigning them to testware versions (concerning responsibilities, please refer to section 5.2.12).

5.2.10   Testing Tasks

Describing test tasks is a dynamic component of the test plan.

In this part of the test plan, test strategy guidelines are broken down into individual activities necessary for test preparation and execution. Responsibilities for these activities, together with their interdependencies and external influences and resources, must also be considered.

It is important not only to list these activities but also to track their individual processing status as well as actual and planned dates. For this reason, we strongly recommend keeping this component of the test plan separate, either in form of a separate test schedule or as several test level plans (see sections 5.1.3 and 5.1.4).

Best would be to have a dedicated test management database. Maintenance, monitoring, and reporting will be described in chapter 6 within the context of the test schedule.

5.2.11   Environmental Needs

Test platform = basic software, hardware, and other prerequisites

We must describe the environmental needs of the project:

- The requirements exist with regard to the test platform (for instance, hardware, operating system and other basic software)
- Other prerequisites necessary for testing (for instance, reference databases or configuration data)

Test interfaces and tools

In addition, the following topics need to be addressed:

- What are the points of control (i.e., which interfaces are used to actuate the test objects), and what are the points of observation (i.e., through which interfaces are the actual responses of the test objects checked)?

▦ What accompanying software and hardware is necessary? Examples are monitoring and protocol environments, simulators, debuggers, and signal generators.

▦ Which approaches to test automation are possible and, if required, should be used in this environment?

Depending on the test level, answers to these questions will turn out quite differently for the same test object. For instance, the software of an embedded system may perhaps be tested in a host development environment during component testing, using a typical component testing environment like CPPUnit [URL: CPPUnit] or Tessy [URL: Tessy]. During system testing, however, hardware in the loop (HiL) environments may be used. For one, the definition of the test environments is influenced by what is technically feasible, while for the other, it is influenced by the test tasks and resulting test techniques. In the end it is also affected by the available and budgetable hardware and software and by the proficiency of the testers.

In addition to the test team, further resources are necessary for test development and execution. Typical resources are test computers and test networks and components as well as special hardware such as hardware debuggers and protocol monitors, but you may also need licenses for test software such as test management or test automation tools.

Resource management of test environment components

Depending on the number of (parallel) users and use scenarios, their management requires different degrees of coordination effort.

Resource management is advisable—be it by means of a simple spreadsheet, resource usage database, or project management tool. Strategies on how to deal with lacking resources must then also be part of risk management (section 5.2.15 and chapter 9).

In addition to resource coordination, the management of software components of the test environment requires integration into test version and test configuration management. Only too often the operability of test environments depends on a precise combination of specific versions of the operating system, test automation tool, analysis tools, and test object versions. For example, testing of software involving medical technology, the aerospace industry, and railroad engineering requires strict accountability concerning the storage of all test environment components for 10 or more years (see section 13.4). This, too, needs to be stated in the test plan.

Part of the test environment must be put under configuration management.

One of the factors in gaining efficiency in testing is efficient test platform management. Using imaging software and an image management environment [URL: Imaging] can help to significantly reduce setup times for test runs in that it allows fast installation of "images" for test hardware across projects with common and often required combinations of operating system, test software, and other platform components (e.g., Office package). In combination with virtualization solutions such as VMWare and Plex86 [URL: Virtualization],

these standard images can be run in virtual hardware and are thus largely independent of short-lived hardware development in the PC sector. In addition, the technology can also be used to make snapshots of the computer states prior to longer test runs, providing points for fallback in case of failing test runs.

5.2.12   Responsibilities

The general responsibilities are test management, test specification, test preparation, test execution, and follow-up.

Further responsibilities concern internal test project quality assurance, configuration management, and the provision and maintenance of the test environment.

The organizational integration of test personnel into the overall project, the distribution of authority within the test team, and, where required, the division/organization of the test teams into different test groups and/or test levels must be defined here.

Responsibilities also comprise document management.

Most of these responsibilities are related to the creation of documents (see section 5.2.9). If responsibilities are only defined at the level of "persons X, Y, and Z are assigned the role of R", it is not sufficient to ensure on-time creation and adequate document quality. Additionally, for each of the documents we must explicitly answer the following questions:

- Who is the responsible author and who participates in which role in the creation of the document?
- How, when, and by whom will the document be released?
- How, when, and by whom will it be distributed after release?

This document plan may either be created in section 5.2.9 or 5.2.12.

5.2.13   Staffing and Training Needs

For each role or responsibility, we must state the resource requirements in terms of staffing in order to be able to implement the test plan; furthermore, it needs to be specified how the role and project-specific training and instruction is to be carried out.

In mature test processes, roles and necessary qualifications are already defined in the test handbook.[6] Based on the list of necessary resources, the test plan simply refers to the predefined role descriptions. The use of a standardized training scheme like that of the "ISTQB Certified Tester" facilitates the creation of this chapter by offering a reference ensuring the qualifications necessary for a particular activity in the test process through standardized training content. At the same time, responsibilities for the standard documents mentioned above can be assigned to these roles. Section 10.2 provides more details on role qualifications.

Using standardized training schemes facilitates specification of the necessary.

In addition to these test-specific qualifications, involved staff frequently need additional, comprehensive, domain-specific qualifications to create good test specifications, to be able to judge system behavior during test execution, and to look beyond their own test specification to recognize, describe, and adequately prioritize anomalies. Other desirable "soft skills" are listed and explained in chapter 10.

5.2.14   Schedule

To begin with, a draft schedule is drawn up of test activities at the milestone level. Because of the inevitable dynamics of scheduling, however, the draft schedule only serves as a starting point for subsequent detailed planning of all activities, which again needs to be updated regularly.

The milestones comprise planned document release dates, due dates for (partial) releases of the test objects, and their delivery dates from development to test.

Based on these milestones, the detailed test schedule is derived; in large projects, this may involve creating several test level plans. This plan or these plans must find their way into the project manager's project plan. Regular coordination between project and test manager must be ensured.

The test schedule (goal) is derived from the milestone plan (implementation).

---

6.   Typically, the definition of and compliance with a standard skill profile is a feature of the SPICE Level 3-compliant test process.

The test manager must be informed about development release delays and react to them in his detailed test planning. The project manager must react on test results and, as the case may be, may even have to postpone milestones because additional correction cycles need to be planned. Chapter 6 describes the interaction between development and test and also explains the test manager's task when controlling and adapting the plan.

5.2.15 Risks and Contingencies

Product risk is a matter for test strategy. Test project risk management is the subject of this chapter in the test plan.

One of the test objectives is to minimize product risk. This is done by selecting a suitable test strategy. A test plan must also address project risks; i.e., all factors that might jeopardize the planned achievement of the test objectives in the test project must be identified, analyzed, and if possible, avoided. The test manager must—not only in this respect—think and act like a project manager. Chapter 9 provides more details on this subject.

The hurdle is high for the introduction of full, formal risk management. One easy way into this topic is to simply list known risks in the test status report, thus making involved staff aware of risks without necessarily having to introduce methods for risk evaluation and risk treatment at that point.

5.2.16 Approvals

List all the names and roles of everyone that needs to sign the test plan as proof of notice. Depending on the signer's role, this has the following consequences:

- Usually the project manager's signature releases the budget necessary for the implementation of the concept—unfortunately, in practice, it too often only shows that notice has been taken of the test manger's statement that the available budget is not sufficient to carry out the measures necessary for achieving the quality goals with all the ensuing risks.
- The development leader's signature confirms that the described tests are adequate and, if applicable, that he agrees to the involvement of the development team and the provision of necessary resources.

▨ The end customer's signature confirms acceptance of the proposed quality assurance measures for his product; it may also mean that the planned acceptance tests are cleared for release.

▨ Last but not least, the test team needs to sign the test plan, thus communicating its "commitment" to joint activities.

5.3 Defining a Test Strategy

The test strategy defines the techniques to be employed for testing test objects, the method of distribution of available resources to components and quality attributes under test, and the sequence of activities that need to be performed.

Depending on the feature, testing of the quality attributes required by the system asks for completely different procedures and test techniques to be applied at the different test levels. Within the context of ISO 9126, testing is a process by which the degree of fulfillment of the quality attributes is to be measured.

Strategy for the selection of suitable test techniques

According to ISO 9126, it is generally not possible to measure quality attributes directly. The standard, however, provides an abstract definition for this evaluation process (see figure 5-3):

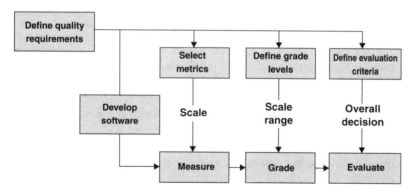

Figure 5–3

ISO 9126 software evaluation process

In this process, testing can be considered a sequence of the following activities:

▨ Select metrics (i.e., define suitable test techniques)
▨ Define classification levels (i.e., define acceptance criteria)
▨ Measure (i.e., execute test cases)
▨ Categorize (i.e., compare actual behavior with the acceptance criteria)

The test strategy correlates each feature to be tested with methods for adequate feature testing and the classification level required for feature acceptance.

In a mature test organization, this task can be done at test handbook level, which then contains information about the general test design strategy and correlates the general quality attributes and test techniques available in the organization with each other.

Examples
for test techniques

The following two examples illustrate how these attributes, methods, and classification levels correlate.

1 "Accurateness"
The functional quality attribute "accurateness" is defined as "attributes of software that bear on the provision of right or agreed results or effects" (e.g., required accurateness of calculated values).

A suitable test technique at the level of system testing is use case testing [Spillner 07, section 5.1.5] with the additional application of equivalence class partitioning and boundary value analysis [Spillner 07, sections 5.1.1 and 5.1.2].

One example of a suitable metric for determining the classification levels is the deviation between calculated and expected value of an output parameter.

Possible classification levels for acceptance are as follows:

- 0 .. 0.0001: acceptable
- > 0.0001:   not acceptable

2 "Operability"
The nonfunctional quality attribute "operability" is defined as "attributes of software that bear on the user's effort for operation and flow control".

A suitable test technique for this attribute is an operability test covering the major use cases of the system. A useful metric is the measurement of the average time spent on each of these use cases for different classes of users (e.g., beginners, advanced users).

It makes sense to define specific classification levels for each of the use cases. For the use case "create new model in the *DreamCar* configuration", we could, for instance, define these classification levels:

- <1 minute: excellently suitable
- 1–2 minutes: acceptable
- 2–3 minutes: conditionally acceptable
- >3 minutes: not acceptable

Strategy for the distribution of
test effort and intensity

Many test techniques are principally scalable; i.e., with more effort one can achieve a higher test coverage. Normally, this scalability ought to be used when spreading available resources across the test activities as not all possible test tasks can be processed with the same intensity.

The test manager bases his considerations on the following aspects:

■ Information on product risk. Chapter 9 exemplifies the necessary basic mechanisms of risk identification, analysis, evaluation, and treatment. Most important in this context is the requirement that the test should minimize product risk[7] as quickly as possible and with the least possible effort, as illustrated in figure 5-4.

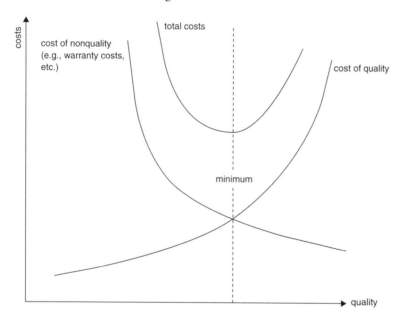

Figure 5–4

Quality costs and risk, according to [Juran 88]

Testing improves the overall quality of products. With increasing quality, however, cost increases disproportionately. On the other hand, the very high product risk before start of testing is successively reduced by the reduction of the expected costs of nonquality. Economically speaking, the best possible time to stop testing is the point where both curves intersect—here the minimum of the sum of cost of quality and nonquality is reached. In order to make risk reduction effective as early as possible, planned quality assurance measures must be performed in the sequence of the product risks addressed by them.

Find the balance between test and failure cost.

---

7. Probability of a malfunction of the products weighted by the damage caused by the malfunction.

To get to this minimum quantitatively and methodically is a very complex task; the section on "precision testing" in chapter 9 provides some approaches.

▪ Consideration of project risks. Injection of defects in a system is influenced by a number of risk factors inherent in the development project. Among such influencing factors are communication problems in distributed teams, different process maturities of involved development departments, high time pressure, and the use of new but not yet properly mastered development techniques. As with product risk, the test manager must try to quantify his knowledge about these factors to be able to use them as a basis for determining the test intensity or test effort for the different test tasks.

Effort distribution, taking risk into account

The test manager must now take all the information on product and project risk into account for his effort distribution. This is best done by using unique algorithmic mapping of all known influencing factors on a particular system feature's product and project risk and calculating one single measurable value for the test effort allocated for testing this feature. Such calculation techniques are, for instance, described in [Gutjahr 95] and [Schaefer 96] (for both, see also chapter 9). The second technique, in particular, is very practical and easy to use. The test manager may, of course, define calculation methods that are perhaps simpler and better suited to his particular project situation.

A general formula for such a figure is expressed as

$$TE(F_x) = f(RProduct_{Fx}, R_1Project_{Fx}, \ldots, R_nProject_{Fx})$$

whereby:

F_x = feature x of the system under test
TE = measured value for the test effort to be allocated
f = mapping between risks and test effort
$RProduct_{Fx}$ = product risk of feature x
$R_yProject_{Fx}$ = different project risks during implementation of feature x

Following are some basic rules for such a mapping:

Basic rules for a pragmatic consideration of risks

▪ In most cases, there are too many influencing factors to consider them all with justifiable effort; some of these factors can easily be quantified, whereas with others, it may not be possible at all with the available knowledge. The basic rule is as follows: It is better to begin with a few, easily assessable factors. In our experience, they cover approximately 80% of all the influencing factors (the Pareto principle[8] applies here, too).

■ In most cases, neither product nor project risk are completely quantifiable. Instead, it is sufficient to work with classifications (e.g., 1 = "little risk", 2 = "medium risk", 3 = "high risk"). The classification should not be too subtle (better to work with three instead of eight risk classes).

■ Avoid using overcomplex algorithms for calculation of risks; in most cases, simple multiplication and addition are sufficient. To improve algorithms, nonlinear weighting may be applied for classification (i.e., 1 = "little risk", 3 = "medium risk", and 10 = "high risk"). Such emphasis on high risks leads to a good differentiation between measured effort values.

■ For practical use of the calculated effort values, a simple mapping between measured value and scaling of test methods must be defined. Assuming the measured effort values to be between 0 and 1,000 (depending on function f), we can give the following example:

- $0 < TE(Fx) < 100$:   no test
- $100 \leq TE(Fx) < 300$:   "smoke test"
- $300 \leq TE(Fx) < 700$:   normal test, e.g., application of equivalence class partitioning
- $700 \leq TE(Fx)$:   intensive testing, application of several test techniques in parallel

Besides determining the test effort, the test strategy must also define the sequence of the test activities and the most suitable dates to start them. From a technical perspective, it makes sense, in principle, to start those test activities first that bring about the highest risk reduction. In most cases, however, additional technical dependencies exist that also impact the planning of the sequence. Last but not least, the sequence of the feature releases by development, too, form an important basis for planning. This basis, however, is of a dynamic nature so that sequence planning is best kept as a separate document or, ideally, integrated into a test management tool (see sections 5.1.3 and 5.1.4).

Strategy for determining sequence and time of the activities

A test strategy that is entirely structured according to formal criteria reduces the probability of finding defects hidden in the "blind spot" of

Including heuristics, creativity, and chancel

---

8.   General observation that in many situations it is possible to achieve 80% of one's objectives with 20% of the total effort.

requirement and risk analysis, i.e., in the area of implicit requirements. At the latest, when the system is put into operation, it is left to the unlimited "creativity" of the end user. Often a massive increase of the failure rate can then be observed. Intuitive and stochastic test case specification should therefore be given enough room within the context of the overall test planning. Well-defined methods exist, which is to say that creative or random-based testing need not mean that the approach is unstructured or chaotic! [Spillner 07] describes these techniques in section 5.3; they are well suited to anticipating end user profiles in a systematic test environment.

This increases the defect detection percentage of those defects that are most visible in the end user environment—a rather effective measure to enhance customer satisfaction. Besides involving creativity and chance, heuristics also play an important role in a good test strategy.

[Spillner 07] mentions and explains several heuristic planning approaches in section 6.4.2; they are therefore not repeated here.

Reusability of test strategies   The development of a suitable test strategy is an elaborate and complex process that, as already mentioned, requires iterative alignment of test objectives, effort, and organizational structures.

It is all the more important that a strategy thus developed is well documented and that it is, stripped of all project-specific data, integrated for reuse into the test handbook of the organization(-al unit). Candidates for such a reusability strategy are, at least, these:

- The definition of test techniques and their assignment to quality attributes
- The methods for the calculation of the test intensity based on risk factors.

5.4 Test Effort Estimation

In most cases, estimating the expected test effort represents an approximate evaluation based on experience values—either one's own or of that of other people or institutions. Depending on the underlying information base and the required precision and granularity of the estimation, different estimation techniques are used. This section considers the following:

- Flat models or analogy estimations
- Detailed models based on test activities
- Formula-based models based on the functional volume to be tested

5.4.1   Flat Models

The simplest method used for test effort estimation is to add a percentage flat rate to the development effort—for instance, 40% for test effort. A simple model such as this is better than nothing and may be the only way—for instance, in case of a new development in a business segment hitherto not covered by the organization—to get to an estimation.

Percentage flat rate as a starting point

What is more, this simple estimation of the test effort causes considerably less estimation effort than more complex methods and may therefore be quite adequate for small projects.

Of course, precondition is that (apart from a consistent add-on factor) the development effort was known or estimated accurately.

Consequent tracking of actual effort and iterative improvements of the estimation model through comparison of actuals against plan after project end are more important here than in all other methods used for estimating test effort. The next test project will then at least be based on a more suitable percentage value for the estimation.

To start with such a flat model, one may take into account experience values from similar projects, technologies, corporate or sector comparisons, or of course general literature sources. Sources with suitable add-on factors are, among others, [Jones 98], [URL: Rothman], and [Rashka 01]. Looking for comparable sources, several factors need to be considered:

Use comparison data

- The source used for comparison must suit the task; i.e., it must take into account the organization's own implemented software technology. For example, sources used for estimating the effort to test an embedded system developed in C are probably inadequate to estimate the effort to test a web portal developed in .NET.
- The authenticity of the source needs to be checked, especially with regard to the fidelity of the data collection.
- It makes sense to use several sources. If the data is contradictory, adjustments can be made using mean value and standard deviation; otherwise, it is better to remain on the safe side and discard the sources altogether.

5.4.2   Detailed Models Based on Test Activities

If the simple estimation method cannot be used satisfactorily, the test project must be considered a concatenation of individual activities and different estimation methods must be used for each individual activity. This

Classic project management approach

approach follows classical methods of project management. There are many different approaches; for orientation, some criteria given below consider the different types of resources required for the execution of the activities:

- Manpower
- Time
- Hardware and software for the test environment
- Testware such as test automation tools

To estimate this effort usually requires a combination of intuition, experience, and comparison values as well as formal calculation methods. The following factors, among others, may enter into the calculation, depending on the desired accuracy of the effort estimation:

Diverse influencing factors

- Number of tests (conditional on the type, number, and complexity of the requirements on the test object but also on the planned test intensity, resulting from risk estimation)
- Complexity and controllability of the test environment and of the test object (in particular during its installation and configuration)
- Estimated number of test repetitions per test level based on assumptions about the progress of defect detection
- Maturity of the test processes and of the applied methods and tools
- Quality of available documentation for the system and test environment
- Required quality and accuracy of documents to be created
- Similarity of the project to be estimated with previous projects
- Reusability of solutions from previous projects
- (Test) maturity of the system under test (If the quality of the tested systems is bad, the effort required to meet the test exit criteria may be difficult to define.)
- Adherence of test object deliveries to schedule
- Complexity of scheduling possible part or incremental deliveries, especially during integration testing
- Results of possible previous test levels and test phases

Different effort types

A typical basic mistake during effort estimation is to take all scaling factors into account but not all effort types that scale accordingly. Essentially, such effort types follow the phases of the test processes. Effort needs to be considered for the following:

- Test planning (among other things, effort required for developing the effort estimation itself).
- Test preparation (reception, configuration management and installation of the test objects, provision of necessary documentation and templates and possibly test databases, setting up the test environment, etc.).
- Staffing (e.g., coaching and/or training of testers).
- Test specification at all test levels. Estimation techniques may differ considerably depending on the quality attributes to be tested and the applied test techniques and test tools.
- If necessary, test automation for selected tests—basically, the same applies here as for the test specification; there are, however, some additional variations regarding the costs for test automation tools.
- Test execution at all test levels, again considering different estimation techniques for different types of tests.
- Documentation of test execution, i.e., reports and incident reports.
- Defect analysis and retests—the latter naturally scaling with the number of detected anomalies, thus requiring a separate estimation of the number of defects: the defect detection percentage and the defect correction percentage.
- Collection of test metrics.
- Communication within the test team and between test and development team (meetings, e-mails, management of incident reports, Change Control Board, etc.).

Within these effort types individual tasks must subsequently be identified and individually estimated. Such tasks must be kept rather small (some person days) and should always be related to a concrete event at the start and at the end to make tracking of the actual effort between these two dates as simple as possible.

Keep estimated tasks small.

The same applies as mentioned earlier: some estimations are extremely difficult. In order to improve on subsequent estimations, the individual applied techniques and assumptions used must be documented; the actual effort must be accurately logged and deviations need to be analyzed.

All these estimation techniques should not lead one to forget that testing is a team process:

Estimations are part of the teamwork.

- A test manager must not perform effort estimation in the ivory tower. Assumptions and estimations should be discussed in the team, with team members being involved in the estimation of activities assigned to them. Different estimations from different people can be averaged out, or alternatively minimum and maximum values can be used for good/ bad case estimations.

▪ It must be considered that later execution of the work is also subject to variation in the same way the estimations are. In our experience, tasks performed by someone not involved in estimating their effort always take longer than expected.

▪ Effort does not only depend on the qualification and knowledge of those involved but also on their motivation!

▪ The quality and test policy—i.e., the importance accorded to testing in the enterprise and in management—affect estimation or at least the risk of false estimation.

▪ The maturity of the software under test has a strong influence, too; immature, defective software can multiply the effort required for one single test by a high factor.

Use experiences values   In this step, too, experiences made in the past can help; the large number of individual estimations, however, also requires a large number of historical data for the individual activities, thus presupposing the previous creation of a practicable set of test metrics (see chapter 11).

It may be of help to carry out a study prior to a complex project, selecting some random sample test cases from the test schedule and logging the effort needed for implementing and executing them. The results can be used for validating the estimation techniques or for extrapolation of the total effort.

5.4.3   Models Based on Functional Volume

This model class is based on the estimation of the scope or functionality of the objects under test and tries to establish a mathematical model by reducing scope or functionality to some few but significant parameters.

Compromise between general   De facto, such models work with experience values, too, mostly in the
and individual estimations   form of fixed coefficients or factors that are used in the formulas. This way, they represent a practicable compromise between the accurate but elaborate models based on single task estimation and the cost-effective but inaccurate and risky flat models.

[ISO 14143] provides a detailed framework, based on which a concrete metric can be evaluated to determine the functional volume of the system to be tested.

As an example of such a method, we shall first look at the

Function Point Analysis (FPA)

This method (see, for example, [Garmus 00]) is generally used in effort estimations and widely applied in system development.

Since the function point analysis starts with system requirements, it can be applied very early in a software development project. The method itself, however, defines only the number of function points of the product; in order to deduce information about the expected development effort for this product, corporate specific experience values relating to the effort per function point is required.

The function point method works in three steps:

Stepwise analysis and estimation

■ In a first step, defined rules are used to count the functions to be realized and all data to be processed; these are divided into the categories input, output, query, interface file, and internal file and then weighed as simple, medium, or complex. The result (i.e., the weighted sum) of this count is called "unadjusted function point value". It is a measure for the functional scope of the system from the user's point of view.

■ Independent of the first step, the system to be realized is evaluated in a second step based on 14 nonfunctional attributes, such as, for example, a measure for the performance or the efficiency of the user interface. Each of these influencing factors is evaluated by a factor from 0 (unimportant) to 5 (very important) and added up. The result is taken as a percentage value. That value is added to 0.65 and multiplied with the result of the first step. Thus we get to the "adjusted function point value", which represents a basic factor for the expected development effort.

■ In a last step, the function points must be converted into effort, i.e., person months and costs, etc. At precisely this point, the method must be adapted to corporate needs because the conversion requires comparisons with figures from past projects.

The test effort can, for example, be deduced by means of the following conversion rule [URL: Longstreet]: Let FP be the number of function points we then get

Test effort is a result of estimates from function points.

■ the number of system test cases = $FP^{1.2}$
■ the number of acceptance test cases = $FP \times 1.2$

Hence, the estimation result is simply the number of test cases; however, in practice this number will not be sufficient to perform a complete effort estimation. In order to use it, we need at least an add-on estimate for the number of test cases with a mean effort for all test activities, or we use the number of test cases as a parameter for an activity-based estimation model.

Test Point Analysis (TPA)

Based on the function point analysis, the test point analysis was developed by the Sogeti company B.V. [URL: Sogeti]. In principle, this method uses all the essential factors already listed in the section on activity-based models as factors by which the number of the system's defined function points is multiplied. The algorithms used are rather complicated and contain several experience-based parameters. For setting up these parameters, we use experience values for the weighting of quality attributes and certain features of the functions, of the environment, experience, and equipment of the test teams, and of the organizational structure.

TPA harmonizes with ISO 9126. The advantages of this method is that the classification of the test points is based on ISO 9126 and that it is therefore well suited to the methods for test strategy development described in sections 5.2.4 and 5.3.

The experience factors map to very many possible influencing factors without confusing the estimation—TPA, for example, can very easily be implemented in form of a spreadsheet. TPA provides a complete effort estimation in test hours; adding additional values as in FPA is not necessary.

Similar to FPA, TPA thrives on the quality of the experience values; it is therefore hardly suitable for initial effort estimation in a new enterprise or business segment. However, if data collection and adjustment between estimation and actual effort is regularly done and if the experience factor is calibrated accordingly, the method will become more accurate with time.

TPA based on FPA. TPA, though, makes using FPA mandatory. In each individual case, we must weigh whether to base estimation on the rather complex TPA or on the simple algorithms for direct derivation of the test efforts from the function point analysis that we just mentioned.

Figure 5-5 shows the test point analysis workflow.

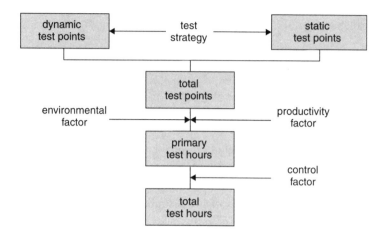

Figure 5–5

Test point analysis workflow

Dynamic test points: for this value we define the following for each individual function:

- The value of the function points for this function
- A factor for the quality attributes required for this function (functionality, safety, integration ability, and performance)
- A factor that comprises the priority of the function, its frequency of application, and its complexity and influence on the rest of the system.

These three factors are multiplied with each other per function and the results are added up. This sum, the dynamic test points, reflects the effort for the dynamic test.

Static test points: For each of the required non-testable quality attributes (flexibility, testability, traceability), the total number of function points is multiplied by a factor and the intermediary results are added up. The result is a measure for the effort of the static tests.

Test point estimation using quality attributes

Dynamic and static test points are summed up and subsequently weighted with environmental factors:

Multiplication with different influencing factors

- With an environmental factor containing as effort reducing or effort increasing influences product documentation, available development and test tools, test documents, testware and test infrastructure.
- With the productivity factor, which allows for staff quality, process documentation, and organizational culture.

■ Finally, the administrative factor is added and grows with increasing team size but will be cushioned in case team coordination tools are available.

The result, as mentioned at the beginning, is the number of test hours required.

5.5 Organization of Test Teams and Test Levels

Once test tasks are identified and estimated, the next important step consists in distributing them in a meaningful way to the several test levels—from component testing close to development to acceptance testing close to the customer. Using the available resources, which test levels can be completed with which test tasks in the most cost-effective way, and which test techniques should be applied?

How can we avoid unnecessary, redundant work—is it perhaps possible to reuse testware components of individual test levels on other levels?

In large software projects and especially in the case of producers of standard software, there will be several test levels and also more than one test team per test level. Typically, hierarchy and organizational team structure is oriented toward the architecture or structure of the system under test.

Figure 5–6

General structure of a test organization

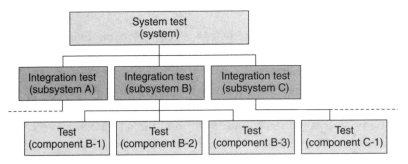

The different test teams must cooperate closely and consult with each other. In order to minimize overall test effort and to maximize achievable test coverage, the test schedules of the different teams should overlap as little as possible. If teams test different test objects and if test teams are at the same test level, this more or less follows automatically. However, as soon as test objects overlap because several teams require the same component(s) for testing, there is a risk of unnecessary duplication, maintenance, and execution of test cases. Such cooperation and consultation is even more important between the different test levels and must be actively encouraged. Here, too, it becomes apparent how important it is to consider testware in configuration management.

The basic distribution of tasks between the test levels and the resulting assignment of test objectives must be clearly formulated in the test plan. Based on the test plan, an overall test schedule is developed that will be broken down into subplans per test team. These plans shall be subject to review by all test managers. Test managers are to agree and to decide which of the tests from lower levels (perhaps in modified form) can be reused at the higher levels, which tests will not be applied at all, and which tests are to remain exclusively at one level. During later execution of the tests, regular coordination meetings between the test managers are necessary to sort out changes in the test schedule. The following example illustrates the workflow across several test levels.

The test team receives a new product release, "*DreamCar* v4.5.001" (Release 4.5, Build 1), from development. To begin with, the test team[9] performs component testing for each component. If defects are detected, the release is sent back to development for rework. Once component testing has been successfully completed (i.e., once test exit criteria have been met), the components are passed on to integration test for integration. Then integration testing is performed. If defects are detected that block integration, "v4.5.001" testing will be terminated. Development will be requested to deliver an improved build (i.e., a release with identical functionality but corrected defects).

Testing of "v4.5.002" again starts with component testing. If the build is stable and good enough to meet the component test exit criteria and if the subsequent integration tests are successful, the build is passed on to system test.

If system testing is successful, "v4.5" will be released. However, if the release is prevented because of defects, development will be asked to create build 3. Testing of "v4.5.003" must again start with component testing.

Example:
One test team for all test levels

In the techniques illustrated here, test levels are completed sequentially, with each build going through a complete regression test cycle.

This means that on each test level all the test cases that exist there are repeated for each build. Figure 5-7 provides a schematic overview of this process.

---

9.   It is assumed that the developers do not perform component testing themselves.

Figure 5–7
Sequentially working test levels

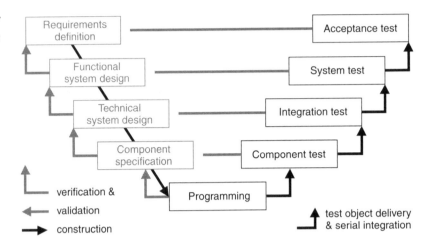

These simple, sequential techniques are sufficient to develop software that contains very few defects. Test duration, however (i.e., the time span between the start of the first component test and product release after the final system test cycle) may be very long and depends on the number of necessary builds.

One test team per test level

As long as there is only one test team, the sequential approach can not be avoided. However, as is often the case in larger software development projects, if there are several test teams (for example, one independent test team per test level with its own tools and test environment tailored to the particular requirements of the test level), parallel working of all test teams and thus all test levels would be possible (see figure 5-8):

Figure 5–8
Parallel working test levels

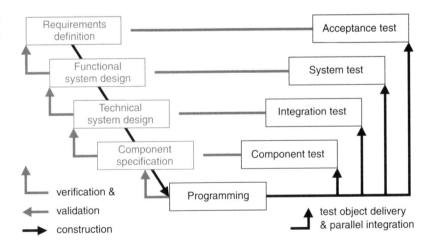

After a build has been completed, it is simultaneously delivered to all the test levels and each test group immediately starts executing "its" test cases.

Since nobody needs to wait for test completion on previous levels, this can be a very fast method. However, since each test level is based on the same untested build, it is very likely that a test level is slowed down or even blocked by defects contained in the build. In a sequential test scenario, such a high proportion of blocking defects would have been encountered and corrected at a lower test level. The higher test level would not have spent any effort on such a deficient build. There is also the very immediate risk that—perhaps even different—failures are simultaneously detected and reported at different test levels, which can be traced back to the same defect.

In practice, this means that with "immature" builds, test levels working in parallel are less efficient than sequentially working test levels.

Parallel testing inefficient with immature builds

At the end of the day, as many build cycles are needed as with the sequential method but the higher test levels waste a great deal of their effort with tests that get blocked and must be repeated on the next build. The tests of the higher levels are inefficient because the test object was delivered too early and in an immature state.

How can several test teams work together efficiently without having to wait too long for each other? We may solve the problem for each test team and test level introducing local "pass tests". To this effect, each test level defines two small subsets from out of its test cases. Thus, the pass test is a subset of all the tests of one test level.

Coordination of test levels through pass testing

The first pass test subset consists of so-called local "acceptance tests". The acceptance test is the pass test of the receiving test level. If the test level contains a new test object, the test level begins executing these acceptance tests. Only if all of these test are passed will execution of the other tests defined for this level start. Acceptance tests are to be selected in such a way as to make it very probable that unstable test objects or objects that do not have the basic functionality required for this test level are identified and rejected.

Acceptance testing at the receiving test level

As a second test subset, each test level defines local "release tests". The →release test is the pass test of the delivering test level. As soon as all test cases marked as pass test have passed the test for the first time, the subsequent test level gives the signal to start testing at that level.

Release tests of the delivering test level

The subsequent level begins with its acceptance testing, whereas the current level carries on testing until its local test schedule has been completed.

During this time, both test levels work overlapping or concurrently. The benefit is obvious: unnecessary test blockages cannot be eliminated completely, but at least they can be considerably reduced. Depending on the size of the acceptance test and release test packages, the amount of overlapping or parallel execution of test activities can be specifically controlled. Compared to the sequential method, the overall time required for testing can thus be reduced.

However, this technique has its price as the need for coordination and resources increases considerably. This method is only beneficial in cases where a short time-to-market period is more important than minimized test costs. This method is also called "triggered" delivery of the test objects to the test levels and illustrated schematically in figure 5-9.

Figure 5–9

"Triggered" test levels

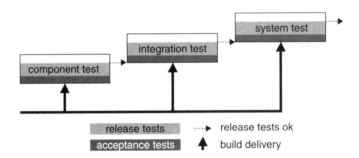

Testing is not a one-off occasion.

- **Acceptance testing:** Select a (small) subset from all the test cases of the test level in such a way that all main functions as well as all functions and requirements crucial to this test level can be tested; automate execution of these acceptance tests so that, following delivery or installation of a test object, they can be executed fast and automatically.
- **Release testing:** In order to determine release tests, we need to consider that certain preconditions may need to be observed. Test cases at one's own test level verifying these preconditions are to be selected for release testing. Test cases that are release test cases are flagged as such and included in the plan for early execution with high priority. This allows giving an early release signal to the next test level.
- **Further tests:** If the release tests have been executed successfully, the test level continues with its test program. The test result of the test level will contain the results and insights of all three tests (acceptance test/release test/further tests).

5.6 Test Planning as an Iterative Process Accompanying Development

Today, hardly any product is developed following a "big bang" waterfall approach, i.e., developed in one go, tested once, and then released. Usually, test and development cycles are interleaved (see chapter 2) in order to use the far too short period until release to the customer and to increase the plannability and ability to respond to changes. To do so, the entire test task is broken down to several subcycles while simultaneously reducing project risk. Test planning thus becomes an optimization task for test management that accompanies the whole of the development and test life cycles.

Selection strategy for pass tests

5.6.1 Begin Test Activities Early and Refine Them Step-by-Step

Test planning can, and must, start very early, in fact in parallel to the early phases of software development (i.e., requirements management and design), even if at that time not all information necessary for the completion of the planning is available (see, in particular, the W-model in section 3.4).

Begin test planning early.

Since further test cycles and test planning phases follow, the first draft test plan can be completed and substantiated in steps. Based on planning data that is already stable, additional activities such as setting up the test environment, drafting the specification, and even partly automating tests may be started.

The test team wins time and can ideally start test execution as soon as the first test objects are available.

Test planning information may be passed on for review to other project participants. It is thus possible to release subtest plans in stages and to initiate actions ensuing from them. Moreover, additional resources or the necessary participation of other parties will be communicated in time; potential problems will become visible earlier and can be resolved.

Interleaved work facilitates mutual coordination of development and test processes as regards content and plan. For example, test planning information can be used to optimally reconcile the delivery sequence of system components under test and the planned strategy for integration testing of these components. Specification documents are to be created in parallel to the system's requirements and design phase. Experience shows that the test design specification can be created based on sufficiently stable versions of the requirements documents and the test case and test procedure specification can be created based on the results of software design. Besides, early creation of test plans and test specifications is an efficient verification measure for the test object and its documentation (see also the documentation for the W-model in section 3.4).

5.6.2   "Plan-Do-Check-Act"-Cycles in Testing

PDCA at different levels   In the 1950s, W. Edwards Deming coined the term "PDCA cycle" for the controlled change of business processes, thus refining a concept of Walter A. Shewhart from the 1920s:

- **P**lan: Examine the present situation, plan the changes, analyze the effects of the changes, and forecast the process results.
- **D**o: Implement the changes in a controlled environment and in small steps.
- **C**heck: Check the implementation and the results of the changed processes.
- **A**ct: If the change has yielded the expected (improved) results, make it become the standard.

In the test process, we find this approach again at different levels:

- At the level of the test project and test level plan, which need to be continuously adapted to the insights gained during test execution. At the starting point are suitable metrics to detect deviations from the plan. Changes in the plan and in particular strategy changes must be communicated clearly and early to the respective persons in charge of the project. All activities connected with this are described in chapter 6. The borderlines between tests control (based on predefined planning) and renewed planning or plan revision are blurred.
- At the level of the test plan, which also needs to be revised in case of plan deviations if these have an impact across test levels, if the project deviates from the test objectives, or if the deviations result from systematic errors in the test plan.
- At the level of the test handbook and test policy, into which gradually enter the experiences and reusable solutions (best practices) from test plans of completed test projects.

5.7   Summary

- Typically, testing is performed in complete test projects involving activities in the form of test cycles.
- The test plan is the concrete application of the test handbook, mapping the strategic requirements of the test policy into the project.
- In addition to the documentation of deviations from the test handbook in the concrete project, the test plan contains, among others, the following:
    - Brief descriptions of all planned test activities as well as of the estimated costs and execution times needed for these activities
    - Necessary prerequisites and provision of manpower or institutions external to the test project
    - The planning of the individual test cycles and their coordination with the software release plan
    - A list and short table of contents of all project results to be generated
- In the test schedule, test plan specifications are translated into concrete resource and schedule assignments.
- In large projects, this may be done by means of several test level plans, representing the requirements of the test plan at each individual test level.
- The IEEE 829 standard provides a structure for the creation of test plans covering all relevant aspects of test planning.
- Essential structural components are:
    - Test strategy
    - Test effort estimation
    - Test organization
- The test strategy's task is to assign the quality attributes required for the system, define the test techniques to be applied for their verification, assign available resources to activities, and structure them in a reasonable sequence. Focus is put on the minimization of product risks.
- For test activity effort estimation, different methods may be applied:
    - Intuition or guesswork
    - Experience
    - Corporate standards
    - A detailed itemization of all test activities
    - Formulae

- Function point method
- Test point method
- A simple percentage estimate relative to the development effort
- Metrics
- Comparable projects (especially for estimating repeated test cycles)
- Calculation of the mean effort per test object or per test case from previous test runs and multiplication by the estimated number in the actual test run

■ Skillful effort distribution at different test levels and test teams helps to optimally use available resources. Success factors are as follows:

- The chosen organizational structure
- Nonoverlapping division of tasks between test teams and test levels
- Delivery of the test objects to the next or previous test level at the right time controlled by suitable entry and exit criteria

■ Test planning does not stop with the start of the first planned activity in the project; it is rather an iterative process running concurrently to development.

■ Planning must begin as early as possible to eliminate as many project risks as possible or at least make them visible early enough and to provide sufficient time to prepare for one's own activities and for the delivery of additional resources. This needs to be done even in cases where at that point not all information is available.

■ Planning must be refined in steps as soon as relevant information is available; it must be possible to start activities such as the early creation of the test specification even on the basis of an initial, "rough draft" plan.

■ It must be possible to use test planning to influence the development planning of the software components; i.e., the dependencies of test activities on other development activities must be made visible.

6   Test Control

The previous chapters explained how test activities are designed and planned. This chapter explains how test managers control test activities during testing to ensure that the test schedule is implemented according to plan. Finally, some hints and tips for an adequate reporting system are given.

The best plan is only as good as its implementation. In the same way a project manager is judged by the final results of his project, a test manager is judged by how well he has performed in actually implementing the strategic specifications of the test plan and the operative specifications of the test project plan.

To do so, the test manager must actively control the test activities. Test control comprises the identification and implementation of all measures necessary to ensure that test activities are performed according to plan during the test cycle and that all test objectives are achieved. This requires timely initiation of the test task, continuous monitoring of the test progress, and adequate response to test results and sometimes to changed circumstances. Based on gained insights, the test manager must then be able to judge if the test process may be completed.

Control test activities actively

Test results and information about the test activities are to be communicated in the test report. Each run through the test cycle usually results in defect correction or change requests for development. When defects are corrected or changes have been implemented, a new software version is created that again must be tested. For this, the test process typically runs through several cycles. Furthermore, the test process runs (perhaps in parallel) at each of the different test levels. Depending on project size, each test level may have its own test manager (see chapter 5).

The following sections explain a test manager's different management tasks from the sometimes simplified perspective of one individual test cycle. In practice, the iterative nature and potentially parallel execution of the test process at several test levels require additional management and control.

6.1   Initiating the Test Tasks

Assign test tasks clearly.   Tasks planned in the test schedule must be initiated, which means the test manager must ensure that planned tasks are assigned to testers, that testers understand the tasks assigned to them, and that they begin performing their tasks in due course.

It would be naive to assume that all task assignments have been effectively communicated to those in charge simply because they have been listed in the plan. In principle, when allocating test tasks to testers, the test manager may choose between two strategies:

- Definite assignment of specific functional or application-specific test topics to individual testers: For instance, one tester can be in charge of the specialist topic "VSR contract management" during the entire test period; i.e., specification and possibly automation and execution of the corresponding test cases are performed by the same tester. The advantage of this strategy is that the tester can and will delve deeply into the test object and gain profound knowledge about the system that he can use in testing. This strategy, however, only works with comprehensively trained testers. Besides, there is a risk that not only the test specification but also the test results could become dependant on individual testers with possibly negative effects on test repeatability and completeness.
- Assignment of testers based on test phases or roles: Test designers specify the test cases, test automaters implement test automation, and testers are in charge of test execution and the creation of incident reports. For this reason, tests must be tester independent and specified with sufficient accuracy and detail. This approach ensures a very high reproducibility and regression test capability. If the expected behavior of the test object is unclear, if the test object changes considerably, or if there is extreme time pressure, it may be difficult or too time consuming to create accurate test specifications. In this case, assigning personal tasks as described above may be more advisable.

In practice, both strategies are used. Dedicated testers, for instance, are employed for technically sophisticated and risky topics, while in order to gain efficiency, general testing is done concurrently using phase- or role-oriented task assignment.

Assigning a task in the plan by no means ensures that the tester is aware of the assignment. The test manager must ensure that each tester understands the task assigned to him, that he accepts it, and that he starts testing in due course. In some cases. a brief phone call will suffice; in others, it will be expedient to arrange for an initiation plan. Perhaps it may be necessary to provide a "free desk" or to remove other organizational hurdles to allow the tester to work productively. Such organizational issues will not be discussed any further in this book; nevertheless, a great deal of the test manager's time will be "eaten up" by this kind of organizational activity. The test manager must allow for this when planning his own work packages.

Ensure that test tasks are undertaken.

6.2 Monitoring the Test Progress

Monitoring the test progress must start as soon as the first draft version of the test schedule becomes available. It is not only a matter of monitoring test execution alone; all test preparation tasks, too, will have to be monitored. Test cases, for instance, must be specified in time (including those that are planned for later versions of the test objects). Test automation for tests that are to run automatically at some later time must be set up early. And last but not least, it must be ensured that the test objects are delivered to test and installed in the test environment.

It is therefore not enough to pay attention to test execution only, since delays in test specification or test automation will inevitably lead to delays in later test cycles. Questions concerning three task categories must be answered:

Test progress versus test schedule

- How many of the test cases contained in the plan have already been specified? How many and which are still awaiting specification? How long is it expected to take ? Will work be completed in time?
- Which tests are fully automated? Is automation still adequate for the current test object version or will it have to be adjusted? Which other fully specified tests are suitable for automation? Does the automation effort pay off? When must the extended automation be available?

Which tests (automated or manual) have already been completed? Which tests are still open, delayed, or blocked?

We should be able at any time to answer each of these questions for each individual test case. To this end, the team must keep the processing status of each test case in the test project plan up-to-date. It is obvious that this is only possible if a well-structured and up-to-date test project plan is available.

Test schedule template

For smaller projects (up to approximately five testers), a spreadsheet may be sufficient. A test plan template is available for download under [URL: Templates].

In larger projects, however, where many testers work in parallel according to the test project plan, technical constraints alone mean that the project will be unmanageable without a database test management tool. An up-to-date test project plan allows a large variety of analyses about the test progress and makes it possible to find answers to questions such as these: What is the percentage of test cases that have reached a particular status (e.g., "completed")? Is work progressing according to plan? If not, to what degree does progress deviate from the plan? How much work is there still left for the team to complete?

Example:
Tracking test progress in the
VSR project

In his test report, the VSR project test manager presents the test progress statistics of the past three test cycles. Each test cycle lasts three weeks whereby a maximum of 250 test cases per week can be performed with the available test team. The evaluation documents the following test progress (see figure 6-1):

Figure 6–1
Test progress
across three test cycles

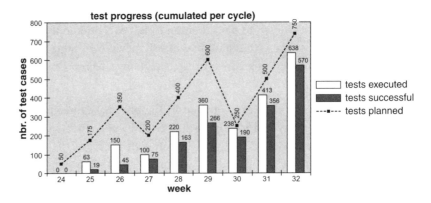

For the first cycle (KW 24–26), the set target was to complete 350 test cases. Certain start-up problems were allowed for in the plan. Due to the functionally incomplete and still very immature test object, only 150 test cases could be completed. Only 45 test cases ran bug free.

The second cycle started in week 27 with an intensively reworked and extended test object. Out of the now 200 planned cases per week, 50% – 70% could actually be completed. The proportion of passed test cases was at almost 75%. In sum, 266 of the planned 600 test cases—that is, 44%—could be completed successfully.

In week 30, cycle 3 received a corrected, stable test object. At the beginning, testing proceeded almost on schedule. Because one of the testers fell ill in week 31, test progress fell below target. In sum, 638 of the planned 750 test cases (85%) could be completed. Thus, 76% of the planned tests ran bug free.

The tracking of the test progress described above refers exclusively to test project plan content (test-schedule-oriented test coverage). One hundred percent test progress thus means that "all planned tests are completed." However, this does not suffice. How do we ensure that all necessary tests are planned and contained in the test project plan? One hundred percent test progress in terms of test schedule does not necessarily mean that the test object has been sufficiently tested.

Test coverage concepts

For this reason, additional, suitable test coverage metrics are required that measure the test progress compared to the product or test object scope (test-object-oriented test coverage). Chapter 11 suggests some corresponding metrics.

Test progress compared to product size

Product size can be considered and measured at different abstraction levels. It is important that the selected metric corresponds with the abstraction level at which the respective test levels are working (compare chapter 3). Thus, the preferred metrics in component testing are code coverage measurements. Architecture-related measurements are particularly suitable for integration testing, whereas in system and acceptance testing, requirements coverage is predominantly measured. If there are any requirements without assigned test cases, it is obvious that tests are missing in the test schedule. However, if test cases exist that cannot be assigned to any requirement (or perhaps only at a level of very vaguely defined requirements), then requirements are missing. In this case, testers have obviously identified use cases to which the person asking for the requirement (e.g., customer or system designer) has not given any thought.

The test-object-oriented coverage can be evaluated analogous to test-schedule-oriented coverage; for instance, to answer one of the following questions:

What is the percentage of the reference units (lines of code, architecture components, requirements) that were covered by the test cases? Is this in accordance with the plan? If not, what is the degree of deviation from the plan? How much work is there still left for the team to complete?

Measurement and evaluation are here more difficult because reference value and test cases must be seen as closely tied up with each other. Modern test management tools, however, will be able to do this.

As mentioned at the beginning, test-object-oriented coverage metrics help in determining if test cases are missing. The test manager should not only check if coverage increases sufficiently with test progress but he should also check all poorly covered software parts to see whether there are any test cases missing in the test design specification. If the latter turns out to be the case, the test design specification must be completed and all added test cases need to be executed.

If this turns out to be true, it must be completed and the added tests must be made up. The "test design verification" metric is helpful in this respect (see chapter 11).

Timing test progress control

Besides the question of how to determine and present test progress, there is the question of timing. The following recommendations can be given:

- The test-schedule-oriented test progress should be evaluated frequently-for instance, on a weekly basis, or in hot test phases, even daily. Delays that become apparent are mostly caused by immature test objects or coordination problems in the test team requiring quick reaction.
- Test-object-oriented coverage metrics should be analyzed at the end of the test cycle. If all planned test cases in the test cycle have been executed and coverage proves to be insufficient, test cases must be added. Either these will then be executed in the subsequent test cycle or the current cycle will be extended accordingly.

Example:
Measurement and evaluation of requirements coverage

The VSR project test plan requires that the achieved requirements coverage is measured and tracked for each test cycle. In order to implement this requirement, the test management tool TestBench [URL: TestBench] is used, providing an interface to the requirements management tool. The test manager imports the requirements list into the test management tool. In order to be able to indicate which test cases validate which requirements, the test designer assigns one or more requirements to each test case.

Figure 6-2 illustrates this in the example of test case "2.1.1. Calculate total price without discount". Four requirements are associated with this test case. Three requirements are already marked "completed," which means that these requirements are actually validated by test case 2.1.1. The fourth requirement is also supposed to be validated by test case 2.1.1. For this to be done, however, test case 2.1.1. still needs to be revised and extended. Thus, the status of the assignment is "not completed".

Figure 6–2

Linking requirements to test cases

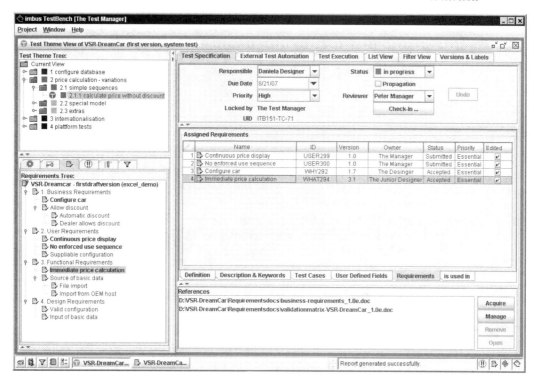

If requirements change or new ones are added, the test manager can synchronize the test schedule with the latest version of the requirements list (baseline). Using a filter query, TestBench shows which test cases have been impacted by changed requirements or which requirements have not yet been assigned to a test case. This is a quick way for test designers to find out which test cases need to be changed or extended. Based on these associations between requirements and test cases or test specifications, the test manager determines after each test cycle which requirements were actually tested and with which result.

Figure 6-3 shows the tool-generated evaluation of the achieved requirements coverage. For example, the table shows that requirement 301 is to be tested by three associated test cases but that one of the three test cases failed. This is not enough to consider the requirement "validated."

Figure 6–3

Evaluation of

requirements coverage

Requirements				Test Cases			
Id	Key	Vers.	Prio	passed	failed	open	total
301	Indication of price and configuration	1.0	1	2	1	0	3
300	No enforced use sequence	1.0	1	1	0	0	1
298	Dealer allows discount	1.0	1	3	1	0	4
297	Automatic discount	1.0	1	1	0	0	1
295	Allow discount	1.0	1	0	0	2	2
294	Immediate price calculation	1.1	1	3	0	0	3
296	Mouse operable	1.0	2	0	0	0	0
299	Continuous price display	1.0	3	1	0	1	2
292	Configure car	1.0	3	2	0	1	3

ok	failed	open

The tools used in the VSR project support bidirectional exchange of data between the requirements management and the test management tool, allowing the test manager to transfer the validation status of each requirement after each test run back into the requirements management tool. This way, everyone involved in the project outside test receives feedback about the test progress achieved in the project.

6.3   Reacting to Test Results

Based on insights gained during progress tracking, test managers may have to initiate specific and appropriate correction measures. For example, if test execution is behind schedule, it needs to be determined how many test cases and which testers are affected. From this a test manager can deduce whether or not tests can be shifted to other testers. If work shifting is not enough, sufficient resources must be provided.

The actual demand on resources can be proven by the data and thus can be explained to management. If neither work shifting nor redistribution are possible, rescheduling of the test cases, new prioritization, or even cancellation of the tests is inevitable.

In any case, it is important to ascertain traceability of and the reasons for changes in the plan in order to learn from these situations through subsequent analysis—for instance, in project reviews or metrics-based evaluations—and to improve planning accuracy in subsequent projects.

For quick allocation or redistribution of tasks, using a tabular view of test schedule data is a suitable option. The test manager may, for instance, filter the plan by the test status "not executed" for tests relating to "contract management". By reassigning the list of test cases thus generated to the tester and by entering new due dates (if necessary), replanning will not cause much effort or many errors.

Task assignment via test schedule tables

Affected testers subsequently receive their new tasks list in the form of a printout, e-mail, or personal spreadsheet in the test management tool.

The identification and evaluation of the test progress based on the test project plan or based on coverage metrics is only one aspect. Since it is the declared target of testing to detect as many defects in the test object as possible, the "quality" of the test objects, i.e., the concrete test execution results, may by no means be neglected. Whoever follows the test schedule regardless of test results and without readjusting the schedule in view of such results will not be able to achieve this goal. In addition to evaluating the data on test progress, the test manager must evaluate test results and use them as control values.

Several defect-based metrics are available on this issue: number of defects detected, number of defects discovered over time or at a given test intensity (defect trend), number of defects based on test object size (→defect density), number of defects based on criticality (defect severity), number of defects per status (progress of defect correction), and others. Chapter 11 discusses these metrics in more detail.

Defect-based metrics

Fundamental to defect-based evaluation and control is the prompt and systematic recording of found defects necessitating a defect or incident management system (incident database). Chapter 8 provides more details. To gain useful evaluations, it must be ensured that all incident reports— irrespective of the author—are classified according to comparable evaluation standards. Only then it does make sense to compare, for instance, the average defect severity in different components and to draw conclusions from them.

In order to ensure comparability, we need, on the one hand, to use practicable methods for defect classification. Chapter 8 describes the IEEE 1044 standard classification for software anomalies. The test manager, on the other hand, is supposed to minimize different author-dependent classifications by post-classifying each report (done either by himself or by an authorized tester). That way, classification outliers can be detected and corrected.

Ensure comparability of incident reports.

In addition, it also makes sense to discuss incident reports with the test team at the start and end of a test cycle to work toward a common evaluation standard.

React to test results.   How can test results or defect data be used for test control? We may postulate three theses:

■ **Where you find defects, there will be even more:** If in certain places in the test object (methods, components, and so on) or in relation to certain test topics we find that there is an accumulation of defects, it is very likely that we shall find further defects in the test object's environment. Perhaps this burst of defects could even be a symptom of completely misunderstood requirements. The test manager's reaction may go in two directions:

- Intensive tests of error-prone parts. The following questions need to be answered: What did the developer understand incorrectly? What is it that he may have implemented incorrectly because of that? Suitable test cases are added that may support or refute these assumptions. The tests are executed on the current test object version and in the defect retest; that is, after the correction of previously found defects. If no further failures are detected, the priority of these additional test cases may again be lowered; however, such test cases should not be thrown away so they do not have to be created again unnecessarily in a similar situation in later project phases.

- Terminate testing of error-prone parts. If too may defects pile up, if many "trivial" or similar defects are found, or if further testing is blocked, it may be reasonable to simply return the test object. Instead of putting more effort into continued testing, we should try to get to the root cause of the problem by using intermediary quality assurance measures such as reviews on entry documents or program code.

■ **Where there are no defects, there are no test cases:** When we consider defect distribution across the test object, we need to look at regions with a defect density below average.

- Perhaps it is not a good product that we see but just a bad test. In order to find that out, we need to look at all associated test cases and talk to the testers in charge. Do they consider the tests useful and sufficient in this position? Which test cases need to be added?

- Of course, the change history of test objects must be taken into account. If the component in question was not changed in the previous version cycle, "no defect" may be good news. In such cases, the controlling reaction could be to lower the priority of all or many test cases associated with this component or to remove them altogether from subsequent test cycles.

▪ **The defect trend curve indicates test completion:** In his evaluation of the defect detection intensity, the test manager must always look at which testing intensity was applied in each case. The absence of an experienced tester on holiday may have a serious effect on the number of defects found during that period. The same applies to weeks with public holidays or to overtime work or weekend shifts. The test manager is therefore advised to deduct from his data variations in test intensity that are caused by resource or workload fluctuations and to establish a normalized trend curve. If the normalized trend curve also shows that with constant test intensity there is a decrease in the number of newly detected defects, it may be taken as a sure sign that the test object is now "stable." If coverage of the test objects is considered sufficient and progress is achieved according to schedule, testing can be stopped.

The different components of the VSR system are designed and developed by different development groups. To be able to compare the maturity and quality of the components, the affected components are noted in the incident reports using the reporting attribute "component." Based on the component thus noted, the incident management system automatically enters the associated development group into the report.

Example:
Evaluation of the defect density per component

If during defect analysis it turns out that the cause of the defect is located in another component, the analyzing developer adds a corresponding comment and corrects the "component" attribute. With this he has passes the report on to the development team that in his opinion is now responsible.

Project and test manager can see the number and status of incident reports for each development group at any time. Furthermore, in order to see which group might have to cope with an above average defect occurrence, the size of the components must be taken into account. This is done by measuring the current code size (e.g., in "lines of code") whenever a new build or release is compiled. The test manager is then able to determine the number of defects associated with each component in relation to its respective code size.

Of course, the "lines of code" metric is only a rough measure, yet at least it provides the test manager with a useful indicator to judge the relative stability and maturity of the components.

Even if test plan, incident database, and metrics ensure perfect formal communication within the test team, the test manager ought to talk to testers frequently. He should "look over their shoulders", so to speak, at what they are doing and ask them for their subjective opinion on test progress and product quality. He should also sit down once in a while in front of the PC and carry out or repeat some test cases on the test object to gain a personal impression of the quality of the test object and tests. This rather selective but personal observation will put the test manager into a better position to evaluate and interpret abstract "measurement data" and test statistics.

6.4　Reacting to Changed Circumstances

The measures concerning test control that we discussed in the previous sections are based on the circumstances and conditions agreed upon in the test plan. They assume that during the test period, the test manager has a designated amount of human resources, suitable system-technical resources (test environment, test workplace, test tools, etc.), and perhaps further financial resources (e.g., for employing external test consultants) at his disposal. Within this context, the test strategy and test schedule were set up in such a way as to achieve an optimal test process.

Circumstances change.　　　Circumstances may of course change—unfortunately, for the worse. The first disillusionment may come even before testing starts because it may turn out that the agreed-upon resources can actually not be made available. The test schedule must then be set up in the light of the actual circumstances and not based on the ideal conception set out in the test plan. Realistically speaking, the test plan, too, must be adapted to these circumstances. This could mean that because of unresolvable resource shortages, test objectives and test exit criteria might have to be redefined.

The test manager must be very open in his reports about the degree by which project and product risks increase as a result of the unexpected cutbacks in test.

In later project phases, too, there may be as many incidences as you like that may lead to worsening circumstances. Test team members may fall ill, be transferred to different departments, or hand in their notice.

Perhaps some testers turn out to be less talented or qualified than expected. The test environment may cause problems. Test tools might not meet expectations, they might be unstable, or maybe they cannot be handled properly. Test automation is not ready in time or is not as stable as it should be.

Hopefully, the test manager has already identified many of these issues in his risk assessment (see chapter 9) at the beginning of the project and has designed some compensatory measures.

Often full compensation (at least for a transition period) will not be possible. The only alternative left is to revise the test project plan, reprioritize test cases, or drop them altogether. This carries the inevitable risk that product defects will be missed. These changes in circumstances, the enforced changes to plans, and the resulting increases in risk must be unequivocally stated in the project reports (see section 6.6).

Risk management

One very essential determining factor has so far not been addressed at all: the release[1] or build plan. The test schedule is always based on a forecast or assumption regarding the number and delivery dates of the test object releases (test object versions planned for internal or external release). From the testing point of view this prediction is often too optimistic. On the one hand, delivery of builds from development to test is often delayed, while on the other hand, test often shifts the release schedule on the grounds that the delivered test objects are not as fit for testing as expected, thus prolonging the time needed for test. And because of the detected defects, more and more work-intensive defect corrections than expected are necessary. In the end, there are more builds or releases than originally planned.

The release plan is a determining factor.

At first glance, this is a comfortable situation for the test manager because the test team wins time. The time left till the delayed release date can, for instance, be used to develop additional tests or to complete test automation. Additional releases and hence additional test cycles can be used to increase (cumulated) test coverage. All this, however, presupposes that test resources must be available for longer than originally planned. Despite the "gained" time, it is precisely this that is often lacking at the end because, in most cases, the external delivery date is kept fixed despite internal delays.

---

1. The release plan defines when specific versions are released to the customer. Moreover, there are, in most cases, additional internal versions (builds) that are compiled for test purposes only, or there are so-called release candidates that cannot yet be released because of unsatisfactory test results. All these versions must be taken into account during planning and test control.

Whenever expensive hardware or software resources need to be shared with other test groups or development, it may only be possible to compensate for shifts in the schedule by working night shifts or weekends.

Due to schedule shifts, it may happen that key people will no longer be available for testing. Often application experts can only be borrowed from their respective departments for a limited period to work as expert testers. A delayed or extended release plan means these experts will have been withdrawn before final tests are completed. Vacations, too, may thin out testing. For example, if development was originally scheduled to be completed before the summer or seasonal holidays, delays in coding may shift test cycles into precisely these periods.

The lessons to be learned for the test manager are to account for release delays (for example, by including a buffer in the test schedule), provide sufficient time when allocating human resources, and assign a stand-in for each tester. Consider each shared resource (staff, parts of the test environment) as a risk factor in risk management. Beyond all planning, sound improvisation is also necessary.

Example:
Compatibility test for an
operating system patch

A large manufacturer of operating systems releases a comprehensive security patch at short notice on a Friday. A little later, the VSR hotline receives the first inquiries about whether the *DreamCar* component is "compatible" with this patch and whether or not customers may install it. Support asks the VSR test manager to have the situation checked by the test group before Monday morning. For many testers, such emergency actions at short notice are nothing out of the ordinary.

That very Friday afternoon, the VSR test manager manages to motivate one of his testers to give up his weekend and together they manage to arrange for an experienced system administrator to be on call by telephone in case system specific questions arise while loading the patch.

The action is successful and on Monday morning support can give the green light to the customers. Of course, "regular" testing continues normally on Monday despite the weekend action and the patch must immediately be considered in the test schedule and test environment as an additional system environment variant.

6.5   Evaluating Test Completion

At the end of each test cycle, the question of test completion arises: Have we tested enough? Has the quality of the test objects been achieved as required or have we missed any serious defects?

Since testing is a spot-check technique that can show the presence of defects but cannot prove that no defects remain in the test object, it is difficult to answer these questions. Even if after complete execution of the test plan no further defects are encountered, it cannot assumed that there are no defects left in the tested software.

Nevertheless, the test manager must decide or at least voice a recommendation as to whether or not the test process may be terminated.

At this juncture, the test manager finds himself in a dilemma: If he stops testing too early, he increases the risk of delivering a product that is (too) defective. If he continues testing and finishes later than would perhaps be acceptable, he prolongs testing, makes it more expensive, and ultimately delays product release. In both instances, customer satisfaction and market opportunities may suffer severely.

Dilemma

In order to arrive at a well-founded and comprehensible decision, so-called "test exit criteria" are being used. Usually, one test exit criterion is a combination of different test metrics, including defined objectives to be achieved per measure. The test exit criteria and the objectives are defined ex ante in the test plan. Reaching or exceeding the objectives (during or at the end of a test cycle) then signalizes the end of the test activities. To satisfy a sound test completion, evaluation of the test exit criteria must cover the following aspects:

Test exit criteria

- **Evaluation of the achieved test progress** based on the test schedule and based on the achieved test object coverage.
- **Evaluation of available test results,** with subsequent (informal) conclusions drawn on product quality.
- **Estimation of residual risks.** A certain number of defects will remain in the system even after testing, either because these defects have not yet been detected or because they (deliberately) have not been corrected. The risks arising from these so-called residual defects have a decisive effect on whether testing can be terminated or not. Based on known data about "test progress" and "test results" the residual error probability can be either informally evaluated by means of test effectiveness metrics such as "Defect Detection Percentage" or analytically, using statistical methods (compare chapter 11).
- **Economic circumstances:** The achieved quality and the (feared) residual risk must be weighed against the available resources, the further development or release plan, the market opportunities, and expected

customer reactions. Ultimately, the decision to complete testing is a management decision.

The test manager's contribution is to provide advice and solid decision supporting data. In practice, additional influencing factors play a role, too: the practical measurability, understanding, and conveyability of the criteria, obligations of accountability resulting from standards, and others (see figure 6-4).

Figure 6–4

Influencing factors on test completion evaluation

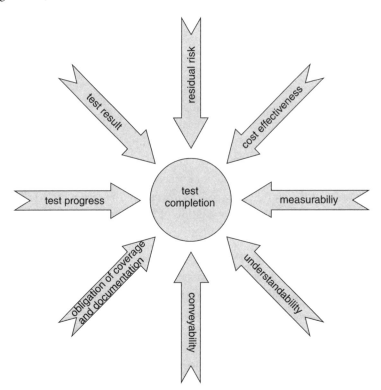

Specific test exit criteria for each test level

Typically, test exit criteria are not defined and evaluated globally but rather specifically for each test level. The metrics used are the same as those used for monitoring test progress at the particular test level (see section 6.2). Instead of giving any additional advantage, the use of other metrics will only waste effort. The trick is to combine the metrics in a goal-oriented way and to provide reasonable objectives per metric.

▪ In **component testing,** test-object-based and structure-oriented metrics are useful if combined with a metric on test scope per component.

For example, the achievement of 100% instruction coverage in "uncritical" components and 100% branch coverage for all components classed "critical" could be a useful test completion criterion.

- In **integration testing,** structure-oriented metrics are the most interesting ones. For each interface, for instance, one could request at least one "positive" (transmission of an allowed data value/data record) and one "negative" (data value outside the interface specification) test case.
- In **system test or acceptance testing,** the emphasis is on test-schedule-based, defect-based, and requirements-based metrics. One exit criterion could be 100% requirements coverage and zero defects in priority 1 test cases.

In the case of test exit criteria. it is true that, as a rule, no simple yes/no decisions can be made but the metrics used provide an acceptance range (see figure 6-5, acceptance range according to [ISO 9126] and [ISO 14598-4]). This results from the fact that data based on insecure knowledge is to be evaluated.

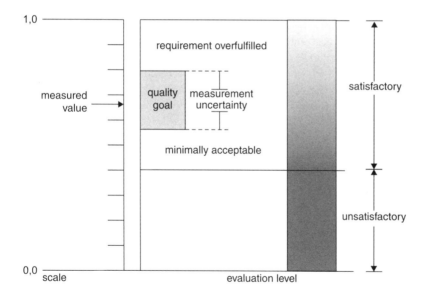

Figure 6–5

Test completion indicator and acceptance range

Test exit criteria are indicators. At test completion, evaluation derived from these indicators is always risky. However, without clear test exit criteria, we always run the risk that testing will be arbitrarily terminated due to time pressure or lack of resources.

Distinguish between test completion and product release.

This way, the test objective, which is to secure a certain minimum product quality, cannot be achieved. After test completion has been declared, the release of the test object does not automatically follow. The decision on when to "release" the tested products is a separate second step not made by the test manager but by project or product management. This decision is again based on objective release and acceptance criteria defined in the test plan (see section 5.2.7).

Example:
Evaluation of test completion in the VSR project

During the system test of the VSR project, the decision on test completion is made based on the two criteria: test progress and test result. Evaluation of data (already shown in parts in previous examples) by the test manager yields the following overall picture:

- Test progress versus test schedule: 112 test cases not yet performed, some of which are priority 1. The test completion criterion requires that "100% of prio-1 tests must be completed".
- Test progress versus test object coverage: If all high-priority requirements are validated by at least one test case, sufficient coverage of all test object areas "important" to the user is assumed. Thus, the analysis of the requirements coverage provides an informal and implicit evaluation of the residual risk. The actually achieved requirements coverage (see figure 6-3), however, shows that this test completion criterion also has not yet been met because some requirements remain untested or associated tests were unsuccessful.
- Test result: performed tests generated "critical" incident reports showing, for instance, crashes during contract storage or price calculation errors. However, the test completion criterion specifies "zero critical defects". As a result, the test manager decides in agreement with the project leader to continue testing in a further test cycle after defect correction.

6.6   Test Report

The test manager must communicate information regarding test progress, product quality, and controlling actions not only within his own team but also within his own line organization (e.g., to test managers of other test levels). To do so he needs to regularly create test reports[2] (also called test progress report or test status report).

---

2.   In the "fundamental test process" (compare figure 2-1) the creation of the test report is an independent process step. Since, essentially, the test report renders findings and results from test control, this is being discussed here in this chapter.

The test report should not be confused with the test protocol, which is created during test execution (often automated) and records the results of each individual test case. It can also record additional data and test object reactions to provide testers with detailed information about test object behavior during the test run. The test protocol documents actual behavior of the tested software, whereas the test report provides an evaluation of the tests. The test report as defined by the [IEEE 829] standard combines the test activities and test results and assesses the quality of the test objects based on the test exit criteria.

Do not confuse test report with test protocol.

It concentrates and interprets the findings of a whole range of executed test cases, evaluated test protocols, and analyzed incident reports. It is advisable to create and distribute a test report at the end of each test cycle but often it is also useful to create (shorter) weekly or monthly progress reports. Often, after test completion or at product release, a more detailed general report is issued. The reporting frequency and distribution list is in each case to be defined in the test plan.

The test report is to contain the following information in concise form:

Content of the test report

- **Context:** project, test object, author, distribution list, reporting period, etc.
- **Test progress:** summary of past test activities; if required, information about the particular focus of the past test cycle (e.g., test cycle with focus on "load test"); the most important indicators and data (test schedule and test object related) pertaining to the actual test progress, ideally supported by charts; the test manager's (subjective, informal) assessment
- **Product quality:** number and severity of detected defects, in particular, the number of new defects detected during the reporting period; progress or problems during defect removal; defect trend and product stability; the test manager's (subjective, informal) assessment or quality estimation; perhaps a statement concerning product release
- **Resources/measures:** resource workload, correction measures and reasons for them (e.g., the requirement of additional resources), perhaps a recommendation to external groups (e.g., development) concerning correction measures
- **Budget:** Overview on spent and still available money and time budget; if required, request of additional means
- **Risks:** Perceived/impending (project) risks (e.g., product release delays), other particular incidents.

- **Further planning:** upcoming tasks and outlook on the next test cycle (e.g., focus of the next test cycle), potential changes in the plan (to address newly identified risks), perhaps recommendations regarding test completion

The scope of the report may vary depending on the target audience. A report to other test groups will be more detailed and also refer to incident reports and test schedules or contain excerpts from them. A report to management will focus on issues such as budget, risks and release maturity.

Ensure comparability of reports.

The structure or form of a report should remain stable and not change from report to report. Metrics presentation, i.e., the way they are presented graphically, should not change. Easy comparison of reports is necessary because most test metrics are significant or only make sense when compared to metrics in previous test cycles. A stable reporting structure makes it easier for the reader to recognize trends in data. A test report template is available for download under [URL: Templates].

The problem with person-related assessments

Data captured for test control provides many possibilities for person-related assessments. It is relatively easy to use the incident management system to identify the "proportion of defect occurrence" per developer. The incident management system also allows easy access to productivity-related data per individual tester (e.g., "performed test cases per week," "number of rejected incident reports," etc.). Such assessments fall under the category "assessment of person-related data" and "human performance assessment".

Right to informational self-determination

In many countries, there are laws ruling the extent to which such data may be collected, stored, and used. The test manager has to be aware of such regulations and respect the employees right to informational self-determination.

Anonymized assessments are unproblematic.

Prior to setting up or even communicating person-related assessments, test managers should familiarize themselves with labor regulations and discuss the issue with affected persons, superiors, and, where applicable, staff association. Unproblematic under data privacy laws are anonymized assessments that cannot be traced back to any individuals. Of course, this does not mean that the unsatisfactory or below-average performance of a coworker needs to be tolerated.

To address this issue, a personal talk is surely better than a report circulating around the whole department. What is more, test managers must never forget to seek personal and informal communication with their staff, especially before preparing their formal report.

6.7 Summary

- The test schedule does not "implement itself." The test manager must actively see to it that planned tasks are assigned to people and that tasks are completed in time. Test progress must be regularly monitored, including all preparatory tasks related to test. Test progress can be tracked in relation to the test schedule and in relation to the test object or product scope.

- During the test cycle, the test manager must assess test progress and test results and use them as control values. Should test progress turn out to be unsatisfactory, additional testers or other resources may have to employed. Depending on the number and criticality of detected defects, the focus of the test may need to be changed.

- If circumstances change fundamentally, the test plan and further course of action in test must be adapted to these changes. The test manager must be very open in his reports about the degree by which project and product risks increase as a result.

- Due to the spot-check character of testing, the decision on test completion is always accompanied by uncertainty. Test exit criteria provide indicators by means of which the decision may be supported.

- The test manager must regularly use the test report to communicate information on test progress, product quality, and control measures initiated by him.

7 Assessing and Improving the Development and Test Processes

This chapter describes different assessment and improvement models that relate either generally to the improvement of processes, products, or services (TQM, Kaizen, Six Sigma), or specifically to the software development or test process. It also explains four appraisal or assessment models: CMMI (Capability Maturity Model Integration), ISO/ IEC 15504 (the "SPICE" model for software development), TMM (Testing Maturity Model) and TPI (Test Process Improvement); the two latter ones are designed specifically for the test process.

A whole range of studies and statistics have shown that many software development projects do not achieve their required objectives at all or achieve them only partly. One of the well-known publications is the Standish Group Chaos Report ([URL: Standish Group]). Over the past years, the percentage of successful projects—i.e., projects that have stayed within the estimated budget and schedule and have delivered the required functionality—has leveled at around 33%. Approximately one fifth of the projects are a total failure. The remaining and largest proportion of projects deliver their software systems too late, at considerably higher costs, and with a functionality unsatisfactory to the customer.

Chaos Report

According to the Chaos Report, the proportion of successful projects has decreased even further over the past years. There is a large variety of different approaches intended to raise the percentage of successful projects. Some of them, for instance Total Quality Management (TQM), relate to the management of projects or the production of goods in a more general way, whereas others concentrate specifically on the improvement of software development processes. Examples are SPICE and Test Process Improvement (TPI). TPI focuses exclusively on the test process.

What all of the approaches have in common is that they are concerned with the solution of the problems exposed in the Chaos Report. As such, they aim at the following:

Improvement objectives

- Realistic project planning and successful implementation of the plans
- Transparency of project status and project progress
- Enhancing the quality of released (software) products
- Lowering of costs during development (and maintenance)
- Reducing time to market

Defect prevention and early defect detection

Defect prevention and early detection may help to achieve or support these goals. Testing makes a substantial contribution to this process in that it appraises quality and enables controlling activities in case of poor quality. Early defect detection and removal lead to reduced costs and shorter development times because defects detected downstream are a lot more expensive and take up much more time.

The following sections look at the different improvement approaches in some more detail.

7.1   General Techniques and Approaches

These approaches to process assessment and improvement can be applied not only to software development processes but also more generally to the development and manufacturing of products. They can also be applied in the service industry.

The following sections introduce a small selection of these approaches—namely "TQM", "Kaizen", and "Six Sigma"—together with their associated practices and possible application in the software development process.

7.1.1   Total Quality Management (TQM)

The International Organization for Standardization (ISO) describes Total Quality Management as "a management approach for an organization, centered on quality, based on the participation of all its members and aiming at long-term success through customer satisfaction, and benefits to all members of the organization and to society".

Total

As the term "total" implies, TQM seeks to realize a really comprehensive concept in which all members at all hierarchical levels in an organization are involved. TQM considers the interests of the customer, of everyone in the organization, and of the suppliers. In short, all are working in concert.

Quality

Quality takes center stage, especially when it comes to customer satisfaction. Moreover, behavioral changes in the organization are supposed to improve employee satisfaction, increase productivity, lower costs, and shorten development and production cycles.

Such a concept requires active planning, development, and mainte-nance; in other words, it's needs to be "managed".

Management

TQM does not provide a plan, nor does it propose detailed practices; instead, it imparts a basic attitude toward quality and economic action. However, TQM does provide a number of relevant principles, which are briefly listed here:

No instructions— it's an attitude.

- Customer orientation: Do not produce what is technically feasible but what the customer requests and desires.

- Process orientation: Software systems are developed based on a defined process that is reproducible and that can be improved. The causes of poor quality lie in an insufficient process. Quality is not a random product but the result of a planned and repeatable process.

- Primacy of quality: Quality has absolute priority. Ambiguity or inaccu-racies that may lead to defects must be corrected or removed immedi-ately before the development process is continued. "We'll solve the problem later!" should never be heard.

- All employees accept accountability or ownership: Each employee is responsible for quality and considers it an integral part of his daily work.

- Internal customer-supplier relationship: Formal acceptance and deliv-ery of interim products are planned during software development and not just at final delivery to the customer. This way employees develop an awareness for their responsibility toward the quality of the interme-diate products. In the end, this helps to enhance the quality of the final product.

- Continuous improvement: We do not need to make revolutionary changes; small step-by-step improvements collectively implemented will bring about the desired results.

- Stabilizing improvements: During the rollout phase of changes, appro-priate measures must be taken to ensure that these changes will not be forgotten again in the daily routine. This is the only way to ensure that they will have a long-term effect.

- Rational decisions: Decisions and changes must be rationalized explic-itly and based on facts. As a prerequisite, this requires a concept con-taining continuous data collection.

A good overview of and introduction to TQM can be found in [Goetsch 02]. The rules and principles provided by TQM can be easily be applied in the test process. In TQM, test managers will find a lot of useful ideas for their daily work.

- Customer orientation: The customer agrees with the test schedule. This involves a customer review of the test schedule as a result of which he provides suggestions stating which test topics, in his view, address important or less important aspects.
- Process orientation: Testing follows the test process described in chapter 2. The process has been adapted in part to the specific requirements of the project and is documented in a system that is easily accessible via an intranet. Each team member assumes a defined role (e.g., test manager, test designer). Role-related instruction and training plans are in place.
- Primacy of quality: Testing stops as soon as the defined test exit criteria have been met, never before. All detected flaws and defects are documented. There is no unclassified or nonassigned incident. The Change Control Board (CCB) decides on correction measures.
- All employees accept accountability or ownership: Each test team member is responsible for the quality of his own work products, from the test plan and the test schedule down to the incident report. These test work products, too, are subject to (peer) reviews and corrected, if necessary.
- Internal customer-supplier relationship: Development delivers its product to component testing. The lower test level delivers the product to the next level higher up. Deliveries are performed in a formal way and accompanied by release, delivery, and acceptance tests.
- Continuous improvement: After completion of each test cycle, the test team meets to perform a postmortem analysis. Weak points that can be improved in the test process, in the application of test methods, or in the test schedule are documented. The most beneficial improvement actions are identified and implemented in the next test cycle (if required, in several steps).
- Stabilizing improvements: Implemented changes are subject to particular monitoring. It needs to be verified whether changes have the intended results and if people abide by them; i.e., whether everybody concerned has changed their working methods accordingly.
- Rational decisions: The test management tool provides an abundance of statistics and metrics. A small number of well-understood metrics (e.g., requirements coverage *new/changed/stable*, number of tests *passed/failed/blocked*, number of defects *low/medium/high*) are analyzed after each test cycle. Decisions on test completion, product release, or test schedule changes are made based on continuous data capture during each cycle and after actual data has been compared with the test exit criteria.

7.1.2 Kaizen

Kaizen is a Japanese concept and a compound of *Kai* (change) and *Zen* (for the better). Kaizen means "continuous improvement". The basic idea is this: As soon as a system or process has been implemented, it begins to degenerate if it is not permanently maintained and improved.

Continuous improvement

As in TQM, Kaizen involves all employees. Improvements are implemented through gradual, stepwise perfection and optimization. The goal of both management approaches is to have employees increasingly identify with the organization and to give it continuous competitive edge. The "Continuous Improvement Process" (CIP) may be considered an essential concept of Kaizen[1].

Everyone is involved.

The foundations of Kaizen are as follows:

Foundations of Kaizen

- Intensive use and optimization of the employee suggestion system[2]
- Appreciation and regard for employees' striving for improvement
- Established, small group discussion circles addressing defects and improvement suggestions
- "Just in time" production to eliminate wasted effort (overproduction or excess inventory)
- 5 Ss process for the improvement of workplaces (see below)
- "Total Productive Maintenance" (TPM) for maintenance and servicing of all means of production

The 5 Ss process serves as a basis for a clean, safe, and standardized working environment in the organization. The 5 Ss stand for the following five Japanese words:

5 S's process

- *Seiri* – tidiness; old and useless items have no place at the workplace.
- *Seiton* – orderliness; "everything" has its place for quick retrieval and storage.
- *Seiso* – cleanliness; keep the workplace nice and tidy at all times.
- *Seiketsu* – standardization of all practices and processes.
- *Shitsuke* – discipline; all activities are performed in a disciplined way.

---

1. TQM can also be considered a comparable concept.
2. The idea is rather less bureaucratic than the term "employee suggestion system" suggests.

Principles   The following organizational key principles are based on Kaizen:

1. Every day, some improvement must be made somewhere in the organization.
2. The improvement strategy depends on requirements and customer satisfaction.
3. Quality is always more important than profit.
4. Coworkers are encouraged to point out problems and to make suggestions for their removal.
5. Problems are solved systematically and collaboratively in groups made up of people coming from different functional areas.
6. Process-oriented thinking is a prerequisite for continuous improvement.

Test management and Kaizen   These principles and concepts are very similar to TQM but show a strong Japanese influence, which might make it difficult for them to be applied fully outside Japan or Asia. Kaizen puts its focus more on the manufacturing of goods than on software development; nevertheless, there are enough ideas and suggestions that are useful to the test manager, such as, for instance, the suggestion system or the employee appreciation program. More details on Kaizen can be found in [Imai 86].

7.1.3   Six Sigma

Static analysis   Six Sigma is another approach or framework for process improvement, using data and statistical analysis to identify problems and improvement opportunities. The objective is to produce faultless products with faultless processes.

σ (Greek Sigma) stands for "standard deviation".   The term "Six Sigma" is derived from statistics and refers to the standard deviation of a statistical distribution. The function of the Gaussian distribution is specified by two parameters: the mean and the standard deviation. A 3×Sigma standard deviation, for instance, means that the process in question is approximately 93.3% defect free; in other words, we get around 66.800 defects out of 1 million opportunities. The 6×Sigma value is only 3.4 defects per 1 million units, which means almost zero defects. Six Sigma thus signifies a systematic reduction of deviations until it reaches the "ideal" state of being almost defect free.

The Six Sigma key statements and concepts are as follows: *Basic concepts*

- Quality decides: Customer wishes and customer satisfaction are of paramount importance.
- Avoid flaws: No product release that does not fulfill customer expectations.
- Ensure process maturity: High-grade goods can only be produced with high-quality processes.
- Keep variation small: Deliver constant quality to the customer. What the customer "sees and feels" is important.
- Continuous workflow: A consistent and predictable process guarantees customer product satisfaction.
- Orientation toward Six Sigma: Customer needs are satisfied and process performance is improved.

Six Sigma practices are based on methods such as DMAIC, DMADV, and   *DMAIC, DMADV, and DFSS*
DFSS. DMAIC stands for "define, measure, analysis, improve, control" and
is used for existing processes, describing a cycle in which the individual
steps are to be performed. DMADV is an acronym for "define, measure,
analysis, design, verify" and is more or less the equivalent of DMAIC but
is used to create new product designs or process designs, as in software
development. Principally, DMADV deploys the so-called Quality Function
Deployment (QFD), which systematically maps customer requirements
into the terminology and (implementation) possibilities of developers,
testers, and (quality) managers. In doing so, the method looks at one or
more possible solutions to determine and quantify their suitability. DFSS
is short for "design for Six Sigma" and is supposed to ensure that new processes
satisfy Six Sigma requirements right from the beginning.

Performing Six Sigma projects in an organization requires training.   *Six Sigma training levels*
The training levels are usually described through the Japanese martial arts
belt system:

- *Master Black Belt*: responsible for project consulting and training
- *Black Belt:* project leader of large and complex projects
- *Green Belt:* project leader of smaller projects
- *Yellow Belt:* has basic Six Sigma knowledge

Six Sigma shows many parallels with TQM and Kaizen, too. The main dif-   *Test management*
ference is freedom from defects, proof of which is provided by statistical   *and Six Sigma*
data collections. Certainly, one of the test manager's goals is to achieve
freedom from defects in the systems he tests. To get there he has to aim

high. However, in no other area of software development is there so much sound data available for statistical analysis as in software testing, which makes statistical analysis and Six Sigma definitely an approach well worth implementing. On the other hand, we need comprehensive and above all comparable data to be able to apply Six Sigma statistical evaluation. In most cases, direct comparison of data from different projects is not that easy; the basic Six Sigma principles, however, can be applied to the test process. Detailed information relating to Six Sigma and corresponding tool support can be found in [John 06].

7.2   Improving the Software Development Process

The following sections address process assessment, improvement methods, and techniques specific to software development.

Chapter 3 introduced different software development processes. Each of the different process models defines a specific approach to software development that can be implemented in projects in many different ways. How good the approaches are implemented can be assessed, we talk about the maturity level of the ("practiced") process.

Best practices   The maturity level refers to the activities or processes defined in the development model compared to so-called "best practices" and their practical implementation. Best practices refer to activities that have, over many years, proven to be successful. The more accurately processes are defined in the development model and the higher the degree of completeness and accuracy of their implementation, the higher is their maturity level.

A process's level of maturity depends on the accuracy with which it is described in the development model and the degree of completeness and accuracy with which it is implemented and performed. The degree of maturity is often specified in maturity levels defining a logical sequence of improvement steps.

We do not wish to place any particular emphasis here on the fact that maturity evaluations are often performed simply to prove maturity "to the outside world" for marketing purposes; instead, we would like the concept to be seen as serving the purpose of "improving the inner processes and procedures" that carry a project through its life cycle.

Maturity level   Higher maturity levels comprise lower ones; i.e., it is useful to adopt a step-by-step approach. For example, level 2 is reached if the software development process is described in more detail compared to level 1 and if it has been implemented accordingly. Process-related planning, monitoring, and control are important factors in the assessment of process maturity. Increasing maturity levels mean that plan dates and the achievement of cost and quality goals can be predicted with increasing accuracy.

To determine maturity levels, "assessments"[3] are performed. During an assessment, actual processes are compared with the requirements of the assessment models[4], improvement potentials are identified, and an appropriate maturity level rating is assigned. The assessment uncovers strengths and weaknesses in the software development process that, together with the identified improvement potentials and the comparison of the assessment results with the target maturity profile, forms the basis for the planning and implementation of the process improvement actions.

Assessments

Assessment and maturity models propose some concrete measures for this purpose. In recent years, several of such models for the evaluation of software development processes have been published. All of them provide guidelines or practices by which an organization or, to be more precise, the processes and procedures of projects in an organization can be investigated, evaluated, and subsequently improved. Thus, these models are management tools for process optimization in an organization.

The following sections describe two well-known assessment models currently adopted by many industrial organizations: CMMI and ISO/IEC 15504 (SPICE).

7.2.1 Capability Maturity Model Integration (CMMI)

Capability Maturity Model Integration (CMMI) Version 1.1 [URL: CMMI] was developed by the Software Engineering Institute (SEI) of Carnegie Mellon University in Pittsburgh and released in 2002, superseding the Capability Maturity Model (CMM). CMM had been developed by the SEI in 1993[5] and had gone through several updates.

The basic idea of the CMMI model and any other assessment model is that improvements in software development processes will inevitably improve the quality of the developed system, lead to more accurate sched-

---

3. In CMMI this is called an appraisal.
4. ISO/IEC 15504 (see section 7.2.2) part 2 defines the maturity level model; part 5 defines the assessment model. CMMI (see section 7.2.1) is an assessment model that can be used in lieu of part 5.
5. 1991 published as a pilot version 1.0, 1993 version 1.1.

ule and resource planning, and make for better implementation of the plans.

Disciplines   In CMMI[6], four disciplines are defined:

- Systems Engineering (CMMI-SE)
- Software Development (CMMI-SW)
- Integrated Process and Product Development (CMMI-IPPD)
- Supplier Sourcing (CMMI-SS)

Staged and continuous representation   CMMI models have two different representations: staged and continuous [URL: CMMI-TR]. The staged representation consists of five maturity levels, whereas in the continuous representation, capability levels are assigned to individual process areas (see the following list). Each maturity level characterizes the whole of the organization. The following list briefly describes the five maturity levels, which belong to a staged representation (see also figure 7-1):

Five maturity levels

Level 1: Initial
Processes are not defined or insufficiently defined. Development processes are ad hoc and chaotic.

Level 2: Managed
Essential management processes are established and applied in projects, though in different ways or degrees.

Level 3: Defined
Standard processes are introduced throughout the organization.

Level 4: Quantitatively managed
Decisions on improvements are made based on quantitative measures. Performance measures are used intensively throughout the organization.

Level 5: Optimizing
This level is characterized by systematic and continuous process improvement. Assessment of success or failure is based on quantitative statistics.

---

6.   Besides the CMMI model discussed here, there are other models (see [URL: CMMI-Models]).

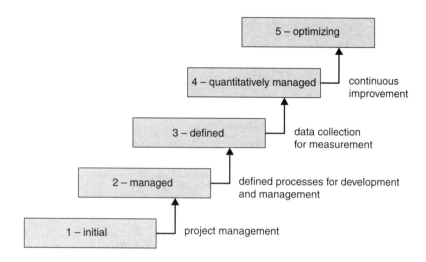

Figure 7–1
CMMI maturity levels

Another important structural element in CMMI, besides the maturity level components, consists of the process areas that cover or combine all requirements relating to one particular area. For each area, a set of goals has been defined, distinguishing between specific goals for each individual area and generic goals describing all the activities that need to be performed in order to achieve long-term, efficient implementation of the specific goals (process institutionalization).

Specific and generic goals

In CMMI, the process areas in table 7-1 are assigned to the four higher maturity levels ([URL: CMMI V1.2 Model], page 44).

Process areas

Level	Process areas
2 – Managed	Requirements Management
	Project Planning
	Project Monitoring and Control
	Supplier Agreement Management
	Measurement and Analysis
	Process and Product Quality Assurance
	Configuration Management

Table 7–1

Maturity levels and process areas

Table 7-1
(continuation)

Level	Process areas
3 – Defined	Requirements Development
	Technical Solution
	Product Integration
	Verification
	Validation
	Organizational Process Focus
	Organizational Process Definition
	Organizational Training
	Integrated Project Management
	Risk Management
	Decision Analysis and Resolution
4 – Quantitatively Managed	Organizational Process Performance
	Quantitative Project Management
5 – Optimizing	Organizational Innovation and Deployment Causal Analysis and Resolution

Continuous representation　CMMI comes with two types of representation: staged and continuous. Staged representation was already used in CMM (see figure 7-1); continuous representation assigns the process areas listed in table 7-1 to the following four categories:

- Process management
- Project management
- Engineering
- Support

Generic goals and capability levels　The continuous representation specifies five generic goals indicating the degree of institutionalization of a particular process. The path to complete implementation is divided into six capability levels (0 = incomplete, 1 = performed, 2 = managed, 3 = defined, 4 = quantitatively managed, and 5 = optimizing). The capability level refers to one process area only. This is in contrast to the maturity level in the staged model, which covers a level-specific set of process areas representing the overall level of maturity of the organizational unit. Continuous representation allows a much more specific description and evaluation of the respective process or process area (see, for example, figure 7-2).

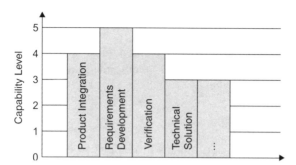

Figure 7–2

*Capability grade of
individual process areas*

Testing in CMMI

The process areas verification and validation are of utmost importance to the test manager. In the staged model, both areas belong to maturity level 3 (defined), whereas in the continuous model, they are part of the engineering discipline. Both process areas will be described in the following sections. Further information on CMMI is provided by [Chrissis 06] and Internet sources (e.g., [URL: CMMI], [URL: CMMI V1.2 Model]).

*Process areas:
verification and validation*

Verification

"CMMI requirements regarding verification are of a relatively general nature, requiring verification to be prepared, that work products are selected for verification, peer reviews are conducted (...) and, generally, verification be executed" (translation from the German book [Kneuper 06], page 56).

To verify the implementation of specifications, the following methods are mentioned: (peer) review, test, and (static) analysis.[7]

Validation

Validation is the process of verifying if customer requirements have been implemented and must be seen in close connection with the requirements development process area (maturity level 3, Engineering discipline).

"The task is to verify constantly and repeatedly if the defined results and requirements actually achieve the intended benefit. For this reason validation is a step within the requirements development process (...).

This also holds true vice versa: If requirements development and verification have gone well, there will not be much left to do for validation

---

7.   All three techniques are described in more detail in *Software Testing Foundations* ([Spillner 07]).

except for the user to accept the system" (translation from the German book [Kneuper 06], page 58/59).

CMMI requires that validation be prepared and performed; however, it does not specify any concrete and applicable (checking or verification) methods.

Test manager and CMMI

The test manager will not find any more detailed descriptions or support than what he already knows about the fundamental test process (see chapter 2). For instance, he gets told what activities are necessary to set up a test environment.[8] What becomes clear, however, is that being a part of the software development process, the test process also profits if the development process has a high maturity level.

7.2.2 ISO/IEC 15504 (SPICE)

In 1993, the Software Process Improvement and Capability dEtermination (SPICE [URL: SPICE]) project was launched to unify available evaluation methods such as CMMI, Trillium[9], Software Technology Diagnostic[10], and Bootstrap[11] and to define an international standard.

Besides other models, the SPICE project group used CMM as a basis to develop a fairly similar approach to the one used in CMMI. The project led to the ISO/IEC 15504 standard, which was published as a technical report in 1998. Currently, parts 1 to 5 are published and further parts are under preparation (see [URL: ISO]).

In contrast to CMMI, the SPICE model consists of continuous representation only and identifies individual process capability levels. To make it possible to assess the different processes used in different business sectors, variants such as "Automotive SPICE", "SPICE4SPACE", "MEDI-SPICE", etc. have been developed. The standard forms the framework for a consistent performance evaluation of the "practiced" processes applied in an organizational unit, comprising process evaluation, process improvement, and performance evaluation (see figure 7-3).

---

8. See [URL: CMMI V1.2 Model], "Establish the validation environment", page 486.
9. Extension of CMM specifically for telecommunications software.
10. For small organizations.
11. EU process improvement program; discontinued.

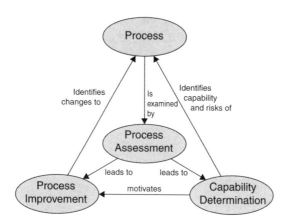

Figure 7–3

Correlation between process, process evaluation, process improvement, and performance evaluation (Figure from http:// www.sqi.gu.edu.au/spice/)

The model defines six capability levels:

The process is

ISO/IEC 15504
Capability level

- ▥ incomplete (level 0),
- ▥ performed (level 1),
- ▥ managed (level 2),
- ▥ established (level 3),
- ▥ predictable (level 4), or
- ▥ optimizing (level 5).

One of the criticisms of the CMM maturity level model was that the step from level 1 (initial) to level 2 (managed) was considered too big. However, the maturity levels in CMM relate to all the process areas of that maturity level. This criticism was taken up in SPICE and CMMI in the continuous representation, and an additional lower level was defined. The upper four capability levels are comparable to those in CMM and the continuous representation in CMMI. The two lower levels are briefly characterized here:

One additional level

- ▥ "Level 0; Not-Performed: There is general failure to perform the base practices in the process. There are no easily identifiable work products or outputs of the process.
- ▥ Level 1; Performed-Informally: Base practices of the process are generally performed. The performance of these base practices may not be rigorously planned and tracked. Performance depends on individual knowledge and effort. Work products of the process testify to the performance. Individuals within the organization recognize that an action should be performed, and there is general agreement that this action is

performed as and when required. There are identifiable work products for the process." ([URL: SPICE doc] Part 2)

Five process areas   Processes are categorized into process categories and organized into nine process groups in [ISO 15504] to gain more clarity within the reference model:

Primary (PLC)

- Acquisition (ACQ)
- Supply (SPL)
- Engineering (ENG)
- Operation (OPE)

Organization & Management (OLC)

- Management (MAN)
- Process Improvement (PIM)
- Resource and Infrastructure (RIN)
- Reuse (REU)

Support (SLC)

- Support (SUP)

Base processes   Each of the process groups is divided even further, amounting to several hundred base processes or base practices. Similarly to CMMI, there are also generic practices that are generally applicable and not assigned to individual processes. Examples are the planning of a process or the training of staff members; such practices are applicable to all processes.

Software construction (ENG.6), Software testing (ENG.8), and System testing (ENG.10) belong to the Engineering (ENG) process category and are of particular interest[12] to the test manager. The same applies to Verification (SUP.2) and Validation (SUP.3) which belong to the Support (SUP) category.

The standard specifies that testing should be performed by persons or teams that are independent from developers. Planning and test preparation is to be started in parallel to the analysis and design phase. SPICE in particular requires full traceability of requirements to test cases already at level 1. Both test process (ENG.8) and (ENG.10) are discussed in the following sections. Internet sources (e.g., [URL: SPICE] and [URL: ISO]) provide further information on ISO/IEC 15504.

---

12. ENG.2 and ENG.3 also address test planning and preparation.

Software Test (ENG.8)

For software testing, the model lists the following activities (practices):

- Develop tests for integrated software product
- Test integrated software product
- Regression test integrated software

Each activity is accompanied by a brief explanation. During test specification for the integrated software system, the different processes (requirements specification, design specification, implementation) are stated and a test specification must be created in parallel.

System Test (ENG.10)

The same activities are listed as in software test (ENG.8), with the addition of

- Confirm system readiness.

Similar to software test, each activity is accompanied by a brief explanation. ENG.10, too, explicitly points out that preparatory tasks are to be performed in parallel to development.

Test Manager and SPICE

The SPICE standard provides test managers with relevant task descriptions and lists and explains all the documents to be developed by them or their test teams. Explanations, however, are not very detailed, but it becomes clear that a structured development process is of advantage for the test process.

7.2.3   Comparing CMMI with SPICE

With the replacement of CMM by CMMI, the differences to ISO/IEC 15504 have become smaller. This is not surprising as it was one of the SPICE project's objectives to harmonize the different evaluation models. The close correlation between the two models is emphasized by the fact that CMMI can be used as a reference model in an ISO/IEC 15504 assessment. Nevertheless, both models contain issues that are not treated in the other model.

From the test manager's point of view, particulars relating to the test process are too general and too imprecise to provide him with concrete assistance in his daily work.

7.3 Evaluation of Test Processes

Since CMMI and ISO/IEC 15504 do not cover the test process sufficiently, evaluation and improvement models have been developed that focus exclusively on the test process. Two such models are introduced in the following section, the "Testing Maturity Model" (TMM) and the "Test Process Improvement" (TPI) model.

7.3.1 Testing Maturity Model (TMM)™

CMM as basis The Testing Maturity Model was developed by the Illinois Institute of Technology in Chicago in 1996 ([Burnstein 96]), using as one of its bases the Capability Maturity Model (CMM). In analogy to CMM, TMM uses the concept of maturity models for process evaluation and improvement.

TMM puts particular focus on testing as a process to be evaluated and improved. Improvement of the process is supposed to achieve the following objectives (according to [Burnstein 96], page 9):

- smarter testers
- higher quality software
- the ability to meet budget and scheduling goals
- improved planning
- the ability to meet quantifiable testing goals

Oriented toward the CMM concept, TMM consists of five identically structured maturity levels containing the following parts (see figure 7-4):

- **Maturity goals**
  are defined for each level except level 1.
- **Maturity sub-goals**
  are concretely specified and provide information relating to the scope, range, constraints, and performance of process evaluation and improvement activities and tasks.
- **Activities/tasks and responsibilities**
  are described in detail and must be performed to reach the respective maturity level. Three groups of people are involved: manager, developer and tester, user and customer.

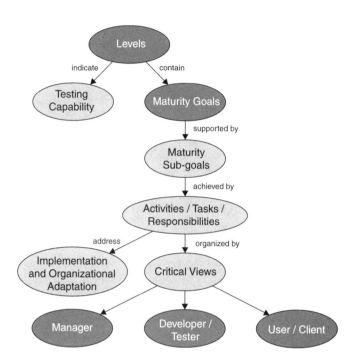

Figure 7–4

Internal TMM level structure

Table 7-2 shows the structure and processes of the five TMM maturity levels.

Levels	Process Areas
1 – Initial	No processes identified
2 – Phase Definition	Test Policy and Goals Test Planning Test Techniques and Methods Test Environment
3 – Integration	Test Organization Test Training Program Test Life Cycle and Integration Control and Monitor
4 – Management and Measurement	Peer Reviews Test Measurement Software Quality Evaluation
5 – Optimization	Defect Prevention Quality Control Test Process Optimization

Table 7–2

TMM maturity models and process areas

Following [van Veenendaal 02], the individual levels are described in the following paragraphs:

1-Initial

At level 1, testing is a chaotic, undefined process and considered to be part of debugging. The objective of testing at this level is to show that no serious anomalies occur during software execution. Software quality evaluation and defect-related risk assessment does not take place and software products are released with poor quality. Within the test process, there is a lack of resources, support tools, and qualified testers.

2-Phase definition

At level 2, the test process is seen as a defined process clearly separated from debugging. Test plans are established and contain a definition of the test strategy. Test techniques are applied to derive and select test cases from requirements specifications. However, test activities still start relatively late—e.g., parallel to the component specification or coding phase. The main objective of testing is to verify that the specified requirements are satisfied.

3-Integration

At level 3, the test process is fully integrated in the software development life cycle. Test planning is performed at an early stage. Test strategy is based on fully documented requirements and determined by risk considerations. Testing focuses on invalid inputs and failure situations. Reviews are performed, although not yet in a consistent or formal way and not yet throughout the entire development life cycle.

A test organization exists, as well as a specific test training program. Testers are perceived as an independent, professional group.

4-Management and measurement

At level 4, testing is a comprehensively defined and measurable process. Individual test activities are well founded. Document reviews are systematically performed throughout the entire software development life cycle using agreed-upon selection criteria. Reviews are considered to be an important supplement to testing. Software products are evaluated using quality criteria such as reliability, usability, and maintainability. Test cases are gathered, stored, and managed in a central database for later reuse and regression testing. Test measurements provide information regarding test process and software product quality. Testing is perceived as evaluation across the entire development process and includes reviews.

5-Optimization, defect prevention, and quality control

At the highest level, level 5, testing is now a completely defined process. Costs and test effectiveness are controllable. Test techniques are optimized and test process improvement is continuously pursued. Defect prevention and quality control are part of the test process.

A documented procedure is in place for the selection and evaluation of test tools. All test activities are as much tool supported as possible. Early defect prevention is the main objective of the test process. Testing has a positive impact on the entire development life cycle.

Maturity Goals and Maturity Sub-goals

To convey a more detailed idea of maturity goals and sub-goals, a sample selection is described here.

The organization has set up a group responsible for the development of the test policy and test objectives. It enjoys full management support and has been provided with sufficient funds. The committee defines and documents goals for testing and debugging and communicates them to all project managers and developers. The test objectives are reflected in the test schedule.

Level 2
test policy and
test objectives

A group for test planning has been established. A test schedule template has been developed and distributed to all project managers and developers. Basic planning tools have been evaluated, recommended, and purchased.

Level 2
test planning

A company-wide test technology group has been set up to develop, evaluate, and recommend a set of basic test techniques and methods (e.g., individual black box and white box test techniques and requirements tracing as well as making a distinction between the different test levels: module test, integration test, system test, and acceptance test). The issue of adequate tool support has also been addressed by the group.

Level 2
test techniques and
test methods

A company-wide test group has been built up with the necessary management support. Test process roles and duties are defined. Well-trained and motivated members of staff could be won to join the test group. The communication channels used by the test group allow direct involvement of users and customers in the test process. User wishes, worries, and requirements are gathered, documented, and incorporated in the test process.

Level 3
test organization

Management has set up a training program, taking into consideration training objectives and plans. A training group has been established in the organization, equipped with all necessary tools, premises, and materials.

Level 3
test training program

The organization has defined mechanisms and objectives for test process control and monitoring. Principal process-related measurements are defined and documented. In case of significant deviations from the test

Level 3
monitoring and control

plan, correction measures and contingency plans have been developed and documented.

Maturity models in CMM and TMM

TMM is intended to complement CMM (or CMMI). The maturity levels of both models correspond to a large extent. Since the test process is considered to constitute part of the software development process, TMM process areas (maturity goals) closely correlate to the CMM[13] process areas (key process areas).

An overview of the corresponding levels of the two evaluation models is shown in table 7-3 ([van Veenendaal 02]).

Table 7–3

Process areas and maturity models in TMM and CMM

TMM	CMM	Process Areas
2	2	Requirements Management Software Project Planning Configuration Management
3	2	Software Project Tracking and Oversight Software Quality Assurance
3	3	Organizational Process Focus Organizational Process Definition Training Program
4	3	Intergroup Coordination Peer Reviews
4	4	Quantitative Process Management Software Quality Management
5	5	Defect Prevention Technology Change Management Process Change Management

TMM Assessment Model (TMM-AM)

TMM-AM is intended to help organizations evaluate and improve their testing practices. Several input documents are required as an evaluation basis in a TMM assessment. Apart from the testing maturity model, three more elements are used in the assessment:

---

13. Since TMM is based on CMM, TMM is compared with CMM rather than CMMI.

- Questionnaire
- Assessment procedure
- Team training and selection criteria

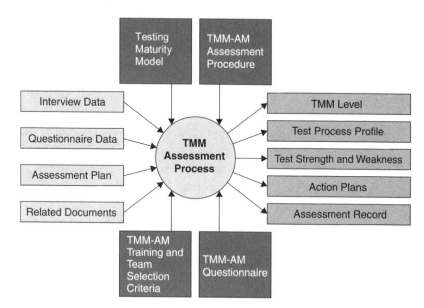

Figure 7–5

TMM-AM: Inputs, components and results

After the assessment, five outputs or results are available (maturity level, test process profile, test strengths and weaknesses, action plan, and assessment report, see figure 7-5). A more detailed description of the Testing Maturity Model can be found in [Burnstein 03].

7.3.2 Test Process Improvement® (TPI)

The Test Process Improvement model is based on Sogeti Netherlands B.V.'s[14] many years of experience in the field of testing ([URL: Sogeti]).

The model serves to assess the maturity of the test processes within an organization and supports stepwise process improvement (see figure 7-6).

Since testing comprises a whole range of tasks and activities that need to be evaluated, TPI has defined 20 key areas. One key area, for example, addresses important aspects related to the use of tools.

Twenty key areas and corresponding level

---

14. Formerly IQUIP.

Figure 7–6

Main elements
of the TPI model

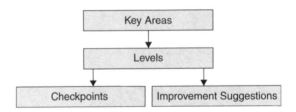

To evaluate the test process, each of the 20 key areas is assigned a particular level. On average there are three levels per key area. So-called checkpoints are used to determine the strengths and weaknesses of a test process. Levels are defined in such a way that improvements from a lower to a higher level have a measurable impact on testing time, required budget, and/or resulting quality. At each level, improvement suggestions are given to help reach the next higher level. Figure 7-6 illustrates the relationship between the main elements of the TPI model.

Similar to SPICE, the TPI has been adapted to meet the needs of different business sectors. "TPI Automotive" covers 21 key areas with a slight bias toward application in the automotive industry. This model variant is suitable in cases where there is a close relationship between a customer and several suppliers, requiring the customer to be the central integrator of different hardware and software components coming from different sources.

Key Areas, Levels, Checkpoints

TPI key areas

This section lists the model's key areas and describes three of them in more detail: "Test strategy," "Life cycle model," "Moment of involvement," "Estimating and planning," "Test specification techniques," "Static test techniques," "Metrics," "Test tools," "Test environment," "Office environment," "Commitment and motivation," "Test functions and training," "Scope of methodology," "Communication," "Reporting," "Defect management," "Testware management," "Test process management," "Evaluation," and "Low-level tests" (TPI Automotive covers the additional key area "Integration testing").

Key area
Test strategy

"The test strategy has to be focused on detecting the most important defects as early and as cheaply as possible. The test strategy defines which requirements and (quality) risks are covered by what tests. The better each test level defines its own strategy and the more the different test level strategies are adjusted to each other, the higher the quality of the overall test strategy" ([Koomen 99], page 35). In order to reach level A, level A must also be achieved in the key areas "Test specification techniques" (informal techniques) and "Commitment and motivation" (assignment of budget and time). Otherwise, the Test strategy will not be able to distinguish between low-level and high-level tests and resource distribution will be insufficient.

"Although the actual execution of the test normally begins after realization of the software, the test process must and can start much earlier. An earlier involvement of testing in the system development path helps to find defects as soon and as easily as possible and even to prevent errors. A better adjustment between the different tests can be done and the period of time that testing is on the critical path of the project can be kept as short as possible" ([Koomen 99], page 36). Here, a dependency exists on the key area "Life-cycle model". The phases planning and preparation are to be differentiated.

Key area
Moment of involvement

"The test staff need rooms, desks, chairs, PCs, word processing facilities, printers, telephones, and so on. A good and timely organization of the Office environment has a positive influence on the motivation of the test staff, on communication inside and outside of the team, and on the efficiency of the work" ([Koomen 99], page 38).

Key area
Office environment

The 20 key areas are organized in levels. Checkpoints are used for the evaluation and assignment of key areas to a particular level.

Levels and checkpoints

For the key area "Test strategy", four levels (A, B, C, and D) have been defined. At the lowest level (A), four checkpoints must be fulfilled:

- A1. "A motivated consideration of the product risks takes place for which knowledge of the system, its use, and its operational management is required.
- A2. There is a differentiation in test depth, depending on the risks and, if present, depending on the acceptance criteria: not all subsystems and not every quality characteristic is tested equally thoroughly.
- A3. One or more specification techniques are used, suited to the required depth of a test.
- A4. For retests also, a (simple) strategy determination takes place, in which a motivated choice of variations between 'test solutions only' and 'full retest' is made" ([Koomen 99], page 85-86). This is also done for further checkpoints of the upper three levels of the "Test strategy" key area.

Key area
Test strategy, lowest-level checkpoints

For the key area "Moment of involvement," there are levels with corresponding checkpoints:

Key area
Moment of involvement,
levels and checkpoints

"Level A – Completion of test basis:

A1. The activity 'testing' starts simultaneously with or earlier than the completion of the test basis for a restricted part of the system that is to be tested separately.

(The system can be divided into several parts that are finished, built, and tested separately. The testing of the first subsystem has to start at the same time or earlier than the completion of the test basis of that particular subsystem.)

Level B – Start of test basis:

B1. The activity 'testing' starts simultaneously with or earlier than the phase in which the test basis (often the functional specifications) is defined.

Level C – Start of requirements definition:

C1. The activity 'testing' starts simultaneously with or earlier than the phase in which the requirements are defined.

Level D – Project initiation:

D1. When the project is initiated, the activity 'testing' is also started" ([Koomen 99], page 98-101).

If all the respective checkpoints are fulfilled, the level of the key area is considered achieved.

TPI matrix

TPI matrix   All key areas with their maturity levels are combined in the test maturity matrix (TPI matrix) to show the dependencies between the different keys areas and maturity levels. The matrix distributes the different maturity levels of each key area across the 13 scales or development levels (see figure 7-7).

	Key area / Scale	0	1	2	3	4	5	6	7	8	9	10	11	12	13
1	Test strategy		A					B				C		D	
2	Life-cycle model		A			B									
3	Moment of involvement			A				B				C		D	
4	Estimating and planning				A							B			
5	Test specification techniques		A		B										
6	Static test techniques					A		B							
7	Metrics						A			B			C		D
8	Test tools					A			B			C			
9	Test environment				A				B						C
10	Office environment				A										
11	Commitment and motivation		A				B						C		
12	Test functions and training				A			B				C			
13	Scope of methodology					A						B			C
14	Communication			A		B							C		
15	Reporting		A			B		C					D		
16	Defect management		A				B		C						
17	Testware management			A			B				C				D
18	Test process management		A		B								C		
19	Evaluation							A			B				
20	Low-level testing						A		B		C				

Figure 7–7

TPI Matrix

The matrix makes it easy to see which key area has reached which level; i.e., at which level of the scale it is situated. Anomalies—either positive or negative—become visible. The goal is to achieve continuous improvement without leaving lower-level key areas behind. The 13 maturity or development scales can be grouped into three categories:

- **"Controlled**:
  Scales 1 to 5 are primarily aimed at the control of the test process. The purpose of the levels is to provide a controlled test process that provides a sufficient amount of insight into the quality of the tested object. (…)
- **Efficient:**
  The levels in scales 6 to 10 focus more on the efficiency of the test process. This efficiency is achieved, for example, by automating the test process, by better integration between the mutual test processes and

with the other parties within system development, and by consolidating the working method of the test process in the organization.

- **Optimizing:**
  (...) The levels of the last three scales are characterized by increasing optimization of the test process and are aimed at ensuring that continuous improvement of the generic test process will be part of the regular working method of the organization" (excerpt from [Koomen 99], page 46-47).

TPI Assessment

A TPI assessment evaluates the test process, using the checkpoints to determine the level of achievement for the 20 key areas. The TPI matrix is also used to determine the next improvement actions and the target situation (see figure 7-8).

Figure 7–8

Current situation ...

Current situation

	Key area	Scale	0	1	2	3	4	5	6	7	8	9	10	11	12	13
1	Test strategy			A					B				C		D	
2	Life-cycle model			A		B										
3	Moment of involvement				A				B				C		D	
4	Estimating and planning					A							B			
5	Test specification techniques			A		B										
6	Static test techniques						A	B								
...																

...and required situation

Required situation

	Key area	Scale	0	1	2	3	4	5	6	7	8	9	10	11	12	13
1	Test strategy			A					B				C		D	
2	Life-cycle model			A		B										
3	Moment of involvement				A				B				C		D	
4	Estimating and planning					A							B			
5	Test specification techniques			A		B										
6	Static test techniques						A	B								
...																

For a test process to achieve a higher level, the checkpoints already provide concrete starting points. Further ideas on how to improve the test process are given in the improvement suggestions. For each transition to a higher level, the TPI model offers a variety of suggestions. These are meant as hints and tips and are, in contrast to the checkpoint criteria, not mandatory. For a comprehensive list of suggestions see [Koomen 99].

Improvement suggestions

Improvement Techniques

The methods of test process improvement are very similar to any other improvement technique (see figure 7-9). Once an awareness has been created in an organization for the necessity for change, improvement goals and the ways in which they are to be achieved can be defined.

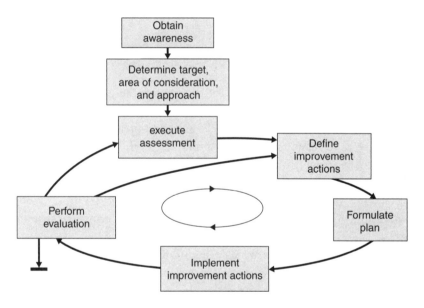

Figure 7–9

Improvement process

A TPI assessment evaluates the current situation. The use of the TPI model is an important part of this activity since they provide a frame of reference for identifying the strengths and weaknesses of the test process. Individual key areas are evaluated based on interviews and documentation and by using checkpoints, determining which of the questions can be answered positively and which not or only partly. The test maturity matrix is used to give a complete status overview of the test process in the organization.

Improvement actions are determined in such a way as to make step-by-step improvement possible. The TPI matrix helps in selecting the key areas

Improvement actions

in need for improvement. For each of the key areas, it is possible to move to the next level or, in special cases, to an even higher level (see figure 7-8).

Planning

A plan is drawn up to implement the short-term improvement actions; the plan contains the targets and indicators as to which improvements need to be implemented at what time in order to reach them.

Implementing the improvement actions

In a next step the plan is implemented. A vital part of the implementation phase is consolidation to prevent improvement actions from remaining once-only affairs.

Evaluation

During evaluation, the test manager needs to determine the extent to which improvement actions have been successfully performed and the extent to which original targets have been achieved. This forms the basis for the decision on the continuation and possible adjustment of the change process. If the intended overall target has been reached, the improvement process is considered completed.

7.3.3 Comparing TMM with TPI

Both TMM and TPI are exclusively focused on the test process. TMM development was based on CMM and leads to an assessment of the entire test process in terms of maturity levels. For a comprehensive evaluation of the software development and test processes, both types of evaluations should be performed.

TPI evaluates 20 (or 21) test-process-related key areas separately, thus resembling the CMMI continuous representation or ISO/IEC 15504, where individual process areas are also assessed in terms of capability levels.

TPI & TMM for the test manager

Both evaluation models are very important to the test manager as they help him to analyze and evaluate the test process and to start relevant improvement activities.

Both models provide useful information and advice regarding the test process. However, which of the two models is best suited for the job also depends on the particular situation in an organization. If a company is going for a CMMI appraisal (staged), TMM may be more familiar since it is similarly structured. Both TPI and TMM, however, are equally suited as complements to all the other assessment models. The TPI description is more detailed and the model appears to be more widely distributed. The results of a worldwide survey on the application of TPI are presented on Sogeti's website ([URL: TPI] Survey).

Detailed descriptions can be found in *Practical Software Testing* [Burnstein 03] for TMM and in *Test Process Improvement: A Practical Step-by-Step Guide to Structured Testing* [Koomen 99] for TPI.

The "Expert Level" program of the ISTQB Certified Tester Qualification scheme will include a training module exclusively dedicated to test process improvement.

Certified Tester – Expert Level

7.4   Audits and Assessments

An audit is defined as a systematic and independent examination to evaluate software products and development processes and determine compliance with standards, guidelines, specifications, and/or processes. Audits are based on objective criteria and documents that accomplish the following:

Systematic and independent examinations

- Determine the design or content of a product solution
- Describe the product's development process
- Specify the methods and techniques used to prove or measure compliance or noncompliance with standards and guidelines

Besides checking compliance with standards and guidelines, audits can also check on the effectiveness of an implementation and evaluate a artifact.

Types of audit

There are three types of audits:

- The system audit examines the quality management system or selected parts of it with regard to structure and workflow.
- The process audit analyzes processes with regard to human resource allocation, process monitoring, and the order of individual process steps.
- A product audit evaluates (part) products relative to their compliance with specification and adherence to standards and guidelines.

Audits usually last one to two days and the audit team is typically made up of two to four people. All audits aim at revealing weaknesses, documenting them, and proposing concrete and lasting improvements. Useful steps are as follows:

Audits

1. Determine the need for an audit (e.g., recognized necessity for internal process improvement or external customer requirement).

2. Plan the audits (content, team, formal basis, resources, dates).
3. Perform the audits in accordance with the plan and determine the achieved results.
4. Discuss strengths and weaknesses and decide whether or not improvement actions are necessary.
5. Implement the improvement suggestions and ensure appropriate reporting and archiving.

Assessments   Assessments are similar to larger audits; they last several days and involve teams that are typically made up of three to five people.

An assessment checks the operational processes and practices against the requirements of an assessment model, analyzing, in interviews, not only the direct artifacts (guidelines, work instructions, process models) and indirect artifacts (protocols, reports, filled-in templates) but also the actually "practiced" processes used in a project. Sometimes the assessment team may even "look over an expert's shoulder" at their workplace to get a clearer idea of applied work practices.

CMMI and SPICE are typical assessment (or appraisal) examples. Maturity or capability levels assigned to organizations or individual processes are determined. Strengths and weaknesses are pointed out as well as improvement potentials, and identifying opportunities for synergies and lead competencies (especially where several organizational units or projects are compared).

Out of the five parts of the ISO/IEC 15504 (SPICE) standard, three deal directly with assessments: "Part 2 – Performing an Assessment", "Part 3 – Guidance on Performing an Assessment", and "Part 5 – An Assessment Model and Indicator Guidance".

The purpose of these detailed descriptions is to ensure that different assessment results can be compared and that different assessors—i.e., the persons actually conducting the assessment—diverge as little as possible[15] in their evaluation results.

TMM and TPI assessments were briefly described in the previous sections (7.3.1 and 7.3.2). More details on how to conduct an assessment can be found in the literature cited there.

---

15. However, only Part 2 is normative, i.e., SPICE assessments results can generally not be compared.

7.4.1   Performing an Internal Audit or Assessment

All of the evaluation models mentioned here contain guidelines on how to conduct assessments. The different steps and activities required during the preparation of an assessment (irrespective of whether external or internal) are more or less the same in all models. The following list of the "assessment input" is based on ISO/IEC 15504 part 2:

- Identify the sponsor. The sponsor provides budget and time for the assessment. He is the person in the enterprise who has a prime interest in the assessment. It is most important to find out about his expectations and to obtain his commitment to perform the assessment with the estimated scope of effort identified in the plan, especially in the case of an internal assessment that may otherwise run the risk of being dismissed as a seemingly meaningless activity because it does not yield any immediate profit.   *Sponsor*
- Identify the purpose of the assessment. Further planning steps depend on the (business) purpose and concern—for example, the selection of the processes and organizational units to be assessed. The sponsor is the primary contact for this issue, but there may be other stakeholders who should also be consulted.   *Purpose*
- Determine the scope. The organizational units, the processes, and the maximum maturity grades to be considered are derived based on the purpose of the assessment and on the actual situation within the company. Background information—such as an organization's size, business sector, and complexity; the type of products or services it provides; and in particular, current problems it may have in projects or with particular products—plays an important role in determining the scope.   *Scope*
- Select assessment approach and model. Depending on the purpose and scope of the assessment, different models can be chosen. The test processes of a manufacturer of medical equipment may, for instance, be assessed using either the "pure " TPI model or the automotive TPI variant, the latter putting special focus on integration testing, a fact that certainly makes sense in a company producing integrated hardware and software solutions.   *Approach*

   In contrast to external assessments, internal assessments enjoy much more freedom—for instance, in combining several models and/ or using only certain aspects of them to address the objectives of the assessment even more accurately. However, this is an approach that can be recommended only to very experienced assessors.

Constraints   Identify the constraints. The most obvious constraint influencing the scope of the assessment is the available budget. Other possible constraints may be the unavailability of interview partners (e.g., because of time pressures in the project), the period scheduled for the assessment, the selected processes and organizational units, and the types and amount of evidence[16] that is supposed to be collected. Unfortunately, in practice, internal assessments suffer more constraints than external assessments. This is an immediate consequence of the often low priority given to internal assessment (e.g., as opposed to the priority given to project work).

Control and confidentiality   Control over assessment results and confidentiality. Assessment partners will give honest answers only if they can be sure that assessment results are treated as confidential. It must be clear to everybody involved in the assessment right from the start to which degree and for which purposes someone will have right of access to assessment results. In internal assessments, this aspect is often sadly neglected.

Involved stakeholders   Identify involved stakeholders and roles. Roles involved in assessed processes must be covered at least by one person participating in the assessment. Representatives from each of the assessed projects must participate. These people must (of course) be available and must have been briefed at the beginning of the assessment about details (purpose, for example) mentioned earlier, the applied assessment, and their role in the assessment. Frequently, in internal assessments, one person assumes several roles; however, what must be avoided at all cost is that during an assessment, an assessor assumes the role of an assessee.

Assessment preparation is decisive for success.   Preparation for an assessment is the most important step because it is the one most critical for the success of the assessment. During this phase the goals of the assessment or process improvement are defined and derived from the organization's business goals, a process that may perhaps raise false expectations or lead to erroneous interpretation of goal statements or to people failing to obtain important opinions. Internal assessments are often exposed to the added danger of having certain preparatory aspects not taken as seriously as they would be for an external assessment—a kind of boomerang that will practically always fall back on the assessment itself because its results will never have the same validity or significance they

---

16. Assessment results that serve as evidence for a particular maturity level; this may be interview statements, documents, data in tool databases, etc.

would have after thorough preparation! Using the preceding list to prepare the assessment input will considerably reduce the risk of error during this phase.

In a next step, planning of the assessment starts based on the information obtained. Among others, the following aspects ought to be considered:

Planning assessments

- Risks that may lead to assessment failure or to adversely affecting utilization of the results
- Interview planning, schedule and resource planning
- Provision of all organizational elements required for the assessment (infrastructure, access to databases, necessary process and project documents, etc.)

After preparations are completed, the actual assessment is carried out; i.e., documents are viewed and evaluated, interviews are conducted and recorded. For the assessor, the focus of this task is on ensuring traceability and completeness of the observations based on sufficient documentation. It makes sense to have the assessment carried out by at least two sufficiently qualified assessors (essentially, people with the necessary model competency, experience, software know-how, and neutrality). Practice has shown that the degree of stringency applied in an assessment is a critical influencing factor in the evaluation process. On the one hand, execution of the assessment may be too lax (it's only an internal assessment); on the other hand, it may be too strict (for example, if one of the assessors gets tied up over some issue that they have always felt to be a real nuisance but has very little priority).

View documents and conduct interviews.

After the assessment is completed and all collected information has been recorded, results are validated. Assessors compare their observations to reach agreement and present their preliminary findings in an on-site presentation to the interview partners. Using the specific assessment criteria, the validated and consolidated results are then evaluated to determine the suggestions for improvement. Assessment findings (in particular the detected strengths and weaknesses) together with the suggestions for improvement are subsequently compiled in a final report that is delivered to the sponsor and assessees (depending on confidentiality agreements and presented results, this may happen on two different occasions).

Validate the results.

7.4.2   Preparing an External Audit or Assessment

In principle, the best preparation for an external audit or assessment is a previous internal audit or assessment. For a learning organization that permanently controls and optimizes its processes, this is mandatory anyway. ISO 9000:2000, for example, stipulates that regular internal audits are held.

Motivation for an external assessment

There may be different motivations for an external assessment, each bringing different stakeholders into play. A customer, for instance, may want (somebody) to assess a supplier's suitability and perhaps be involved in improving the quality of the supplier's products.

It is quite conceivable that a customer imposes an assessment on a supplier to evaluate its processes with a distinct bias on the supplier's obligations toward him as the customer without considering his own obligations toward the supplier, and then even expect the supplier to pay for it all.

As a supplier, you should always proceed on the assumption that the assessment will provide you with useful information that will more than compensate you for the seeming disadvantage of the customer having imposed it upon you. Do not let yourself get pushed into a passive role, especially not during the preparation phase, but get actively involved in the planning process and defining the objectives. This is the only way to protect your own interests and to ensure that you can use the findings of the assessment to your own advantage.

Self-initiated assessments

An organization can initiate an external assessment itself—for instance, to obtain certification for a particular maturity level and to be able to identify improvement potential.

Assessor quality

Assessors are pledged to observe absolute neutrality at all times, and it must be ensured that the assessment is not used to pursue any political purpose or to obtain short-term monetary gains. The professional competence of the assessor, too, must be guaranteed. In this respect, CMMI and SPICE offer better opportunities than TMM and TPI because these models provide relevant certification and qualification training programs. For SPICE, this is INTACS (INTernational ISO/IEC 15504 Assessor Certification Scheme [URL: INTACS]), and for CMMI, it is SCAMPI (Standard CMMI Appraisal Method for Process Improvement [URL: SCAMPI]).

Pursuing different objectives may be a danger.

In a next step, it is important to obtain clarity about the inputs for the assessment (see list of the "assessment input", section 7.4.1). Especially in cases where the assessment is initiated by the customer and where it is performed by the organization itself or by some third party, there is a risk that the contractor, assessor, and organization hold very different views on the objectives of the assessment.

If this risk is not recognized, or even worse, if it is recognized but ignored, the consequences will be similar to those resulting from badly prepared internal assessments; i.e., unreasonable expectations, cover-up of problems, inaccurate results, and suboptimal improvement activities.

If an external assessment is carried out based on a process model unknown to the internal participants, a certain familiarity with the model needs to be established prior to the assessment. An assessor aware of his duties will ensure that this is done and brief all participants in good time.

While the assessment is being held, the assessed organization puts its main focus on making all the necessary information available; i.e., providing all the necessary documents and ensuring the availability of interview partners. What is equally important is that the infrastructure has been sufficiently prepared; i.e., that rooms, whiteboards or flipcharts, video projector, beverages, etc. are available.

Infrastructure is important.

A good idea is to assign a local organizer exclusively to the task of infrastructure and interview scheduling. That person is to work in close cooperation with the assessment team and accompanies it during all the assessment dates.

The following example of a "lightweight assessment"[17] for the support of a platform test strategy illustrates the major components of the assessment input and conclusions drawn by the assessor.

A manufacturer of commercial PC software introduces a strategy for software reusability by combining all modules belonging to the current product range (which up to now have been developed independently from each other in different business areas) into a comprehensive software platform that can be used across application boundaries. In the future, further development of this platform is to be performed independent of individual products (but of course in close cooperation with the product teams). The company expects substantial savings during development while at the same time improving quality.

Example:
Lightweight assessment

Changes in the development process

In support of this strategy, a platform test process is defined in parallel to the requirements engineering, design, and implementation of this platform. This platform test process is located between the testing of individual modules and the testing of products using the platform.

During integration of the first platform releases in product development, product teams—in particular their test departments—notice that a considerable

Too many defects

---

17. Describes a rather simplified and informal type of assessment.

number of defects are localized in the platform. In their opinion, these should have been detected during platform testing or even earlier in module testing. The large number of defects causes significant delays in product development. As a result, the platform development leader asks an external consulting company to address this issue.

Assessing affected processes

The consultant suggests carrying out an initial assessment of the module and platform test processes. In an introductory workshop with all involved staff of the different development levels, the following hypotheses are jointly developed:

- One possible cause for the low defect detection percentage (see chapter 11) is that there are insufficient module and platform test cases.
- Another possible cause is obviously due to the fact that there are no sufficient test completion and exit criteria (see chapters 6 and 11) to evaluate if the platform software is mature enough for release. As a consequence, platform software may be released to product development too early.

Assessment input

At the end of the workshop, the consultant summarizes the findings in an assessment input statement:

- Sponsor: This role is assumed by the person responsible for platform development.
- Purpose of the assessment: Improve the efficiency of module and platform testing in order to significantly increase the defect detection percentage at these levels.
- Scope of the assessment: Since at that stage the assessment's objective is only to gain a first insight, helping to either support or reject the hypotheses, its scope in terms of effort will be limited. Five out of the 17 modules are to be sample-checked; it is agreed that for each module and platform integration test, interview time with project members will be limited to a maximum of 4 hours. It is also agreed that the scope of the assessment will be limited to the test process.
- Since it is obvious that the root cause of the problems lies in the test process, the consultant chooses TPI as the appropriate assessment model. He ensures the availability of two assessors with longstanding experience in TPI and basic knowledge in commercial data processing.
- In order to test the first hypothesis, it is decided that the TPI key areas "Test strategy" and "Test specification techniques" will be examined. Weaknesses in either of these areas can be the cause for the presumed testing inefficiency.
- The second hypothesis prompts the consultant to include the key area "Metrics" in the assessment since the presumed lack of suitable test exit criteria may have its origin in missing or wrongly applied product quality metrics.

Starting with this input and based on the TPI documentation, the assessors carry out an analysis to see up to which level the individual key areas need to be examined and whether or not other key areas need to be taken into account due to internal dependencies.

Key area / Scale	0	1	2	3	4	5	6	7	8	9	10	11	12	13
1 Test strategy		A					B				C		D	
2 Life-cycle model		A			B									
3 Moment of involvement			A				B				C		D	
4 Estimating and planning				A							B			
5 Test specification techniques		A		B										
6 Static test techniques					A		B							
7 Metrics						A			B			C		D
8 Test tool					A			B			C			
9 Test environment				A				B						C
10 Office environment				A										
11 Commitment and motivation		A				B						C		
12 Test functions and training				A			B			C				
13 Scope of methodology					A						B			C
14 Communication			A		B							C		
15 Reporting		A			B		C					D		
16 Defect management		A				B		C						
17 Testware management			A			B				C				D
18 Test process management		A		B								C		
19 Evaluation							A			B				
20 Low-level testing					A		B		C					

Figure 7–10
TPI target profile

The target profile serves as a guideline for the depth of the investigation in the subsequently planned and performed interviews and document reviews.

7.5 Summary

Evaluation and improvement models have been introduced, discussed, and applied for some years now. Some of them cover general processes, but some are especially designed to cover the software development process. Several of these models were described in this chapter:

▨ TQM, Kaizen, and Six Sigma are models that are not limited to the software development process but are supposed to be generally applicable to the improvement of processes, products, and services. They provide many ideas and suggestions that can be applied to software development and test.

- The Capability Maturity Model Integration (CMMI) has evolved out of the Capability Maturity Model (CMM). Using the staged representation, an entire organization can be evaluated in terms of maturity levels, whereas the continuous representation is used for the evaluation of individual process areas in terms of capability grades.

- To the test manager, the verification and validation process areas are of particular interest. However, CMMI does not provide very detailed descriptions of these areas and offers few concrete hints on improvements.

- ISO/IEC 15504 (SPICE) provides a more detailed differentiation of the capability levels. Similar to CMMI, they correspond to individual processes.

- Some processes are of particular relevance to the test manager. The processes are divided into individual steps, each of which is briefly described.

- The Testing Maturity Model (TMM) was developed based on CMM and is used exclusively for analysis and enhancement of the test processes. Five maturity models and different process areas are defined.

- Test Process Improvement (TPI) is not based on any existing model but was developed by a company with many years of experience in this field. Twenty key areas are used for estimating the test process. The capability grades (levels) of all key areas are clearly arranged in a matrix.

- TMM and TPI are well suited to critically analyze the test process and to expose a process's weaknesses and strengths. Both models provide concrete indicators as to which actions should be taken to improve the process.

- An audit is a systematic investigation to examine products or processes based on objective criteria, not just in software development. It assesses compliance with standards, guidelines, and specifications.

- Assessments are used to determine the maturity or capability levels of organizations or individual processes. They are closely connected to the maturity models. Evaluation models can be used in very different types of companies or organizations.

- It is up to the individual company or organization to decide how well a particular model is suited to its own specific circumstances; a general recommendation cannot be given.

8 Deviation Management

The added value of testing lies mainly in the detection and reporting of a system's deviations from its requirements. To be able to correct a deviation, development requires as much detailed information as possible about symptoms, reproduction, and consequences of abnormal system behavior. The test process must therefore place particular focus on accurate documentation and tracking of deviations. Part of this process is a risk estimation of the consequences of defects remaining in the system. This chapter explains the requirements of the documentation as well as categorization techniques and the prioritization and status tracking of deviations.

8.1 Terminology

Generally speaking, all software contains defects. A defect is a widely used synonym for a software system's deviation or divergence of actual from expected behavior. However, it is advisable to establish a more accurate distinction between the different stages in the development chain of deviations (see also [Spillner 07]):

- An **error** is an erroneous act of a person or group causing a defect in the system.
- A **defect** is a fault in the system that, with a certain probability, will lead to a failure.
- A **failure** is the visible deviation of a system's operational behavior from the requirement specifications.

Error, defect, failure

According to these definitions, testers do not detect defects, they find failures. Finding out which defect caused a particular observed failure must be considered a separate and subsequent activity in which test and development must cooperate. In this context, people typically speak of debugging.

Different failures may well be traced back to the same defect, while it is also possible that defects may remain in the system and not lead to a failure.

"It's not a bug—it's a feature." Probably every programmer and tester knows this phrase expressing the differences of opinion that may well exist between development, test, and users as to whether or not a particular system behavior is to be seen as a failure, a tester's wrong interpretation of the requirement documents, or an (justified or unjustified) enhancement or change request. A neutral, generic term for all these types is the term "deviation" (of a system's behavior from the user's or tester's expectations; common synonyms are "anomaly", "incident").

Incident reports are mostly based on differences between the specification of a particular test case's expected result and the actual behavior of the tested system. The reasons for such differences can lie in abnormal system behavior but also in an inaccurate test case specification. The correct answer often becomes clear only during the ensuing resolution activities. Many projects use a common management system to deal with incident reports written against the tested system and incident reports written against the testware; i.e. test plan, test specifications, and test automation.

8.2 Documenting Incidents

The people who detect anomalies are normally not the same as those who analyze and correct them (see section 8.3.1). Because of this situation, detected anomalies require careful documentation and clear communication.

First, when communicating an incident report it makes no real difference whether it is documented and communicated via email, spreadsheet, or a specialized database (deviation management system). However, in order to support efficient treatment, the documentation of an incident must meet certain requirements independent of the medium used:

- The description of the incident must allow simple and accurate reproduction of the failure:
    - The test run and required input parameters are to be succinctly described so that the test run can be reproduced. Ideally, the incident report refers directly to a test case specification and/or an auto-

mated test procedure based on which development can reproduce the failure.

- The report shall address only one single, clearly defined problem and not a combination of several anomalies.

- The environment in which the test was executed must be clearly documented—for example, the version of the test object, platform, tested component, necessary reference data, etc.

- It must be possible to prioritize a number of anomalies relative to each other in order to resolve them according to their assigned priority. To do so, the presumed failure potential must be evaluated from different perspectives, such as, for instance, from both the end user's and the tester's point of view.

- Since typically more than one person is involved in the resolution of an incident, efficient control must be supported. This can be done by assigning a unique status to the report and by assigning people responsible for debugging, defect resolution, and retesting (see section 8.3).

- Date and time the incident was detected is documented. For one thing, time may well be a relevant aspect regarding the cause of a failure; on the other hand, it allows some helpful analyses based on the total number of reported failures.

These requirements necessitate the use of a fixed format for communicating anomalies. Depending on the reporting method used, this may be in form of an e-mail, document template, or database scheme. Completing his report, the author must take sufficient care; he can do this best by putting himself into the position of those who have to read and evaluate his report later on.

Some basic rules regarding incident reports

It should not be forgotten that each incident report carries a certain political and emotional potential as in most cases it (implicitly) criticizes someone else's work (namely, that of the affected software developer).

Dogmatism, malice, and displaced humor are inappropriate. Chapter 10 provides further advice on how appropriate forms of communication can help to avoid unnecessary disputes or putting up mental barriers.

Table 8-1 illustrates an incident report template that, due to its different attributes, satisfies the above mentioned requirements (see also [Spillner 07], section 6.6.2).

Table 8–1

Sample reporting template

Identification	
Number	**Incremental, unique number of report**
Test object	Identifier of the test object (system or impacted component or components)
Version	Exact version identifier (tested build) of the test object
Platform	Identification of the hardware/software platform or test environment where the problem occurred
Reporting person ID	Unique identification of the person who detected the incident
Responsible corrector ID (developer)	Unique identification of the person responsible for correcting the defect
Date of occurrence	Date and time the incident was first observed
Classification[1]	
Status	Current processing status of the report[2], possibly historical information allowing tracking of status changes with corresponding change dates
Class	Severity (e.g., crash, malfunction, deficiency, nice to have, change request)
Priority	Urgency of defect removal
Requirement(s)	Reference(s) to the requirement(s) violated or not fulfilled by the incident
Source	Phase of assumed defect injection: coding, documentation, design, etc.
Problem description	
Test case	Test case reference (identification) or direct description of the steps necessary for the reproduction of the failure
Problem/symptom	Accurate description of the incident stating the differences between target and actual behavior
Comments	Comments by involved staff on the report; possibly historical information
Correction	Details concerning correction measures
References	References to other, related incident reports; if required, additional references to background information, etc.

---

1.   For a more detailed classification scheme, see section 8.4.
2.   See section 8.3.2.

8.3   Incident Handling

In principle, each incident goes through the following life cycle: the anomaly is detected, documented, analyzed and corrected. Alternatively, the incident report is discarded or rejected because it is thought to be unsubstantiated.

The incident life cycle

Different people with different roles participate in the correction process. In order to coordinate these roles and to ensure orderly communication, it is necessary to define a deviation management process.

The most important components of such a management process are a suitable incident status model, an adequate workflow for the execution of status changes, and a definition of the roles and responsibilities pertaining to incidents within the status model.

8.3.1   Roles and Balance of Interests in Deviation Management

The following roles and functions contribute to incident resolution. These roles have partly overlapping and partly contradictory interests in the resolution of incidents:

- The **tester** reports incidents, documenting them following a well-defined pattern of input data necessary for analysis and management. He performs retesting after defect correction.

Interests of tester and test manager

- The **test manager** leads the test group and organizes the deviation management, tracking the incident occurrence and the correction measures and using this as a basis for the planning and control of his test activities.

Both tester and test manager are interested in quick defect resolution, particularly of those potential "showstoppers" that might jeopardize or even stop the test activities altogether.

- The **developer** analyzes the incident reports, perhaps jointly with the tester, and resolves defects. (Since the cause of a defect does not always lie in the system's implementation phase but can also lie in the requirements or design phases, the term developer applies to programmers, designers, and requirements specifiers / requirements modelers.) The developer also implements approved change requests.

Interests of developers and development leader

■ The **development leader** is in charge of the development project and leads the development team; he is also responsible for the success of the defect resolution process. He estimates and is accountable for the effort required to perform the necessary resolution activities.

In order to reduce the stack, developers and the development leader are interested in correcting failures first whose resolution requires the least effort.

■ The **product manager** is responsible for product developed in the project. He approves change requests and is responsible for the prioritization of the correction activities.

It is in the product manager's interest to achieve the highest possible customer satisfaction with the least possible cost. For this reason, it may be that in some cases change requests are given priority over defect resolution.

The interests of the customer   ■ In some project situations, especially where individual software is being developed, the **customer** may be closely involved in the development process, evaluating new incidents with regard to their relevance for the operational use of the system. He may even report incidents himself that in many cases turn out to be change requests.

The customer expects a high-quality product, i.e., one that shows as little behavioral deviation from the expected quality profile as possible.

In order to balance these different and partly contradictory interests, the following board is established in a deviation management process:

Change Control Board   ■ The **Change Control Board** (CCB) regularly tracks the progress of deviation detection and resolution and decides on prioritization of defect resolution and change requests. Typically, this body is made up of the development leader, the test manager, and the product manager. The (sub)project leader, customer representative, or end user may also be part of it.

The better and more qualified the information is on reported incidents, the easier the task is for the CCB. [IEEE 1044] (section 8.4) provides a lot of classifiable information. How information is used in concrete projects is up to the organization. The test manager in charge or the CCB must make a reasonable decision.

It also makes sense to introduce suitable defect metrics to be able to support CCB decisions with quantitative data. Chapter 11 provides some examples.

8.3.2   Generic Deviation Management Process

Figure 8-1 ([Spillner 07, section 6.6.4]) shows a model including incident statuses, events that lead to status changes, and the roles allowed to perform status changes:

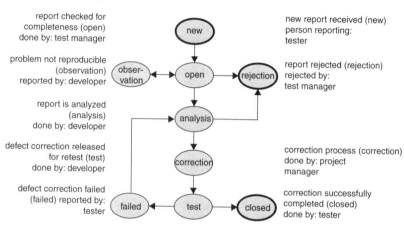

Figure 8–1

Incident status model

The status model needs to be adjusted to satisfy organizational requirements, for instance by introducing the following:

- A different number of final states—e.g., rejected, deferred to next "minor" release, deferred to next "major" release, deferred to release xy
- A different number of "analyses states", which help development show different workflow phases from reception up to the provision of a correction
- Different roles and customized rights for individual roles—for instance, additional rights for the test manager to change the report status to "closed"
- The transfer of activities of individual roles to the CCB, together with rules stating criteria based on which the CCB can make decisions regarding status changes

Table 8.2 illustrates an incident report from VSR system test. Based on data recorded in the standard incident report template (see section 8.2), developers and tester process the report, documenting the different processing steps:

Example of an incident report with history data

Table 8–2

Sample incident report

Identification	
Number	**VSR-Systest 03347**
Test object	VSR Component DreamCar
Version	Build 02.013 – 04.27.2006
Platform	Windows XP – Standard-Client-Configuration
Reporting person	G. Myers
Responsible corrector (Developer)	K. Beck
Date of occurrence/ reporting	04.30.2006 10:17
Classification	
Status	**Status** **Date** **Set by** **Comment** closed 05.14.2006 G. Myers successful re-test test 05.12.2006 K. Beck Recorrected check failure 05.06.2006 G. Myers Discount = 100% still possible test 05.04.2006 K. Beck Checking function corrected correction 05.03.2006 K. Beck Correction in callback function analysis 05.02.2006 K. Beck source code review analysis 04.30.2006 CCB class 3->2 new 04.30.2006 G. Myers
Class	2 (critical malfunction)
Priority	2 (correction prior to release)
Requirements	CC-Sys-CalcPrice-01/037 rebates
Source	Validation procedures for rebates entry
Problem description	
Test case	TC-Price Calculation/0313 rebated purchase price
Problem / symptom	Irrespective of the selected model, special edition, and accessories, it is possible to enter a discount of $\geq 100\%$. As a result, a negative purchase price is displayed.
Comments	CCB, 04.30.2006: high classification as wrong calculation will leave an extremely bad impression with the customer

8.3.3   Using Deviation Management Tools

Reporting template, storage, and management process are best implemented in form of a database—i.e., a so-called deviation management system (or a deviation or defect database[1])—to obtain additional efficiency
gains and benefits over simple "pen to paper" or spreadsheet solutions:

Deviation management systems

- Users and user-assigned roles can be granted defined read and write
  access rights to ensure observance of the status model. Especially in
  chaotic projects, this will help control the workflow.
- In case of status changes, the system can automatically inform affected
  people (e.g., via e-mail). This way, for instance, the tester will be automatically informed if an incident that he reported earlier is up for
  retest, thus saving him effort and time because he does not have to look
  for it in the reporting list.
- It is possible to connect the deviation management system to other
  tools used in the software development process via suitable interfaces,
  which will enable traceability and provide considerable process support:
  - An interface to a test management system (link between test cases
    and anomalies detected by them) will make typical test management
    tasks a lot easier for the test manager—for example, allowing him
    during retest planning to filter for all test cases linked to incidents
    that are reported closed.
  - An interface to the configuration management system (linking devi-
    ations to changes in documents and source files that are necessary
    for the resolution of the problem) supports traceability during a
    development project's consolidation phase. It may, for example, be
    required that in case of newly checked-in source code, the configu-
    ration management system must refer to a deviation addressed by
    the code changes.
  - An interface to a requirements management system (relating devia-
    tions to requirements, often implemented by linking requirements
    to test cases in the test management system and linking the same test
    cases to deviations) allows a direct evaluation of the current product
    quality based on the requirements. The number of requirements in

---

1.   Several other terms are widely used for such systems, such as, e.g., "bug tracking
     system" and "problem database".

the system with status "untested," "successfully tested," or "tested with deviations" can thus be determined.

 Reporting and statistics functionality allow consolidation and visualization of data, facilitating the evaluation of product quality and the indication of risk and improvement potentials.

Sample statistics and their application

The sample statistics in figures 8-2 and 8-3 are derived from the VSR system test deviation management system, showing the current state of the database at the end of the third system test cycle.

Figure 8–2
Status reporting

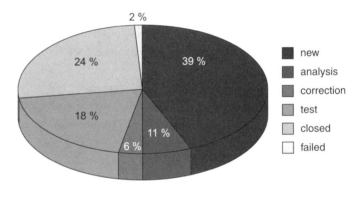

Figure 8–3
Reporting according to correction priority

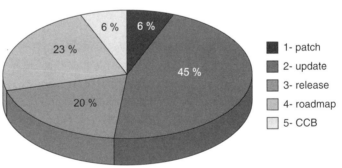

Test manager and development leader discuss the statistics generated out of the deviation management system. Based on the above diagrams, in the final report of the third system test cycle, they make the following observations:

 The diagram relating to the status of the reports (see figure 8-2) shows that a large number of open reports have been newly recorded but not yet processed. The test manager voices his concern that this carries a high risk and asks the development leader why so many reports have been left unattended by the development team.

▪ The development leader sees in the diagram on correction priority (see figure 8-3) that his team needs to cope with a large number of urgent defect correction activities. More than half of all reports must be processed prior to the next system test cycle (priorities 1 and 2) so testing won't be jeopardized. This hardly leaves any room for the analysis of newly registered reports.

Both deliberate on how to improve the situation. The development leader could provide the team with some additional staff to remove the bottleneck but requires some more information on where to put them to be most efficient. To answer this question, the test manager creates another statistic, filtering the database for the newly created reports in the third test cycle and categorizing the reports according to the impacted VSR components (see figure 8-4).

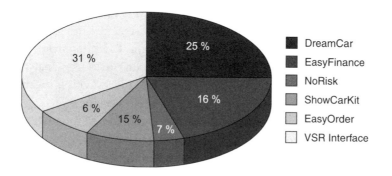

Figure 8–4

Reporting according to impacted component

The evaluation by components indicates that the majority of the new defects are localized in the two components *DreamCar* and VSR interface.

▪ Consequently, the development leader decides to provide additional developers for the two components.
▪ The test manager, on the other hand, updates his test planning for the fourth system test cycle, intensifying testing of these two components following the rule of thumb "If you've already found lots of failures, expect to have missed a lot more".

As the example illustrates, a database-supported deviation management system is a very useful instrument for controlling a project. In order to establish such a system, a well-organized approach is needed that may well take a long time to realize (see chapter 12). In practice, we can see that with regard to deviation management, organizations often adopt an evolutionary improvement approach that goes hand in hand with other process improvement activities and has a sustained and positive impact on the efficiency of the test processes and on the achievable product quality:

Step by step from bits of paper toward a deviation management system

■ People often start reporting incidents or anomalies rather informally via e-mail. There is no control over the content and over processing the report. As a result, analysis, prioritization, and retesting are time-consuming and inaccurate.

■ As a next step, most organizations introduce a reporting template for their e-mail system. A project agreement is drawn up saying that in the future, copies of new reports are to be sent to the project or (if there is one) test manager. This will considerably improve traceability. The project or test manager can start with prioritizing, ensure that reports get actioned, and gain an overview of project progress based on simple statistics.

■ In the course of these activities, most managers start organizing storage of the reports—for example, in a directory structure in the file system or in a central table in a spreadsheet program. The latter makes report-related information machine readable so that it can be analyzed or evaluated in the form of status reports and statistics. This is the preliminary stage to a proper deviation management system.

■ The last step in this process is transferring all the information held in tables into a proprietary or commercial database system. Actioning of reports is now controlled by the status and rights system incorporated in the deviation management system. Sophisticated reporting and statistics functions, in combination with interfaces to the requirements and configuration management systems, open up the way to develop even further potentials.

Often the deviation management process is the first or the only (halfway) formally defined process in an organization and the tools used are the only available process-related tools. Gradual, step-by-step improvements in this area are often seen as a precedent for other improvements in the overall project, leading to medium-term improvements in other areas such as requirements or project management.

8.4   Standardized Classification for Software Anomalies According to the IEEE 1044/1044.1 Standard

The [IEEE 1044] standard describes a classification of anomalies, the documentation of the attributes of an anomaly, and the associated process. This standard serves as a good basis and is briefly explained in the following section.

Standard techniques for the classification of anomalies (incidents)

8.4.1   Overview of the Classifications Process

For classification, IEEE 1044 defines a sequence of four steps:

1. Recognition
2. Investigation
3. Action
4. Disposition

Essentially, each of these four steps consists of the execution of three parallel activities:

- Recording
- Classifying
- Identifying impacts

Applied on each step, the three activities classify and document the features of the incident from different perspectives.

The focus of this workflow is clearly on report classification. The standard does not describe a complete management process and does not, for instance, consider how to deal with rejected reports or ineffective corrections. A reasonable management process is based on a status model similar to the one illustrated in figure 8.1 above, integrating the classification steps according to IEEE 1044 (see figure 8-5).

It is important to classify in each step; i.e., to classify not only the severity and impact of an anomaly defined during analysis but also the circumstances that have led to its detection, the necessary resolution actions, and the report's disposition after closure.

Figure 8–5

Classification according
to IEEE 1044

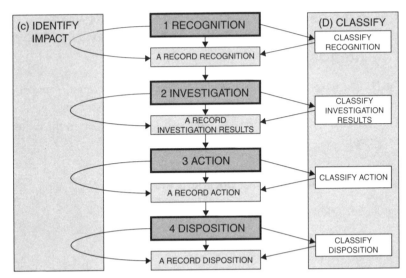

Figure 8–5

Classification according to IEEE 1044

8.4.2   Data Model: Categories, Classifications, and Supporting Data Items

Classification is done using a selection of predefined values, so-called "classifications", and attributes of assigned "categories". The standard considers some of these attributes mandatory and others optional. Each classification and each category is clearly defined to ensure uniform recording and processing of anomalies even in large projects. Classifications and categories are combined in "classification schemes" and applied to each of the classification process steps.

The category *recognition classification scheme – project activity* serves as a good example. It is used to determine the activity (e.g., review or test) by which an incident is detected (see figure 8-6).

Figure 8–6

Example: Recognition classification scheme – project activity

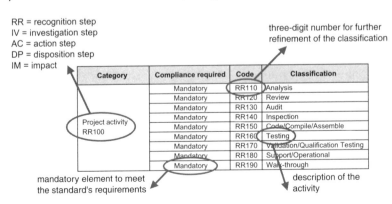

RR = recognition step
IV = investigation step
AC = action step
DP = disposition step
IM = impact

three-digit number for further refinement of the classification

Category	Compliance required	Code	Classification
	Mandatory	RR110	Analysis
	Mandatory	RR120	Review
	Mandatory	RR130	Audit
	Mandatory	RR140	Inspection
Project activity RR100	Mandatory	RR150	Code/Compile/Assemble
	Mandatory	RR160	Testing
	Mandatory	RR170	Validation/Qualification Testing
	Mandatory	RR180	Support/Operational
	Mandatory	RR190	Walk-through

mandatory element to meet the standard's requirements

description of the activity

RR100 implies that this scheme is to be applied to the recognition step of the anomaly. "Mandatory" in each line indicates that in order for the classification process to comply with the standard, the category as a whole and each of the possible activities in the associated classification table must be applied.

Based on this scheme, an anomaly found during system test is assigned code "RR160", whereas an anomaly detected during review has "RR120" assigned to it.

Besides categories, the standard also defines so-called "supporting data items", which can be applied in the description of the anomaly and the environment in which it occurred. This can be exemplified by the "investigation supporting data items" in figure 8-7, which support the anomaly analysis step.

Acknowledgement	Verification
Date received	Source of incident
Report number assigned	Data from recognition process
Investigator	
Name	
Code or functional area	
E-mail address	
Phone number	
Estimated start date of investigation	
Estimated complete date of investigation	
Actual start date of investigation	
Actual complete date of investigation	
Person hours	
Date receipt acknowledgement	
Documents used in investigation	
Name	
ID number	
Revision	

Figure 8–7

Example: Investigation supporting data item

During the analysis step this table is used to enter organizational pieces of information. They can serve a variety of purposes:

- To support subsequent classification steps as well as the actual treatment of the anomaly. Stating the "source of incident" provides direct help to the person assigned to resolve the anomaly.
- To help in analyzing data in different ways, keeping process improvement in mind. For example, if estimated and actual times used for the analysis step regularly show substantial deviations, the issue may be addressed by introducing improved estimation models or more highly qualified staff for the job.
- To have better traceability of the different processing steps. For example, should one of the people in the processing chain drop out for some reason, it will be a lot easier for someone else to continue processing a particular step. In the example in figure 8.7, the information "documents used in investigation" provides an overview of the documents that have already been checked and those that still need to be analyzed.

8.4.3   Classification Steps in Detail

Recognition

Recognition   Each project member can report anomalies. The following activities of the recognition step are performed as soon as the anomaly is encountered:

- **Documentation** by collecting *recognition supporting data items*. These items comprise all data related to the environment in which the anomaly was detected. Data such as hardware and software environment and test supporting software (e.g., test automation tools) and also the contact ID of the reporting person are recorded here, together with the time of occurrence and the documentation used during the operation of the system. Note that the standard considers the attributes list it provides as optional and incomplete.
- **Classification** via selection of values out of the *recognition classification scheme*. It consists of six categories (three of which are mandatory) that are supposed to help provide accurate reporting—for example, project phase, symptom, and system status after the anomaly has occurred.
- **Identifying the impact** by means of the *impact classification scheme* and the *impact supporting data items*. This data is to be used by the per-

son who encountered the anomaly to report his observations (or assumptions) on the impacts of the incident: urgency and severity of the anomaly, effects on product quality, customer value, safety, project cost, risk, and project schedule.

Analysis

Each reported anomaly must be investigated. The aim of the investigation is to be able to evaluate the anomaly. Usually this step is carried out by development, but important information may also come from testers or other project members.

Analysis (investigation)

- **Documentation:** The *investigation supporting data items* are collected here to confirm the existence and reproducibility of the anomaly and to identify possible workarounds and correction measures. The standard considers this list, too, as optional and incomplete.
- **Classification:** Selection of suitable data out of the *investigation classification scheme* to describe the actual cause, the impacted documents, and the nature of the anomaly. In addition, classifications made in the first step are checked and, if necessary, corrected.
- **Identification of the impact:** The assumptions made on the impact of the anomaly documented in the first step are checked and, if necessary, corrected. The tables used in the first step are used as a basis.

Resolution

Based on the analysis results, resolution actions are planned. This step may comprise both the direct resolution of the anomaly itself and process improvement actions designed to avoid further, similar incidents. In this step, development is primarily involved, but other roles may also be involved, such as the product manager or the quality assurance department.

Resolution (action)

- **Documentation:** To begin with, *action supporting data items* are collected; for example, planned resolution date and product delivery status, a description of the resolution activities, and the names or functions of people responsible for correction or retesting.
- **Classification:** This is done using the *action classification scheme*, describing the type of the action (e.g., code or documentation changes) and their priority (ranging from "immediate" to "no resolution"). Optionally, the scheme also describes additional countermeasures of a

more strategic nature, such as process improvement and research activities.

■ **Identifying the impact:** Again, impact categories documented in the previous steps are reviewed and, if necessary, updated.

Disposition

Disposition   In the disposition phase—i.e., after all resolution activities have been completed or at least after long-term correction actions have been initiated—the removal of the anomaly is to be documented. The main actors involved in this step are usually testers, in some cases support staff, and the product manager.

■ **Documentation:** The *disposition supporting data items,* for instance, document that the customer has been informed about the resolution. They are also used to document verification (e.g., retest) results.

■ **Classification:** The *disposition classification scheme* documents the final version of the anomaly report (e.g., "resolution completed" or "duplicate problem").

■ **Identifying the impact:** A concluding consideration is made and previously documented impacts are reviewed and updated, if necessary—again based on the same reference tables as in the previous steps.

8.4.4   Tailoring of Standards

The sample tables and the descriptions of the individual categories show that the standard is very comprehensive, covering the entire software life cycle. In practice, however, it will not be applied in its entirety but rather tailored and reduced to the concrete needs in the project in the following manner:

■ By means of omission of redundant attributes or categories
■ By integrating the steps of the classification processes into one's own deviation management process

Influencing factors   Generally, the reasons for this so-called "tailoring" are found during a cost-benefit analysis—more detailed data collected during incident treatment means more data is available in subsequent process steps; however, it also amounts to more effort required for collection and maintenance. The following list includes some of the factors that may possibly influence the standard's scope of use:

The intended area of influence: Is the process to be applied across the different test levels, projects, or even the entire organization? Is it to be restricted to development and test or is it also to be applied in product support?

The evaluation of collected data for process improvement purposes: Accumulation of particular incident categories is an indicator that can be used for focusing on and removal of weaknesses in the development and test process.

The applicability of categories in the concrete project environment. *Supporting data items* such as databases and firmware only make sense in particular settings.

Documentation and obligation of accountability required by customers and/or licensing authorities. These may possibly require more detailed data than what is needed in the development department.

Supplement IEEE 1044.1 to the standard provides valuable support for the tailoring and customization of standards to suit one's own requirements, providing the following:

Tailoring support

Support for the decision if, and within which scope, the standard can and should be applied in one's own organizational setting

Detailed explanations and examples of categories and classifications

Additional *supporting data items* not mentioned in the standard

Guidelines for correct tailoring; i.e., particulars and examples of stand-ard-compliant and noncompliant adaptations and omissions of categories and classifications

A sample status model for anomalies (similar to the one in section 8.3.2)

Methods to map the standard into commercial and in-house developed deviation management systems

Examples of incident metrics, their analysis, and application to project control, product evaluation, and process improvement

---

It is easy to draw a line from the contents of this supplement right back the beginning of this chapter. Both the sample incident reporting template (section 8.2) and the status model (section 8.3.2) were derived from, though not necessarily in compliance with, the IEEE 1044/1044.1 standard to be applied in software development and testing during development at the project level. Both have been successfully tried and tested in many projects.

Hint

These examples may serve as a starting point to readers establishing their own deviation management system. Nevertheless, we would recommend that the standard be used to critically scrutinize the examples for applicability.

8.5 Summary

- On the one hand, anomalies require consistent and complete documentation to provide maximum support for their evaluation and resolution; on the other hand, they require a management process that reflects the life cycle of the incident reports and coordinates the roles involved in the processing of the deviation.
- In practice, a large variety of different systems is used for incident reporting, ranging from simple management techniques to sophisticated deviation management tools, from the simple exchange of e-mails to deviation management systems spanning an entire organization with comprehensive databases that can be used for a wide range of different statistics. If such systems are linked to other corporate configuration, test, and requirements management systems, they can considerably increase efficiency in the development process.
- To provide for a common basis for this historically grown heterogeneity, the IEEE defined a standard for the classification of anomalies (IEEE 1044), containing mandatory and optional attributes of anomalies as well as a description of a generic processing workflow.
- IEEE 1044 arranges the documentation, monitoring, and classification of deviations into four process steps:
  - Recognition
  - Investigation
  - Action
  - Disposition
- The IEEE 1044 standard is very comprehensive and allows application in test not only during development but also throughout a system's entire life cycle. For this reason, however, the standard in most cases requires customization to suit the concrete requirements in a particular environment. A supplementary document (IEEE 1044.1) provides valuable information on this issue.

9 Risk Management and Risk-Oriented Testing

In software development, problems may arise during the course of a product's development and later during operational use. We therefore distinguish between project and product risks. Early risk-identification, analysis, evaluation, and control combined with a risk-oriented test plan and test prioritization enables test management to help control risks.

9.1 Introduction

Countless examples show that IT projects carry inherent risks (e.g., [Standish 04]). A risk is a problem that could occur in the future with undesirable consequences. The severity of a risk is made up of the likelihood of the problem occurring and its collateral damage. Peter G. Neumann ([Neumann 95]) publishes and regularly updates a list of risks or damages resulting from the use of IT products.

IT project = risk!

Test managers must face these facts. In principle, there are two ways in which to react:

- Ignoring risks ("ostrich-like" behavior)
- Tolerance and proactive risk management

The first option does not necessarily prevent the project from being successful, yet it does leave those involved in the dark about what could perhaps happen "tomorrow." The second option may not always secure the project's success, but it enables those involved to at least get a glimpse of a possible future so that they can act accordingly and with precaution.

The reliability of individual actions increases with better risk handling. Risks can be kept low if potential risks are recognized early and if countermeasures are initiated in time to lower the probability of occurrence or the extent of damage.

The intention of risk management

This is the purpose of risk management. To put it crudely, →risk management is the conscious and deliberate planning of failures and their consequences ([DeMarco 03]). It comprises the systematic identification, analysis, evaluation, control, mastering, monitoring, and communication of risks in order to effectively minimize losses and optimize the benefits ([IEC 62198], [ISO 16085]). The objective of risk management is to identify risks that could massively endanger project success or lead to very poor product quality because of, for example, drastic cost overruns and schedule delays and to prevent their occurrence with suitable measures.

The intention of risk-oriented testing

Within the given constraints (effort, time, availability, etc.) the intention of risk-oriented testing is to design software testing in such a way as to minimize as much as possible previously identified risks, i.e., →project risks relating to development or →product risks relating to the product's operational use ([Spillner 07, section 6.4.3]). A product risk, for example, may be an undetected defect that could lead to a system failure, whereas a project risk could be failure to meet a delivery date.

The IEEE 1008 Standard for Software Unit Testing ([IEEE 1008]), for example, considers the identification of risk areas addressed by testing as an inherent step in test planning. Systems with a high risk potential must be more intensely tested than systems that do not cause much damage if they fail, whereby risk estimation must be done for individual system parts or even individual defect potentials. Thus, test managers always also act as risk managers.

Ideally, all participants in a project are involved in all the phases and steps of risk management. The most important parties involved in this process and their responsibilities are listed here:

- The customer: He demands project risk management and provides information regarding acceptable risks and product environment.
- The management of the contractor (i.e., the project sponsor): Management requires and promotes project risk management and provides information regarding the project environment and corporate risk management.
- The project manager: He takes into account in his project budget the costs of risk minimizing activities and of risk management itself. He is in charge of risk management and provides, if necessary, further resources (e.g., sufficiently experienced engineers).
- The test manager: He actively participates in risk management and optimizes test strategy and test effort to reduce product risks.

Developer, tester and users: They provide information related to project and product risks.

A comprehensive risk management process (see also [Charette 89], [ISO 16085], [IEC 62198]) involves specific activities that will be discussed in more detail in the next sections of this chapter:

- Identification of the risk context
- Risk identification
- Risk analysis and risk evaluation
- Risk control and treatment
- Risk verification and monitoring

These activities cannot be performed without effective communication between all the parties involved. It is part of the general management activities to learn from completed projects and to critically assess risk management during project wrap-up.

In order to gain maximum benefit from risk management, risk management activities are to be started as early as possible in the project and continued throughout the project's life cycle.

Start risk management early and keep on doing it.

9.2   Context Identification

The risk context must be defined right at the beginning of the risk evaluation. It comprises the project's stakeholders, the agreed-upon project goals and results, and the scope and delimitations of risk management within the project context. Within this context, interfaces and overlaps with other projects need to be identified together with all organizational and strategic constraints regarding the project or product. According to the [ISO 16085] standard, these are external goals and constraints that may limit the project, throw it off course, or jeopardize product deployment. Examples are technical, corporate specific, commercial, political, financial, legal, contractual, and market political developments (see figure 9-1).

Listing all the project goals defined to satisfy project, corporate, and customer requirements helps with later risk identification and risk prioritization. Moreover, all the general criteria for risk acceptance and risk tolerance are to be listed for use during the evaluation of identified risks in later process phases.

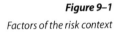

Figure 9–1

Factors of the risk context

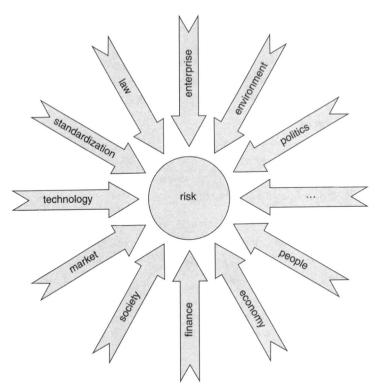

It is also important for the test manager to know the project environment and to be familiar with the project and product characteristics. The latter need to be quantified in the form of quality goals (see also [ISO 9126]).

9.3   Risk Identification

Risk management revolves around maximum identification of all relevant risks. →Risk identification should be process oriented and individual risks should be combined into risk categories to provide a better overview. This will be described in the next section. Section 9.3.2 introduces some techniques and means for risk identification.

9.3.1   Risk Categories

A rough but in most cases sufficient risk categorization differentiates between external and strategic risks as well as between project and product risks that are of particular importance to the test manager.

External risks, for example, are natural events (lightning damage, water damage, earthquake) or political, legal, or social changes, but there are also macro-economic risks such as market shifts, the evolution of new sector trends and new markets, technical changes, and changes in customer behavior. These risks cannot really be influenced. Additionally, some of these risks cannot even be predicted (at least not in the medium term).

External risks: cannot be influenced and are difficult to predict

Strategic risks subsume micro-economic risks such as changing market shares, the company's liquidity, takeovers, and outsourcings (for instance, of the IT department). In addition, there are organizational risks, such as changes in the corporate organizational and operational structures, associated uncertainties with respect to strategic investments, project control and planning, and resource shortages due to competing projects. Insufficient corporate crisis management, as well as communication barriers concerning "bad news" for upper management rate among these, too. Strategic risks cannot really be influenced by the project or test manager, but often they are at least fairly easy to predict.

Strategic risks: difficult to influence but often easy to predict

Among the project risks (operational risks), we find potential problems in logistics and sales; for instance, if a supplier drops out or if a licensing agreement for a third-party software product cannot be concluded in a way that satisfies the needs of the development department. Further project risks are staff fluctuation, contractual risks, supplier problems, and overly optimistic effort estimations and schedules. A risk may also be a company's excessively aggressive pricing policy, as a result of which resources become very limited.

Project risks: predictable and relatively easy to influenc

Technical project risks, too—such as insufficient IT safety (e.g., outage of the project servers due to viruses), insufficient requirements management, product line uncertainties, and required use of new and immature technology and development tools—frequently end up in project failure. Especially in complex, distributed development projects, we find a whole vista of different risks arising out of the project structure itself: communication problems, differences in organizational process maturity, deadline pressures, and the application of new, not sufficiently mastered development techniques.

Defect correction risks, too, are project risks, because additional time is required for defect analysis and correction, regression testing, renewed delivery, and installation. Sometimes this even needs to be accompanied with time-consuming corrective customer training. With new products, delays may occur because developer capacity is tied up in the maintenance area. The project or test manager can, in principle, influence and predict such risks in most cases.

Product risks are a result of problems with the delivered product. Such risks lead to many different types of damage, depending on who is affected:

- The manufacturer incurs mostly indirect nonconformity or failure costs. These are costs or losses in sales due to nonperformance of the contract or product liability claims, increased effort for customer hotline and support, and loss of image that may lead to losing the customer altogether, as well as a declining "brand value" due to insufficient functionality, poor quality, or even violations of the law enabled or supported by the product (viruses, phishing, etc.).

- For the customer of the system, product risks are often reflected in direct failure costs incurred by him as a result of software failures (and for which the manufacturer may be liable, see [Spillner 07], section 6.3.1). Among these are, for instance, costs of computation errors, data loss, accounting errors, hardware damage.

- If the customer uses the system to provide some kind of service to one or more end users, the end user, too, may suffer damage through the product risk. This may range from unwanted commercials to administering wrongly delivered medication as a result of a failing logistic system.

- The "safety" issue must be considered as a further risk class (e.g., in systems such as an irradiation device in a hospital). Here we may have a product or user risk even with a faultlessly running system; an operating error could cause the system to inflict damage (e.g., using too high a radiation dose) or external circumstances could change the operating conditions or the system environment (e.g., a power cut). With regard to safety risks, we need to take into account issues such as usability, redundancy, and error tolerance, and we need to make sure that the system is endowed with functions or features appropriate to its risks.

Applying suitable methods and techniques will make product risks relatively controllable for the project or test manager. Together with quality metrics or tests, such risks are also measurable and predictable.

Product risks can be further differentiated into the following two categories:

- Business (functional) aspects (particularly critical functions or business processes)
- Technical (nonfunctional) aspects (e.g., technological, platform, performance, safety, and usability aspects)

Assumptions made at project start regarding the project environment and the operational use of the products represent a risk source and must be regularly checked with regard to their validity.

9.3.2   Techniques and Utilities

In order to be able to identify risks, the following techniques and utilities can be applied and fine-tuned to the specific project situation:

- Expert interviews and questionnaires
- Independent estimations (audits, assessments)
- Risk workshops
- Risk brainstorming
- Use of risk templates and checklists
- Experiences from completed projects

Different roles, ranging from executives, external consultants, and experienced project or test managers to former, already retired top managers may be invited to participate in expert interviews and independent risk evaluations.

Premise of risk identification: Think the unthinkable!

What is important is that these people are not influenced in their statements by predefined project goals and stakeholder wishes and that they are well and objectively informed about the project situation and specific project and product characteristics.

Risk workshops can be planned and performed similar to reviews (see [Spillner 07, section 4.1.3]). At the beginning, the risk manager informs everybody involved, whereby next to the team members (architect, developer, tester), members of the steering committee or, should the need arise, external experts are to be informed, too. All participants of the workshop receive sufficient information about the project and its context (customer requirement specification, project plan, risk checklists) and each of them individually define possible risks. Before the workshop, the risk manager

Performing a risk workshop

ensures that workshop aids such as pin boards, presentation material, and a video projector are available. It also makes sense to reserve one separate pin board for each of the main risk categories.

Normally, the risk manager also moderates the workshop. At the beginning of the workshop, all participants are briefed about the workshop schedule and all (or those that have not done so yet) are given approximately 30 minutes to draw up an individual risk list. Risks are written down on note cards and then arranged on one of pin boards according to their risk category. All perceived risks are subsequently discussed per category and consolidated, and duplicates are removed. In some cases, more suitable terms may be found or some more risks added.

At the end of the workshop, some initial ideas are collected for the evaluation of each of the remaining risks (see section 9.4.1) and possible occurrence indicators are listed. Examples are a high number of staff on sick leave and frequent changes of particular functions (see section 9.4.2).

Scenario-based worst case brainstorming

In order to counteract possible uncertainties and anxieties that might prevent people from naming critical risks ("showstoppers"), techniques such as catastrophe brainstorming based on scenario building may be used (see DeMarco and Lister [DeMarco 03]). In such a session, participants may voice their worst project-related "nightmares." Additionally, the moderator can, for instance, predict that the project will fail after x months, whereupon all participants must name possible causes that could lead to the disaster. In many cases, a change of perspective turns out to be helpful, starting out with the question of what would be the best possible project outcome. Then possible causes that might prevent the project from reaching that goal are determined. All in all, the workshop will try to consider many different scenarios leading to possible project failure. After all the "nightmares" and scenarios leading up to them have been collected, underlying causes are analyzed and associated risks identified.

Checklists pool earlier experience

Checklists for risk identification pool the experiences of earlier projects. These experiences need not have been made in the same company and help to avoid known errors and forgetting important, frequently occurring risks.

General risk checklist for software projects

The "Top Ten" lists of the software development risks ([Ould 99], [Standish 04], [Pol 02]) may be used to set up an initial checklist for risk identification. They regularly contain risks like those listed here:

- Insufficient top-level management support
- Unrealistic schedules and budgets

- Lack of user involvement; hence. incompletely defined requirements and continuous requirement changes
- Plans either missing or not detailed enough
- Development of wrong functions and features
- Development of a wrong or poor user interface
- Unnecessary "gold-plating" of already sufficient functions and features (overshooting the mark)
- Insufficient qualification or poor productivity

The following checklist contains particular test-related risks relevant to the test manager (see also [Pol 02]):

Risk checklist for test

- Test basis insufficient or not available in time   (business workflow methods, instructions for use, and design specifications)
- Qualitatively insufficient test basis
- Overly optimistic or "aggressive" delivery date preventing completion of all test activities
- Testers not available or not available in time (quantitatively and qualitatively)
- Productivity problems due to lack of test expertise or premature introduction of new test techniques
- Efficiency losses due to missing or poorly established test management processes
- Effort overruns and schedule delays in test if estimations and planning are done based on experience values only
- Delayed availability of the necessary test environment
- Incomplete control over the test environment and associated elements (hardware, software, data, etc.)
- Poor test coverage or ignorance of defects and risks still hidden in the software due to the use of test specification techniques that are inadequate for the test object
- System failure or unwarrantable performance of individual functions due to skipped or missing performance and load tests

These checklists should in due course be adapted to the organization's concrete circumstances and be made applicable to all projects; furthermore, they should be substantiated with added notes and risks relating to concrete experiences and possible occurrence indicators (see section 9.4.2) and measures taken together with their impacts and effects.

<table>
<tr><td>

Example:
Risk identification for VSR

</td><td>

To identify the risks in the VSR project, the test manager draws up an initial risk list. After some pondering and going through status reports of former projects, he comes up with the following list:

</td></tr>
</table>

- Chief tester drops out
- Late requirement changes
- Delays in development
- Overly optimistic test planning
- Insufficient entry quality of the test object
- Poor quality of the test basis
- 64-bit version of the test tools available too late or not at all
- Configuration and versioning problems
- Loss of the configuration management database

In a second step, this list is distributed to the project and subproject leaders and some of the testers and developers for review and possible supplementing. A risk brainstorming meeting is felt to be too time consuming.

Based on the returned feedbacks, the test manager revises and consolidates the risk list, identifying the following additional risks:

- Planned changes to the user interface could adversely affect the automated GUI tests.
- A change of the database system could adversely affect system performance and require further performance testing.
- The auto manufacturer's early model change could result in having to move the latest delivery date up to an earlier one.

The current list does not yet contain statements regarding risk probability or occurrence indicators since these will be identified later during risk analysis and risk evaluation.

 Hint

Typically, all minor problems and those for which a solution has already been found or that can be easily averted are meticulously listed and tracked, whereas the really big, major problems are often not mentioned at all.

Dare to speak the unspeakable and risk using in your risk workshops words like "failure, technology revolution", and "flu epidemic"!

9.4 Risk Analysis and Risk Evaluation

During →risk analysis, recognized risks are quantified or at least qualitatively weighted and then evaluated. There are many different approaches with different degrees of precision, reaching from simple assignments to risk classes to precise probabilistic calculations.

Qualitative analysis can be performed early in the project's life cycle even though only little or shaky data may be available. Quantitative techniques can be applied if and as soon as more data is available.

The outcome of risk analysis and evaluation is a comprehensive risk inventory in which all risks are described and listed together with estimations on the probability of their occurrence over time and the expected damage incurred. Moreover, each risk has occurrence indicators assigned to it, based on which an impending risk can be recognized early and objectively. The following sections explain both aspects in more detail.

9.4.1   Analysis Techniques

Depending on circumstances, risk analysis uses quantitative and qualitative techniques. Quantitative analysis quantifies risks based on statistical data and fuzzy mathematics, system and sensitivity analyses, and error tree or incident sequence analyses. Should quantitative techniques reach their limits, qualitative techniques or techniques such as scenario-based analyses similar to those used in risk identification (see section 9.3.2), Pareto or ABC analyses, scoring models, and risk matrices (see section 9.4.3) are used.

Quantitative or qualitative risk analysis

As already explained in *Software Testing Foundations* [Spillner 07, section 6.4.3], a risk can be quantitatively calculated if the probability of occurrence (P) and the associated damage (D) can be quantitatively estimated. Risk R is calculated as follows:

Risk = occurrence probability × accrued damage

$$R = P \times D$$

Estimating risks with very large damaging effect, the maximum possible loss (MPL) and the probable maximum loss (PML) are frequently determined together with the probability with which a certain amount of damage is going to be reached or exceeded.

In most cases, however, probability of occurrence and incurred damage are not accurately quantifiable and can only be estimated qualitatively in terms of trends. The risk is then defined as a gradation within a number of classes or categories. If no reliable data is available, analysis is performed based on subjectively felt probabilities and damage estimations.

In such cases, the results depend on the experience of the evaluating person and must therefore be based on independent evaluations of several people. Results are then averaged.

Project managers, developers, test managers, testers, and users all have different viewpoints when it comes to risk evaluation. Whereas project managers tend to evaluate project risks as high, developers will direct their attention to product risks and are inclined to use caution, although they are prepared to take chances when it comes to using the latest technology. Test managers and testers, too, concentrate on product risks, in particular on possible failures and associated indirect failure costs. Test managers also consider project risks that could jeopardize the test process. For the user, product risks and especially direct failure costs are the focus of their risk evaluation.

In practice, the probability of occurrence is often weighted in terms of classes such as "neglectable," "low," "medium," and "high," and "very high" mapped onto values ranging from 1 to 9 to calculate the risk. Similarly, the amount of damage can be stated qualitatively, whereby the mapping onto (monetary) values should be based on a nonlinear scale, such as, for example, 1, 10, 50, 100, and 1,000. Particularly risks that are difficult to quantify as regards market or image loss can thus be mapped more easily.

Risk profile for functional requirements

For a risk analysis based on functional requirements (and also for test effort estimation), the following criteria can be used to establish a risk profile for the functions:

- The frequency of execution or use: F indicates the mean frequency with which a function is executed. With frequently executed functions, the probability of software defects impacting program execution and causing failures is very high. On the other hand, direct failure costs grow with the number of occurred failures.

- Criticality: C represents the (worst) possible effects of a function not working at all or working erroneously. Criticality is defined in subsequent evaluations together with the customer and with the possible assistance of technical experts. In addition, it is often evaluated in monetary terms; i.e., with regard to its financial consequences.

- The project risk: R_P (to what extent will nonfulfillment of a function at a given time put project progress at risk) results, for instance, from the number of functions dependent on the function under consideration.

- The technical product risk: R_T (how complex is the implementation of the function?) is derived from the complexity of the description (textual description, perhaps activity diagrams and sequence diagrams).

- The commercial product risk: R_B (to what extent are sales/acceptance of the application system put at risk in case of nonfulfillment of the function) can, for instance, be determined by consulting commercial experts.

The assignment of concrete values is a result of experiences made in earlier projects and based on current metrics (chapter 11). Three values—"low," "medium," and "high"—are usually enough to be able to quantify the individual factors that, incidentally, are not independent of each other (see, e.g., [Lyu 96]). Mapping these three values onto the natural numbers 1, 2, and 3, each function F is assigned one risk factor $R(F)$:

$$R(F) = (R_T + R_B + R_P) / 3 + F \times R_B + C \times R_T$$

9.4.2   Risk Occurrence Indicators

It is important to assign each identified risk to indicators that will signal its imminent occurrence. To keep the structure simple and concise, indicators for individual risks of a risk category may be condensed to one indicator for the entire category. They form, as it were, the data material for the control panel allowing the risk manager to evaluate, control, and prevent the risks.

State occurrence indicators for each risk!

Each indicator is accompanied by one or more metrics, a calculation specification for the overall value out of the individual metrics, and a threshold value (trigger or alarm level), based on which measures for risk mitigation or risk prevention must be initiated.

Whereas the data underlying the metrics will still be sketchy at project start and will not be sufficient to allow accurate occurrence predictions, the data material will become increasingly more comprehensive and accurate in the course of the project's life cycle. "False alarms" will decrease with the project progressing. Concrete metrics on this issue can be found in chapters 5 and 11.

To monitor the risks identified in the VSR project, the test manager adds occurrence indicators and possible metrics to the risk list:

Example:
Occurrence indicators for risks in the VSR project

R1: **chief tester drops out:**
Bad tempered; too much overtime per week; frequent short-term sick notes per month

R2: **delays in development:**
Delayed milestones; low defect correction percentage; e-mails are not answered; too many overtime hours; frequent sick leave

R3: **overly optimistic test planning:**
Defect rate too high shortly before test completion date; too many overtime hours; many blocked tests

R4: **insufficient entry quality of the test object:**
Entry tests fail; initial defect rates are very high

R5: **64-bit version of the test tools available too late or not at all:**
No preliminary version available; manufacturer postpones/does not set a delivery date

R6: **poor quality of the test basis:**
Frequent document changes; many incidents reported in reviews

R7: **loss of the configuration management database:**
Increasing response times despite constant data volume; nonrepeatable database error messages; frequent recoveries

9.4.3   Risk Inventory

All the findings gained during risk analysis (risk identification and risk evaluation) are entered into the →risk inventory (risk profile), arranged by their financial consequences and their occurrence probability.

Risks are chronologically recorded and listed in the inventory in a condensed and clearly structured way and can be illustrated by a risk diagram (figure 9-2) or a risk matrix (figure 9-3) to give decision makers an overview about the risk situation and particularly about their significance for the project.

Figure 9–2

Risk diagram

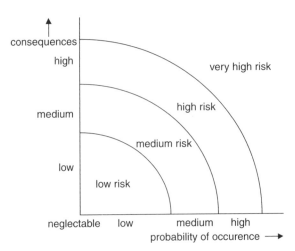

Depending on the actual value of the occurrence indicators, risks can be color- and size-coded and may, for instance, be shown as circles. Green and small, for instance, may indicate low indicator values; yellow and medium may indicate that the indicator value is below the threshold value; red and large may mean that the indicator value is equal to or above the threshold value.

The results of a risk analysis must also indicate the degree of uncertainty that accompanied the risk evaluation. Besides quantitative indicators, for example in the area 0% (absolutely uncertain) to 100% (absolutely certain), we may also classify by categories such as "very uncertain," "uncertain," "medium," "certain," and "very certain."

Risk estimations are repeated periodically. The progression of the estimations and indicator values of the different risks or risk categories must be captured in the risk inventory.

If, in the course of time, we observe increasing values, the planned measures have to be initiated (see section 9.5).

The VSR test manager has entered the most important risks in the following risk matrix.

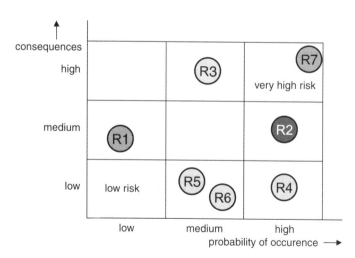

Example:
risk inventory in the VSR project

Figure 9–3
Risk matrix

The occurrence indicators of risks R1 and R7 are far away from their threshold values, those of risks R3 to R6 are only just below the threshold values, and the occurrence of risk R2 is imminent (indicator values already above the threshold value).

9.5   Risk Control and Treatment

→Risk control and treatment plays a key role in risk management. It comprises all measures that are taken in response to identified and analyzed risks.

Response to perceived risks   Possible responses to perceived risks can be as follows:

- Unconditional acceptance of the risk, which means doing absolutely nothing at all and waiting to see if the problem occurs or not
- Risk mitigation, which means lowering the risk potential; e.g., through outsourcing of specific corporate functions or by establishing appropriate emergency plans
- Mitigation of damages through corrective compensatory measures prior to problem occurrence; e.g., by taking out liability insurance or including a nonliability clause in the license contracts
- Total risk avoidance; e.g., through discontinuance of the project in order to completely avoid any associated risks.

The choice of a suitable response to a risk depends on the benefits associated with its removal or mitigation and the cost of the risk reducing measures.

In particular, technical and organizational measures that can be taken to reduce risks ought to be considered here. Among these are workplace ergonomics; protection of the infrastructure (e.g., smoke detectors, air-conditioned server rooms, and uninterruptible power supply); protection against procurement, development, sales and liability risks; protection against embezzlement, betrayal of confidence, fraud by staff, and not to be forgotten, computer abuse and industrial espionage.

We also need to think of how to prevent burglary, theft, and vandalism, for example through the installation of appropriate alarm systems, contracting of a plant security service, or conclusion of a transport insurance policy.

The current status of the project's risks needs to be published regularly, for example in a risk list as shown in figure 9-4, taking into account all relevant information. We must also bear in mind that risk control and solution can itself create new risks. These also need to be taken into account.

Risk List					Project: VSR		Version: 1.8e		June 15th 2006	
	Risk Evaluation						Risk Status			
ID	description/ owner	P	D	R	indicator	alarm level	act. value	measures	respon- sibility	initiated on
R7	loss of the confi- guration manage- ment database /Sc	9	500	4500	response time	5 sec	1	new server	Mi	–
					recovery	2/d	0.1			
R2	delays in develop- ment / Me	9	100	900	milestone delay	14 d	7	adjust schedule	Sc	06.10.06
					sick leave	3	3	reassign test staff	Wy	06.15.06
R4	insufficient entry quality of the test object / Sc	9	10	90	failed entry test	3/d	2/d	intensify code reviews	Me	–
					defect rate	15/d	12/d			
...	...				...			...		

Figure 9–4

Risk matrix

The risk list in figure 9-4 tells the VSR test manager that the current R4 occurrence indicator values (insufficient entry quality of the test object) are getting alarmingly close to their threshold levels (2 resp. 12 per day vs. 3 resp. 15 per day). In order to mitigate the risk, permitted value specifications of the complexity metrics are tightened, the complete source code is scanned with a static analyzer, and code reviews are carried out for all software modules with a cyclomatic complexity greater than 8.

Risk list

Risk review in the VSR project

- If risk identification and analysis is not or only insufficiently performed, a large part of the overall risk may hide in the pseudo category "non-identifiable risks," thus preventing proper and effective risk control and solution.
- It is also important to plan measures and contingency plans in preparation for unexpected risks.

9.6   Risk Review and Risk Monitoring

During risk review and monitoring, new risks are perceived and measures are taken to ensure that risk control and treatment remains effective. Attention needs to be paid during risk reviews throughout the project's lifetime to keeping relevant documents, standards, techniques, and action lists up-to-date and maintained. Risk monitoring shall be performed during the whole of the project's duration and shall include the review of the project budget, the project plans, and additional project information.

More elaborate monitoring activities can be performed at the project's milestones or if there are considerable changes to the project environment.

The VSR test manager checks the risk list (figure 9-4) and notices that the R2 (delay in development) mitigation measure "temporary reassignment of testers to the development department" increases the occurrence probability of all the risks in risk category "poor product quality."

This means that part of the risk is passed on to the user because of nonliability and warranty rules stipulated in the general terms and conditions or in the licensing agreement. Because of the high product liability risks and in order to avoid the risk, the decision is made not to launch the product in the U.S. Another alternative is to conclude an insurance policy against liability damages and regression claims.

An early start of risk management works like a "safety net" for the project. Furthermore, the findings form an essential basis for the creation of the test plan and for the prioritization of the specified test cases applied to reduce the product risks. Both aspects are discussed in the following section.

9.7 Risk-Oriented Test Plan Creation and Test Prioritization

A complete test means that the system is installed in all possible environments, operating systems, parameter constellations, etc. and that in each case tests are performed that completely cover all possible input/output constellations and system internal states. Even for very small software systems, this would mean that we would have to conduct an astronomically large number of combinations or test cases (test case explosion). It is one of the tasks of test management to keep the test effort in reasonable proportion to the achievable results. [Pol 02] states, "The test strategy is directed toward finding the optimal balance between the test effort to be exerted and the coverage required for the risks ... Testing should continue for as long as the costs for finding and correcting defects during testing are lower than the costs connected to the defect occurring in production."

Even without a precise quantitative identification of the optimal relationship between test costs and test benefit, test managers should keep this general principle in mind at all times and use it subjectively in their decision making.

In this context, the results of risk management can be used to perform risk-oriented testing, comprising:

- Target-oriented testing: applying appropriately different test techniques and test intensities to cover system functions with different risks
- Prioritized testing: giving areas with higher risks higher priority and testing them earlier
- Residual risk awareness: identifying the residual risks that remain in the delivered software and are due to reductions in test or nonperformance of planned tests

Test managers use their knowledge of risks to define a suitable test plan, using the nature of the risk to determine suitable test techniques. This way, product risks associated with the user interface of a software product may be mitigated by performing intensive usability tests. Incorrect storage of a complex computer game may pose a very high risk to the manufacturer (although it does not cause him direct costs) because the faulty game will not be appreciated by the customers. This may possibly cause large losses in sales, affecting perhaps all the other games of that manufacturer.

Target-oriented test plan creation

Project risks, too, can be addressed in the test plan, for instance by starting test activities early enough or subjecting code written by inexperienced programmers to reviews.

Since, as a rule, the test budget is limited, test cases are usually prioritized (see, e.g., [Amland 99], [Schaefer 96]). If we succeed in associating tests or test cases with particular risks, the prioritization of the risks also implies a prioritization of the tests: tests covering a large risk are then executed earlier.

Risk-based test prioritization

A simple tabular technique for risk-based test prioritization is described in [Schaefer 96]. First, some general risk factors are defined. For example, the three factors r_i, $i=1..3$ may delineate product risks (i.e., they determine the impact of the risks) and the three factors f_i, $i=1..3$ delineate the test risks (i.e., the probability with which failures can be expected in the product). In addition, each risk factor is assigned a weight, $g(r_i)$ or $g(f_i)$, $i=1..3$.

The test manager then focuses his attention on individual risk aspects, such as, for instance, particular functions or nonfunctional requirements like performance or usability.

Each risk aspect t and each of the above mentioned general risk factors r_i or f_i has a value $r_i(t)$ or $f_i(t)$ assigned to it. In the end, one factor $I(t)$ for each test aspect evaluates the quality of the current test strategy; i.e., the effectiveness of the current test plan with regard to this particular risk aspect.

[Schaefer 96] recommends the use of only three values for the weights $g(pi)$ and $g(fi)$, and for the quality factor $I(t)$, namely 1 (small), 3 (medium) and 10 (high). For the risk factors $r_i(t)$ and $f_i(t)$, values are to be defined ranging from 1 (very low) to 5 (very high).

The priority $P(t)$ of a test aspect t is then calculated as

$$P(t) = [(\textstyle\sum_{i=1..3} r_i(t) \times g(r_i)) \times (\textstyle\sum_{i=1..3} f_i(t) \times g(f_i))] / I(t)$$

Figure 9–5

Schaefer's test prioritization

Test aspects and corresponding test cases are subsequently prioritized using a spreadsheet as illustrated in figure 9-5.

Risk aspect	Product impact			Test risks / probability			Test quality	Priority
	visibility	impact	frequency	time delay	staff	complexity	current	
Weight	1	3	10	1	3	3		
usability	1	4	5	1	5	5	1	1953
performance	0	1	1	1	1	4	1	208
safety	5	1	2	3	1	5	1	588
function A	2	2	2	2	2	5	1	644
function B	1	1	1	1	1	2	1	140
function C	1	2	1	2	1	1	1	136
integration comp. A–B	2	1	2	1	2	2	1	325
...	1	2	1	2	2	1	1	187
	2	1	2	1	1	1	1	175
	2	2	2	1	1	1	1	196
	1	1	1	1	1	1	1	98
	2	4	2	4	2	4	1	748
	2	2	5	2	5	1	1	1160
	1	1	1	1	1	1	1	98
	5	5	5	5	5	5	1	2450
	1	1	1	1	1	1	1	98
	1	1	1	1	1	1	1	98

A purely risk-based assignment of test resources may lead to an absence of coverage of low-priority test risks if the project runs out of budget or time. This issue can be addressed in two ways.

Defining the test intensity

First, the intensity of the tests to be performed can be derived from the degree of risk. Most safety standards, such as [DO 178 B] or [EN 50128] (see chapter 13) use this approach and prescribe for each safety level the test procedures to be used as well as adequate test exit criteria.

For components belonging to the highest safety level, for instance, 100% branch coverage is frequently required. One method to define test intensity is described in [Gutjahr 95].

This method assigns an execution probability p, a failure probability f, and a defect-costs factor c to each function and uses this approach to determine the number of executable tests (see figure 9-6).

number	Function	p [%]	f	c	f[1/F]	C[money]	g	p*g	t	# tests
		1,000					25,953	5,675	1,000	100
1	enter model	0,080	N	H	0,0010	100	3,162	0,253	0,045	4
2	change model	0,100	M	H	0,0100	100	10,000	1,000	0,176	18
3	delete model	0,050	N	N	0,0010	5	0,158	0,008	0,001	5
4	price inquiry	0,390	M	H	0,0100	100	10,000	3,900	0,687	69
5	print	0,180	N	M	0,0010	20	0,632	0,114	0,020	2
6	list of models	0,200	M	M	0,0100	20	2,000	0,400	0,070	7

Figure 9–6

Gutjahr's test intensity

Level code	meaning	f	c
NN	very low	0,0001	1
N	low	0,001	5
M	medium	0,01	20
H	high	0,05	100
HH	very high or catastrophic	0,2	1000

Second, risks that are poorly covered by tests or not covered at all are known as a result of the correlation made between test cases and risks. Against this background, the test manager or the steering committee must decide whether or not the software product is ready for release and whether the residual risk can be accepted.

Estimation of residual risks

Thus, testing can be used to mitigate risks since the detection of defects in the product and their removal is a considerable contribution toward risk reduction. Project risks, too, are reduced by the application of a suitable test plan—for instance by detecting defects in interim products with an early test case well before they can affect later software development activities. In addition, the test will show the current risk status because in certain areas of the software product, high or low defect rates can be used to improve the quality of the risk analysis.

Tests inform about the risk evaluation.

Finally, risk management and risk-oriented testing are permanent processes spanning the entire life cycle of a project. Test results may be used as input for risk management and may lead to a reevaluation of risks. Levels of uncertainty can be reappraised and may require a redistribution of the remaining test budget.

9.8   Further Possibilities

This section introduces two further possibilities for risk based testing: the Failure Modes and Effect Analysis (FMEA) and risk-based precision testing.

9.8.1   Failure Modes and Effect Analysis (FMEA)

→FMEA is a method used to identify potential error types and their effect on a system and to classify the error types with regard to their criticality or persistency (see [IEC 60812]). Defects are to be prevented and possible weaknesses, for instance in design, are to be detected as they might pose a danger to the system or the user of the system during operation.

Furthermore, the FMEA is supposed to provide results for corrective design activities and help in the definition of test cases. The FMEA can, in the end, be used to show operational problems and usage constraints of the system or software.

FMEA uses the following means of representation (examples):

- Sequence descriptions of critical functions
- Functional and reliability block diagrams
- Error trees
- Error classification lists
- List of critical functions and modules

What happens when?   The basic principle is to look at the functional hierarchy and the programming logic (in case of software) and systematically (functionally and chronologically) ask, "What happens when?" using defined success or failure criteria. This analysis and evaluation is to be done for all operating phases and operating possibilities. In this connection, the "6 Ms" illustrated in figure 9-7 are of help, as each of the Ms is covered by one or several queries relating to possible failure or error causes.

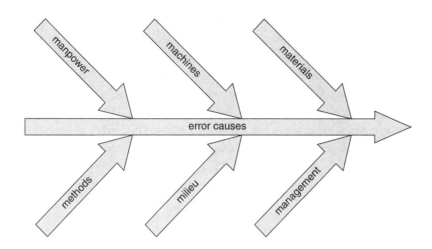

Figure 9–7

The "6 Ms" definition

Using FMEA in risk evaluation, the procedure is as follows:

1. Generate a list of all the risk factors.
2. Specify the type and probability of failures for each factor.
3. Investigate the effects of failures on other factors, applying, e.g., simulations.
4. Investigate the effects on project planning.
5. Identify possibilities for detecting the failure.
6. Identify possibilities for compensating the failure.
7. Identify possibilities for preventing the failure.
8. Define measures to avoid defects.
9. Evaluate the effect of the proposed measures.
10. Document the results.

Similar to risk evaluation discussed in section 9.4.1, risks are quantified according to their probability of occurrence O and expected damage E. In the FMEA, we optionally have the additional analysis of the probability of detection D; i.e., the quantitative evaluation of the quality of the identified risk occurrence indicators. From a risk perspective, the probability of detection is reciprocally evaluated; i.e., a high evaluation of D signifies a lower probability of risk occurrence (in particular, of a defect) prior to the delivery of the (interim) product. Using these three factors, the →risk priority number RPN is calculated as

$$RPN = O \times E \times D$$

FMEA defines the risk priority number (RPN).

The FMEA is used for prospective and retrospective risk analysis. Prospective risk analysis is a continuous process focusing on the current situation regarding deadlines, staffing, and resources in order to detect and resolve problems early, whereas retrospective risk analysis analyzes past problems in order to extract information that will help to avoid similar problems in the future.

FMEA only in case of stringent reliability and safety requirements

As regards risk analysis, the use of the FMEA is limited to projects with highly restrictive safety specifications or stringent requirements regarding system reliability; a general application of the FMEA, however, does not appear adequate considering the effort to be invested and its possible results.

9.8.2   Risk-Based Test Effort Optimization

One of the fundamental problems facing the test manager can best be described by the question: How can more tasks be accomplished with less resources? Risk-based test effort optimization (see *Precision Testing*, [Schettler 06]), which goes beyond pure test prioritization (compare with section 9.7), can provide a possible answer to this question.

The basic assumption is that risk reduction through testing is limited and that test effectiveness decreases with increasing effort. Figure 9-8 illustrates this under the assumption that the test effort remains constant over a specified period of time (compare with [Sherer 91]).

Figure 9–8

Test effectiveness

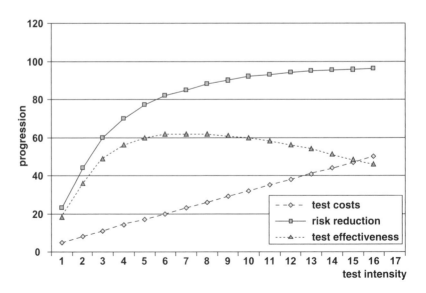

The basis of precision testing is a frame model describing the cost and benefit parameters (and their interdependencies) relevant in test management and quality assurance. Figure 9-9 ([Schettler 06]) provides an overview.

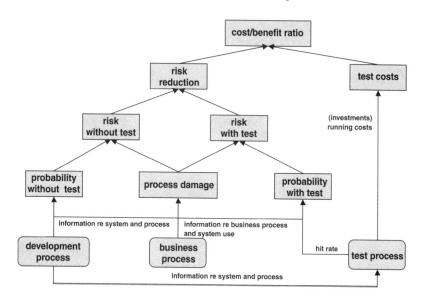

Figure 9–9

Frame model for precision testing

If a certain budget is to accomplish the least possible residual risk, the test plan must be optimized with regard to risk reduction. The test cost/benefit ratio is one of the central planning factors: The benefit is defined as the risk reduction achieved through testing (and defect correction) and calculated as the difference between the risk resulting from untested software and the forecasted residual risks after testing. If it turns out that the risk can be tolerated even without testing, further testing against that risk is not necessary.

Relative to risk quantification, the risk without test arises from the probability with which a function may behave abnormally and from the amount of damage for the business process that may result from the failure.

The prediction of the residual risk (after testing) is based on the probability with which failures will occur despite tests. It is a result of the probability with which certain failures or defects are detected with the test techniques applied. As a rule, residual risk is initially estimated by test experts and then adjusted on the basis of experience data.

In the end, the cost of testing is for the most part determined by the defined test procedure and the system's functional scope.

Figure 9-10 illustrates the operative procedure during planning in *Precision Testing* ([Schettler 06]). The result is a test plan that defines for each function one out of several possible test design techniques for test execution.

Figure 9–10

Test planning with

precision testing

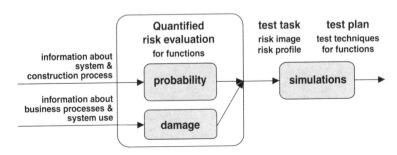

As a first step, the risk for each system function is evaluated, querying quantitative, basic indicators representative of the risk and evaluating them to a relative risk index. The work split into probability and damage evaluation matches the work split in software development quite well. Probability indicators deal with the construction process, whereas damage indicators deal with the affected business process. In practice, probability evaluation is typically done by evaluating function specifications or requirements specifications, whereas damage evaluation can be done by means of expert interviews or questionnaires and the possible support of statistical data.

Simulation of test scenarios based on the evaluations provide the projections of the test benefit and test effort parameters, which can now be assessed based on the targets and the optimization and test scope specifications. Test planning ends with the selection of the optimal test scenario. This is followed by schedule and resource disposition, whereby the risk image also supports the prioritization of the test activities. It is relatively easy to react to schedule or budget changes during the project's lifetime by simply resuming the test scenario simulations.

9.9   Summary

■ A risk is a problem that may arise in the future and may have negative consequences. Its severity is made up of the probability of its occurrence and its associated damage. Risks may be divided into product and project risks.

- Some of the core activities of risk management are risk identification, accurate risk analysis including specification of risk occurrence indicators, the definition of suitable measures for risk avoidance, risk control and solution, and the monitoring of risk management activities themselves. Risks can be evaluated qualitatively and quantitatively.

- Testing is a preventive measure, reducing risks through the detection and removal of defects. Risk-oriented testing uses the knowledge about risks to define the content of the test plan in such a way that under the given circumstances, risks (effort, schedule, availability) can be minimized as quickly as possible. Moreover, testing can yield information about the risk evaluation itself. High or low defect rates in certain areas of the software product may be used to improve the quality of the risk analysis.

- Based on the most important risks, suitable test techniques are to be selected, and tests are to prioritized to allow tests covering high risks to be executed early and with the appropriate effort.

- Prioritization and risk estimation criteria, as defined during risk analysis and in the test plan, can be applied to test objects during test object definition and to test cases during test case design. The intensity of the test to be executed is to be derived from the degree and type of the involved risk.

10 Staff Qualification and Skills

This chapter discusses the professional and social competencies expected of testers and points out factors critical to a successful test team.

10.1 Individual Skills

The "perfect" member of a test team has excellent knowledge and comprehensive experience in several domains: he possesses profound IT expertise; has knowledge about, and experience in, the application domain of the application or test object under test; brings with him a thorough professional qualification in software testing; and has high social competency.

Only very rarely do we find people who fulfill all these requirements equally well. Depending on training and professional career, most candidates are highly qualified IT experts (IT specialists) or they have comprehensive knowledge in the application domain under test (application or technical engineers).

A banker, for example, will fully understand the finance-related aspects of the VSR vehicle financing system. However, since he probably possesses little or no IT-specific qualifications, we may assume that his ability to comprehend system behavior or to notice technical flaws and system anomalies is rather limited. In contrast, an IT specialist will have only limited understanding of the banking system and its processes and may perhaps not be able to recognize banking-related anomalies.

Test managers must take the different educational backgrounds of their team members into account and assign to members of their team tasks and roles that best match their individual profile. Furthermore, knowledge gaps are to be closed through appropriate training and qualification measures.

The IT know-how comprises not only aspects of software development but also software testing and knowledge in system administration. In order to be able to work at test levels close to development (component testing, integration testing) or to be able to carry out certain nonfunctional tests (e.g., load or stress test), we need testers that have the required technical test and development skills. The same holds true when it comes to tasks such as structuring, formalizing, and consolidating test ideas provided by the domain experts. Other typical IT domains in the testing area are tasks concerned with test tools and the establishment and maintenance of the test environment.

In general, we can say that professional experience in coding, software design, system analysis, etc. will give testers a better feeling for potential sources of defects and frequent coding or logic errors. A tester with long-standing experience in these domains will be more likely to detect corresponding anomalies than someone without this background.

However, IT experts are unlikely to have sufficient knowledge of the application domain. Hence, if they are working as testers, they must be willing and prepared to familiarize themselves with the respective application domain and to acquire the necessary knowledge.

Test managers must keep an eye on IT experts in their team because they tend to pay too much one-sided attention to the optimization of test automation, enhancement of the test environment, and similar, technically challenging tasks. There is a certain danger that they lose sight of the application that is to be tested and that test resources are not deployed as they should be.

Application or domain experts know the technical and operational background and context (business processes, workflows, work products/results, work instructions, etc.) of the system under test. They often have in-depth knowledge of nonfunctional requirements such as system usability or performance because they may have worked with a previous version of the system for some time. They have a good understanding of how the system performs its tasks, in which areas system failure or operational errors have severe consequences, and what normal system behavior should be. They are experienced PC users but not IT experts. They can assist in the specification and execution of technically relevant test cases and can therefore do a good and useful job in system or acceptance testing.

There is a certain danger of developing a blinkered attitude that may lead to the acceptance of complex or strange system workflows "because it's always been that way" (in previous versions of the system). A domain expert can rarely judge whether a workflow or feature could be implemented by an IT expert in a simpler or more elegant way. Sometimes people just lack the courage to ask a seemingly stupid question or to show a weakness in front of IT experts.

Some companies consciously delegate user-oriented tests to "laymen"—for instance, by providing temporary part-time jobs for a group of students of different disciplines to execute the system tests. As a rule, these people have neither test nor user application-specific know-how.

Laymen as testers

This only works if the test specification is up-to-date and very detailed and if testing is accompanied and supervised in detail by an experienced test manager. In all other cases, this approach will yield suboptimal results. Especially when it comes to detecting failures, experience has shown that laymen do not have the necessary perception.

One of the few exceptions is the "usability test". In this case it makes sense and sometimes it may even be imperative to work with "laymen". However, tests are performed under guidance and follow a predefined plan, such as, for example, a usability test specification.

No matter which group a member of the test team belongs to, a sound education or training in the area of software testing makes sense and is in most cases necessary. All members of the test team should have at least obtained the "Certified Tester – Foundation Level" certificate. Some members require additional, role-related in-depth knowledge provided by the "Advanced Level"—for example, the "Certified Tester – Advanced Level – Test Manager". This also applies to testers with long-standing experience, since this is the only way to guarantee that test terminology, for instance, is interpreted in the same way and that people develop a uniform understanding and comprehension of the methodology.

Software test training

In order to be successful and in addition to his IT-, application-, and test-specific skills, the tester is required to have social competence. The following are some important and helpful character traits for the tester:

Social competence

- The ability to familiarize himself quickly with complex domains and applications.
- The ability to detect defects. This presupposes a certain basic skepticism and willingness to challenge apparent facts, paired with creativity, curiosity, and analytical thinking ("professional pessimism").
- The ability to cope with and voice criticism adequately (political and diplomatic aptitude).

- The ability to distinguish essentials from nonessentials and the courage to leave out what is less important ("courage to leave some gaps").
- Discipline, exactitude, patience, perseverance, frustration tolerance, determination.
- The ability to work in a team and ability to communicate.

Although the ability to work in a team and to communicate are listed last, both qualities are highly important. Because testing is teamwork, only those who are able to work in a team and communicate with colleagues and customers alike will have lasting success in their work as testers. The following sections will look at the different aspects of the test team work in more detail.

10.2 Functional Team Roles

The different tasks in the test process are reflected in the different roles within the test team:

Functional team roles and qualification profiles

- **Test manager**: The test manager leads the test team. He is responsible for the creation of the test schedule and its technical and on-time implementation. He reports test status and test results to the project manager, product manager, or development leader. The test manager is experienced in test planning, test control, and test process improvement. Of course, he has knowledge and practical experience in general methods of software testing. It is also desirable that he should have knowledge and experience in quality management, project management, and human resource management. And last but not least, he should have knowledge of applicable standards and of corporate- and product-related software development and test processes.
- **Test designer**: The test designer is responsible for the creation and maintenance of test specifications. His role involves identifying the appropriate test methods and the definition of a suitable test environment. He supports the test manager in the creation of the test plan and test schedule. He requires know-how in the areas of software testing, test specification techniques, and general software engineering. He must be able to familiarize himself quickly with complex application domains, requirements documents, functional specifications, and system prototypes. Furthermore, he must be able to comprehend the function and expected behavior of the system under test. Using this

information, he derives appropriate test cases and documents them in such a way that they are fully traceable. One of his most important character traits is that he is able to distinguish important from less important information and set priorities. Some practical experience as a tester is necessary.

- **Test automator**: The test automator is the test team's programmer. He has comprehensive programming experience, general software engineering know-how, and a very good knowledge of the test tools and script languages applied in the project. Basic knowledge of testing techniques and practical experience as a tester are of great advantage. With sufficient experience in test automation, the test automator can specialize further to become a developer of test frameworks and test tools.

- **Test administrator**: The test administrator is responsible for the installation, operation, and maintenance of the test environment. Among other responsibilities, this involves installing and setting up the system software (operating systems, database systems, application server), installing and configuring the test object, installing and setting up the test tools, and creating, managing, and restoring system configurations (images), e.g., by means of imaging or virtualization software.[1] The test administrator has necessary system administrator know-how (see also section 5.2.11). Since he is a troubleshooter and firefighter who can solve complex installation or configuration problems even under stress, he is an indispensable member of the test team.

- **Tester**:[2] The tester is responsible for the execution of the tests and the documentation of the test results. He executes the test cases according to the test schedule and test specification. If he notices a deviation from the expected system behavior, he writes an incident report. The necessary qualifications for this job are test fundamentals, IT basics, ability to operate applied test tools, and a basic understanding of the test objects. The tester's work style is characterized by concentration, accuracy, and perseverance. In addition, a good tester must be able to go beyond the limits of a test specification and apply his own ideas and creativity in a systematic manner. Depending on the test specification's

---

1. Overviews of tools and explanations of associated concepts can be found at [URL: Imaging] and [URL: Virtualization].
2. The term "tester" is also used as a generic term for all of the roles listed above.

degree of detail and the maturity of the software under test, it is almost always necessary during testing to fill gaps in specifications and to add additional test cases in an ad hoc fashion to isolate presumed or identified failures. A good tester also distinguishes himself in writing brief, succinct incident reports containing correct and traceable information.

- **Experts** (load test expert, database expert, network expert, etc.): Their duty is to support the "core" roles mentioned above in technically sophisticated matters or in problem solving.

Role combinations   Ideally, each of these roles is exercised by a specially trained member of the team. If in smaller teams several roles must be combined into one, the following combinations are best suited: test manager/test designer, test designer/tester, test automator/test administrator.

10.3 Social Team Roles

Besides their professional role, be it consciously or unconsciously, willingly or unwillingly, each team member assumes a social role in the team. The role one plays in the team depends on the individual's personality, his experience in his role, and how well he can fill it. [Belbin 93][3] distinguishes nine typical team roles (see table 10-1).

---

3.   A large number of concepts relating to team roles can be found in the literature— e.g., DISGModel [URL: DISG] or Myers-Briggs Type Indicator [URL: MBTI]. Belbin's model is considered here in more detail as representative of such team role models.

Type	Descriptors	Strengths	(Allowed) Weaknesses
Monitor Evaluator	Sober-minded, strategic, and discerning	Good power of judgment, discrete,	Lacks drive and the ability to inspire others
Shaper	Dynamic, open-minded, edgy, result oriented	Lots of drive, fights idleness and inefficiency, exerts pressure	Prone to provocations and irritations, prone to hurt others
Planter	Individualistic, unorthodox	Brilliant, creative, lots of intellectual power	Often absent-minded, inclined to ignore practical details and instructions
Completer	Meticulous, straight, conscientious, anxious	Ability to see things through to completion, perfectionism	Inclined to worry unduly, reluctant to delegate
Team worker	Cooperative, mild, sensitive	Ability to cope with different situations and people, promotes team spirit, calms the waters	Indecisive under pressure, can be easily influenced
Implementer	Conservative, dutiful, calculable	Hard-working, turns ideas into practical actions, disciplined	Somewhat inflexible, rejects unproved ideas
Co-ordinator (chairperson)	Self-confident, mature	Quick at recognizing individual talents in team members, knows how to use their strengths unreservedly, good at clarifying goals	Not necessarily a high-flyer, has limited creativity
Resource Investigator	Extrovert, enthusiastic, communicative	Likes to develop internal and external contacts, picks up new ideas, reacts to challenges	Overly optimistic, inclined to lose interest after initial enthusiasm
Specialist	Single-minded, self-starting, dedicated	Provides knowledge and skills in rare supply	Contributes only a narrow front, dwells on technicalities, overlooks the "big picture"

Of course, the specific features or characters of real people are much more complex and multilayered, but knowing about these personality profiles may help when it comes to employing new members that need to "fit into the team". It also helps us understand the success or failure of an individual team member or even a complete team and may help improve team performance.

If new team members are to be selected or employed, care should be taken that already available knowledge and personality profiles are sensibly complemented by the new team member. Belbin's investigations on

Table 10–1

Personality types[4] according to [Belbin 93]

Selection of team members

4.   None of the team roles should be considered positive or negative, despite the fact that some role descriptions, such as "pessimist," may have negative connotations in everyday language.

group psychology show that regarding the different personality profiles, lopsided teams work[5] less successfully than properly mixed teams.[6] Teams, for example, that are entirely made up of "Implementers" will only perform well in the completion of routine tasks. However, when it comes to solving complex issues, such teams will lack the ingenuity and skills necessary for creative problem resolution.

Conversely, if we have too many "Planters" in the team, it may be extraordinarily creative but will lack the ability to implement and utilize its ideas with the necessary perseverance and endurance. Teams composed entirely of people with exceptionally high intelligence (Belbin calls them "Apollo teams") do not necessarily turn out to be successful. Such teams are difficult to control; they are prone to destructive debates and have difficulty making decisions. Despite a whole bunch of highly intelligent people, the team flops.

Getting the task distribution right

It is therefore important to find a suitable combination of different characters or personalities; it is equally important that the distribution of tasks in the team is appropriate to the test constellation. Especially when it comes to team forming for software testing, it is difficult to get professionally qualified staff. In that case, selection based on somebody's "personality profile" is of only secondary importance. However, it can help in the correct distribution or, in case of problems, redistribution of roles or tasks in the team.

Examples: task distribution

It is certainly of advantage if "Planters" or "Monitor Evaluators" work as test designers. Yet testing in complex system environments or testing of "immature" systems, too, asks for "Planters" with analytical skills. They should at least be available as coaches because as soon as technical problems arise, their know-how and creativity is required.

Completers, Implementers, and Teamworkers will feel comfortable working as testers, especially in regression testing. A "Planter" will find this a rather boring affair. Consequently, he may not observe the test specification to the letter and will try to find his own test variants. This, however, is not required in regression testing.

---

5. The success of software development projects depends to a large extent on social, nontechnical factors. Worthwhile observations on this issue and the management of software development can be found in, e.g., [DeMarco 95] and [DeMarco 97].
6. [Belbin 93] originally considers management teams, i.e., teams made up of executives. His findings, however, can be applied to other forms of sophisticated teamwork.

Despite all these considerations, we must not forget that the personality types just listed are "constructs" only and that in reality we hardly ever encounter them in pure form. One and the same person can quite often slip into several roles, for instance, if the preferred role in the team is already occupied. The role concept and the idea of personality profiles help us in our understanding and analysis of problems in the team or of the reasons for low achievement and weaknesses of individual team members as a whole.

Stop thinking in stereotypes.

Care must be taken not to carelessly pigeonhole people. Other factors, too, ought to be taken into account, such as personal antipathies, career thinking, or factors pertaining to the team as a whole, like company climate or current project situation.

10.4 The Communication Factor

Testing does not only involve finding and documenting as many defects as possible. It is equally important to communicate identified problems or defects in the right way and to the right people. If there is interest in quick defect resolution, the way a defect is communicated is often more important than the content of the report itself.

Communicate problems accurately

Test-Team-External Communication

Generally speaking, members of a test team and especially the test manager have to communicate with three main team-external groups:

- **Communication between testers and developers:**
  A tester detects a failure in the software or in a colleague's work result. He writes an incident report and thus lays open the defect in more or less forthright terms. The ways in which the incident report is written must always be factual and problem oriented. Personal or unobjective criticism or even finger-pointing must strictly be avoided.

  Tester → developer

  A diplomatic communication style is an indispensable precondition for the acceptance of incident reports (hence, testing as a whole) as a positive contribution to the project effort and is the only way to contribute to the improvement of the product and its quality.

  The same applies for communication in the opposite direction. Nobody can "blame" the tester for the fact that failures occur, and he is entitled to receive a well-conceived answer to each of his reports. It

  Developer → tester

really makes good sense if developers inform testers about which system parts require particular attention—for instance, because of their high degree of complexity or because they are newly conceived. Conversely, it helps if testers pass test cases on to developers in support of early testing within development.

Example:
"Well" and "badly"
formulated incident reports

The following examples illustrate a "well" and a "badly" formulated incident report.

Bad Style:

"... Tried to save a purchase contract but application still crashes. This has been known for weeks; see reports 264 and 253. Can't somebody come up with a decently coded program? ..."

Good Style:

"Crash after attempt to save purchase contract:

Description: *ContractBase* crashes when trying to create new purchase contract.

Impact: Contract data is lost; system needs to be rebooted.

Reproduction:

- Call up *ContractBase*
- Select customer
- Select new purchase contract (compare attached screen shot)
- "Save contract"
- → crash
- ..."

Test manager →
project manager

Communication between testers and project management: The test manager regularly reports test progress and observed software quality to product or project management. The test (status) report needs to be open and direct. The same holds as before: solution-oriented, constructive contributions and formulations will facilitate things. Statements concerning individual team members and personal finger-pointing are not acceptable.

Project manager →
test manager

Conversely, product/project management informs the test manager about changes in the project plan and delivery dates; new, changed, or deleted features; system environment changes; staffing changes in the development team; and new software suppliers.

Tester → user

Communication between testers and users: Testers, and in particular test designers, should try to stay in close contact with users, developers, and other stakeholders involved in the system under test. Requirements specifications are hardly ever detailed, complete, or up-to-date enough to do without additional talks with the people who originally wrote them. Here, additional background information may be gained about the system's application domain or information that will help set testing priorities. In order to prioritize, remove, or contain failures it may be necessary or helpful to explain test results to system users (e.g., pilot customers).

Test-Team-Internal Communication

Besides external communication, the test manager must also pay attention to team-internal communication. Scheduling regular team meetings is an important measure in support of team-internal communication. In order to be efficient, the meeting must have a fixed agenda and must be moderated. In practice, the following agenda has proved useful:

Hint

Test team meeting: agenda

- General project situation
- Current status of test progress versus plan
- Test object quality, defect rate, defect correction percentage (bug fix rate)
- Release planning and upcoming release test cycles
- Current staff planning
- Necessary changes to the test schedule
- Quality of the test process and improvement potential
- Status tracking of other tasks outside the test schedules (e.g., expansion of the test environment)
- Newly identified tasks documented and assigned to a member of the team

10.5 The Motivation Factor

Effective and productive testing not only requires the right technical and social skills, it also requires the full commitment and motivation of the testers involved. No matter how good the process, and no matter how well people are trained or how experienced they are, without the right motivation the end result will be bad or at best mediocre.

Motivation checklist

How can motivation be achieved and how can it be sustained at a high level? What are the factors that can dampen or even kill motivation altogether? "The motivation checklist" [URL: Templates] contrasts motivating versus demotivating factors. Using this list, it may be helpful to once in a while check the motivational situation in the team.

Of course, not every circumstance that may have a demotivating influence on the tester or the test team can be influenced or even eliminated by the test manager; however, there are many possibilities or opportunities where he can actively intervene.

Some of the measures that a test manager can take are listed below:

- Plan realistically. Communicate clear objectives and provide for a clear task distribution. Track the plans and respond to deviations.
- Ensure management support. Promote testing and show the benefits of testing to everybody. Present test results regularly and make sure they're well prepared. Present the costs of testing in an unvarnished and honest way and compare them with the benefits of testing (see [Spillner 07]).
- Provide for a professional, adequate working environment (facilitating communication, test laboratory). Provide for interesting tasks that will relax the inevitable test routine. Allow and encourage specialization within the team. Point out opportunities for further personal development and careers.
- Provide feedback to the test team about its contribution to the project's success or product quality (by way of feedback from management, development, support, and the market).
- "Propagate" the accomplishments of the test team within the organization. Present the successes of the test and development teams as a collective success that will be collectively celebrated.

10.6 Summary

- A member of the test team needs to possess IT knowledge, knowledge of the application domain of the system or test object under test, and knowledge and experience in the area of software testing.
- In addition, in order to be successful, a tester needs to have social competence.
- The different tasks in the test process are reflected in the different roles within a test team: test manager, test designer, test automator, test (laboratory) administrator, and tester.

- Besides their professional role, each team member also plays a social role in the team. Not only professional qualification but also the suitable combination of different personalities and a suitable task distribution within the team are vital to team success.

- Detected problems or failures must be communicated to test-team-external addressees (developers, project management, users). The style of communication must be objective, solution oriented, and focused on improving quality. Personal or unobjective criticism or finger-pointing must be discouraged.

- Regular test-team-internal meetings summoned and chaired by the test manager contribute to good communication.

- The test manager is to provide for a motivating working environment and professional working conditions for his team. Part of this task is to adequately represent the role and contribution of the test team within the organization.

11 Test Metrics

Test metrics allow quantitative statements regarding the quality of a product and its development and test processes. They must therefore be built on solid measurement theoretical foundations. Metrics form the basis for transparent and traceable test process planning and control. Based on different measurement objects, we can create test-case-based metrics, test-basis and test-object-based metrics, defect-based metrics, and cost- and effort-based metrics. One added value of such metrics is that statements can be made regarding the best possible test finishing date, using on the one hand experienced-based estimates on the probability of residual defects and on the other hand statistical failure data analysis and reliability growth models.

11.1 Introduction

Performing test management activities such as test process planning and control or test end evaluation, qualitative statements such as "We must do extensive testing" are by no means sufficient. On the contrary, required are quantitative and objectively verifiable statements such as "All components from safety requirement level 2 onward must be component tested with 100% branch coverage". This is also reflected, for instance, in the Capability Maturity Model Integration (CMMI [CMMI 01], see chapter 7) and the ISO 9000 family of standards, which require quantitative statements about planning and control.

However, how do test managers obtain quantitative statements or specifications regarding products and processes? The answer is, they do it in the same way as, for example, someone specifying the floor area or the wall thickness of a new house—through measurement values.

And how do we verify that the specifications have been met? Through measurement! In *Software Testing Foundations*, it was explained that quality attributes can be measured with measurement values or metrics and that McCabe's cyclomatic complexity metric can be taken as a possible measure for the evaluation of program code complexity ([Spillner 07, section 4.2.5]).

Measure

Hence, evaluation and measurement are central test management activities and must be put on sound theoretical foundations. The most important ones are explained in section 11.2. Section 11.3 describes how metrics are defined and evaluated, and section 11.4 shows how measurement values can be visualized by means of graphs and diagrams. Based on this, section 11.5 sets out to describe the most important test metrics. Section 11.6 deals with residual defect and reliability estimations.

11.2 Some Measure Theory

Measurements relate features of objects to values.

A measurement is generally understood as a number of symbols, identifiers, or figures that can be assigned to specific features of a (measurement) object by means of a measurement specification.

Observations on objects can be carried out with or without technical aids. If technical means are used, we talk about a →measurement. In most cases, measurement in the technical, physical sense means comparing and assigning measurement values. Going back to the previous example, the thickness of a wall can be compared with the values of a measuring system, for example, a yardstick or a tape measure. The measurement value is expressed as a number and unit, e.g., 25 cm or 250 mm.

Measurements can be direct or derived.

If a measurement relates directly to an object or its features, we talk about a direct measurement; otherwise, we talk about a derived measurement. A derived measurement cannot directly measure the feature that is in the focus of our interest but instead measures one or several directly measurable features that we assume bear a specific relation to the feature we are focusing on.

Models for indirect measurements

Often, indirect measurements are formulated with the aid of models that help to explicitly express the relation to the actual measurement object or features that we are interested in.

In the first instance, information gained through indirect measurements is valid only within the context of our model assumptions, and the quality of the interpretation or transfer of such information from the model back to the real world is dependent on the quality of the model.

For instance, if in our house-building example a model such as the architectural drawing is not to scale, we cannot infer from measurements taken from the drawing that one room is "larger" than another.

Instead of the general term "measurement", we sometimes casually speak of "metrics"—Greek µ, (the art of) meter, relating to measurement. In mathematics, this term is defined as a function that describes the "distance" between two elements of an arbitrary (vector-)space. For example, the Euclidian distance between two points a and b with the Cartesian coordinates x_a, y_a and x_b, y_b is formulated as a function

Measurement = metric?

$$d(a, b) = \sqrt{\left[(x_a - x_b)^2 + (y_a - y_b)^2\right]}$$

and is a metric in the mathematical sense.

In software engineering and in testing, the term "metric" is used for both the measurement techniques and the measurements values used to measure certain features of the measurement objects. The IEEE standard 1061 ([IEEE 1061]) defines a software (quality) metric as a function that maps specific properties of software development processes, or of interim or end products, to values of a predefined value range. The resulting values or value combinations are interpreted as the degree of fulfillment of specific (quality) features.

In software engineering metric is used to denote measurement as well as measurement techniques.

Measurement objects, therefore, are software development projects or underlying processes (figure 11-1a) or concrete products such as a program text, design model, test case, etc. (figure 11-1b).

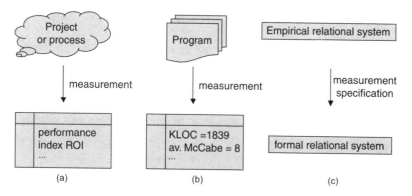

Figure 11–1

Measurement and measure

Generally speaking, a measurement relates specific features of objects of a so-called empirical relational system[1] (e.g., some property of a software artifact) to specific values of a formal relational system (e.g., the natural numbers, by means of a measurement specification).

---

1.   A relational system comprises the number of (measurement) values and associated allowed operations (see [Zuse 98]).

An empirical relational system, for instance, can be the number of all programs written in a particular programming language together with the attribute "comprehensibility." A possible measurement counts the lines of code, and the associated formal relational system consists of the (value) set of the natural numbers 0, 1, 2 … and the larger-than-or-equal-to relation. The measurement values are then interpreted as "a larger value corresponds to lesser comprehensibility".

Measurements associate empirical with formal relational systems.

A measure (or metric) is thus made up of the following elements: an empirical and a formal relational system, the measurement specification to map specific attributes of elements of the empirical relational system to values in the formal relational system, and the interpretation of the relation in the formal relational system with respect to the observed features in the empirical relational system. This general relationship is illustrated in figure 11-1c.

It is important to understand clearly that the results of metrics are, to begin with, hypotheses that need to be validated. It is therefore necessary to define or select metrics that are relatively simple and easy to reproduce and adequate to the project's needs. It is equally important to continuously verify the quality and target orientation of these metrics

11.3 Metrics Definition and Selection

Metrics and metrics collections are not an end in themselves but meant to provide a quantified, objective basis for decision making. This section explains how metrics can be accurately defined and methodically selected.

Selecting suitable metrics

Before thinking about concrete measurement objects and associated measurable features, we need to be clear in our minds about which fundamental objectives we really want to achieve and track through measurement.

Major objectives such as quality or productivity targets are broken down into subobjectives until we can assign one or several measurement objects and a small number of practical and applicable metrics to each of them.

This method, known as the "factor-criteria-metrics" (FCM) method (see figure 11-2) forms one of the bases of the quality model of the ISO 9126 family of software-quality-related standards. There, quality attributes are broken down to subattributes and further to measurable quality factors that can be assigned to concrete metrics.

A distinction is made between internal and external metrics, the former measuring the product itself and the latter measuring attributes that can be observed during the use or operation of the product.

The ISO 9126 standard, for instance, decomposes the quality attribute "efficiency" into the subattributes "time behavior" and "resource utilization." With regard to the subattribute "time behavior," the external metric measures the response time T as the difference between the system's response and the completion of the corresponding command.

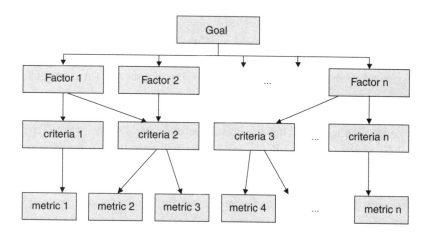

Figure 11–2
Factor-criteria-metrics- (FCM) method

In order to arrive at individual factors and finally at metrics, Basili and Weiss ([Basili 84]) in their "Goal Question Metric" (GQM) method recommend starting with the definition of goals. For each goal we should then think of questions we would have to answer to see if we are reaching that goal. Roughly speaking, we must first ask what we actually want to find out. Subsequently, we construct simple hypotheses and consider which kind of data or measurement values we need to confirm or disconfirm these hypotheses.

The Goal Question Metric (GQM) method

It may, for example, be our goal to gain better control of the test process. We may want to ask, for example, the following questions: Which tasks have been completed within the planned time? Which tasks have not been completed? Which tasks are delayed? Possible measurements would, e.g., be product completeness, already used-up resources, or already agreed-upon delivery dates.

Measurement objects in test management are test basis documents (e.g., requirements and design specifications) and the test objects themselves as well as corresponding test case specifications, test scripts, and

Measurement objects in test management

test reports. In addition, similar to the above GQM-example, the test process itself serves as a measurement object whose attributes such as progress of plan, effectiveness, and efficiency can be quantified with one or more measurements.

The scale indicates which operations are allowed with the measurement values.

Once we are certain which attributes or factors of a measurement object are to be measured (empirical relational system), the measurement specification and the value range of the measurements (formal relational system) are defined. It is important to accurately define the so-called scale or scale type as it limits the operations allowed on the measurement values.

If, for example, we take two programs, A and B, and measure their number of lines, with A resulting in 250 lines and B in 500 lines, we may rightly assert that B is twice as long as A. However, if program A were classified 1 (equivalent to "short") and program B as 2 (equivalent to "medium"), it would not tell us anything about the ratios of the lengths of A and B. But if, in the latter case, test cases executed 100 lines of code each in both programs A and B, we could infer that A was structurally "better" tested than B.

Formal measure theory knows the five scales listed in table 11-1 ([Zuse 98]) and distinguishes between metric and non-metric scale types. For software measurements, we ought to look for metric scale types, since otherwise the measurement values will not (or only in a very limited fashion) be open to mathematical operations and statistical evaluations.

Table 11–1
Features of the five scale types

Scale type	Expression	Attributes / permitted operations	Possible analyses
non-metric	Nominal scale	Identifier	Comparison, median, quantile
		Renaming	
	Ordinal scale	Rank value with ordinal numbers	Classification, frequencies
		All F with $x \geq y \Rightarrow F(x) \geq F(y)$	
metric	Interval scale	Equal scale without natural zero point	Addition, subtraction, average, standard deviation
		All F with $F(x) = a \times x + b$	
	Ratio scale	Equal scale with natural zero point	Multiplication, division, geometric mean, variation
		All F with $F(x) = a \times x$ and $a > 0$	
	Absolute scale	Natural number and measurement units	all
		Identity $F(x) = x$ only	

In the above example, the number of lines of code resembles an absolute scale, whereas the (subjective) classification would have been on a nominal scale where the values cannot be divided. The scale for the above mentioned response time metric T to measure the quality subattribute "time behavior" is of scale type "ratio scale" and has the natural zero point 0 seconds, which at the same time is its lowest value because negative response times would violate the principle of causality.

The following requirements or criteria help to evaluate the quality of measurements or metrics:

Requirements for "good" metrics

- A good measurement must be easily calculable and interpretable and must correlate sufficiently with the attribute it is supposed to measure (statistical validation!).
- Measurements must be reproducible; i.e., the measurement values must be objectively obtainable (without being influenced by the person taking the measurement).
- Measurements must be robust against "insignificant" changes of the measurement object; i.e., the measurement value must be in a continuous functional relationship with the measured attribute.
- A further requirement is the timeliness of the measurement values or measurements. Measurements must be taken early enough to enable you to make relevant decisions that can positively influence target achievement.
- A question closely associated with the scale type of a measurement is whether, and how far, measurement values can be compared and statistically evaluated. Expedient in this respect are the ratio and absolute scales.

If a measurement has been successfully used in several different projects, we may, as it were, take this as empirical evidence that is has been reasonably defined and that it is usable. In the end, for reasons of documentation, all measured values must be traceable and reproducible.

In test management (see figure 11-3), metrics are defined based on the quality requirements and incorporated in the test plan: based on the metric definitions tests are planned and designed as measurements. During execution of the tests, the test object is measured, classified into the selected classification scheme, and evaluated with regard to its quality attributes (see also section 5.2.6).

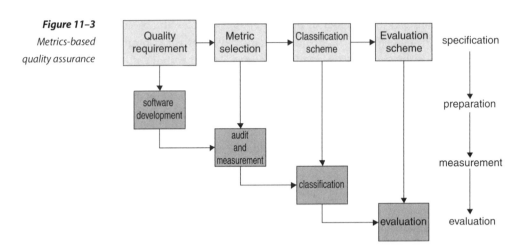

Figure 11–3

*Metrics-based
quality assurance*

Table 11–2

Metrics definition template

For cataloguing, distribution, and application, it is best to document metrics consistently, using the template provided in table 11-2 ([Ebert 05]).

Field	Description
Name/identifier	Name or identifier (filename; ID number)
Description	Brief, succinct description
Motivation	Goals and issues that are to be accomplished or addressed
Base data	Product attributes or other metrics taken as a basis
Scale type	Scale (nominal, ordinal, interval, ratio, absolute)
Definition	Calculation algorithm
Tools	References and links to support tools
Presentation	Visualization; i.e., possible chart types
Frequency	Frequency/interval in which metric must be created
Costs	One-off, introductory costs, and regular metrics collection costs
Method of analysis	Recommended or permitted statistical operations
Target and boundary values	Specified range of values for product, project, or process evaluation
Storage location	Configuration management system, project database
Distribution	Visibility and access control
Training	Available training opportunities (training, documentation)
Examples	Application examples, including graphs and data collection

Templates and concrete metric definitions as well as up-to-date measurement values should be made available via an intranet, allowing all project members immediate access to associated documents, data collections, and analysis results.

With increasing maturity level of the test processes, the selection, collection, and evaluation of metrics becomes a clearly defined test management activity. Figure 11-4 shows the metrics-based feedback loop structure for test management.

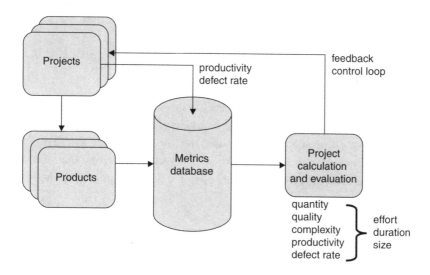

Figure 11–4

Metrics-based test management feedback

For a more detailed illustration, see [Ebert 05] and the ISO 15939:2002 standard ([ISO 15939]), which defines a software measurement process.

11.4 Presenting Measurement Values

A variety of different charts or diagrams can be used to display measured values. Popular are bar or column charts to show metric values for several measurement objects (right, figure 11-5) as well as line charts to show the chronological progression of a measurement object or of one or several metrics (left, figure 11-5).

Circle or pie charts are favored for presenting portions of several measurement values or measurement objects from a certain total size onward (left, figure 11-6). Lesser known are so-called cumulative charts, which

Diagrams help you to visualize measurement values and their progression.

can be used to show the sum of several measurement values in their chronological progression in the form of stacked line charts.

Figure 11–5

Line and bar charts

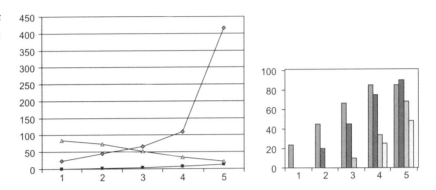

The chart to the right in figure 11-6 shows the cumulated efforts of component testing, integration testing, and system and acceptance testing in person days. Component testing ends at the beginning of the fourth month so that allocated cumulated effort remains constant from that month onward. All in all, approximately 295 person days were spent until the fifth month.

Figure 11–6

Pie chart and cumulative chart

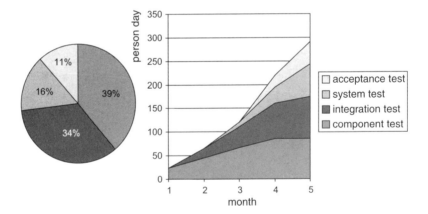

Kiviat charts illustrate values of many metrics in a concise way.

For most of the measurement objects, several metrics are collected simultaneously, each highlighting different features or aspects of the measurement object. In order to be able to evaluate a measurement object as a whole, it may not be sufficient to consider the measurement values of only one metric in isolation. It is the overall view that is of interest. As figure 11-7 illustrates, Kiviat diagrams combine measurement values of several metrics with a corresponding number of concentrically or rotation symmetrically arranged axes, each indicating the measurement value of one metric. The associated points on the axes are bounded by a closed polygon so that, with some experience, the evolving pattern can be used to deduce features of the measurement object as a whole.

The VSR test manager studies the Kiviat diagram illustrated in figure 11-7, showing the metric values for one class of the object-oriented implementation. The value for the weighted count of methods (WCM) is at approximately 80%, and the depth of inheritance (DIT) is 9, hence rather deep. Since the other values are relatively high, too—i.e., the values for the average complexity of the methods (CMPL), the errors found (ERR), and the Halstead metrics (HLSTD)—the test manager recommends a refactoring of the class.

Example:
Kiviat diagram in VSR

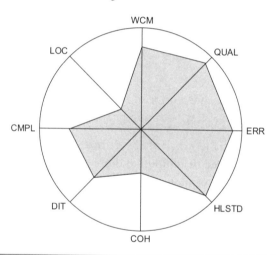

Figure 11–7
Kiviat diagram

11.5 Several Test Metrics

After our more general discussion on measurements and metrics, this section introduces concrete →test metrics, which are useful for the measurement of the test process or the evaluation of product quality.

Test metrics can be distinguished according to the different measurement objects under consideration, resulting in the following:

- Test-case-based metrics
- Test-basis- and test-object-based metrics
- Defect-based metrics
- Cost- or effort-based metrics

As already suggested in the metrics examples above, there are many metrics in which both absolute numbers (number of tested X) and ratio values (number of tested X / number of all X) are of interest.

11.5.1 Test-Case-Based Metrics

Test-case-based metrics focus on a large number of test cases and their respective states. They are used to control progress of the test activities with reference to the test (project) plan or its different versions. Here are some examples for metrics with absolute scales:

- Number of planned test cases
- Number of specified test cases
- Number of created test procedures
- Number of test script lines

And here are a couple of examples of test-case-based metrics with ratio scales:

- Number of test cases with priority 1/number of planned test cases
- Number of specified test cases/number of planned test cases

Measure the unexpected, too!   During the course of a test cycle there are many instances where new test cases must be developed in addition to those planned; for instance, if particular coverage targets cannot be reached with the available test cases.

In most cases, requirement changes, too, require new tests or changes in current test cases, or even make old ones obsolete. Metrics with absolute scales are as follows:

- Number of unplanned new test cases
- Number of changed test cases
- Number of deleted test cases

If, for example, the number of unplanned new test cases rises above a particular value, this may be an indication of insufficient requirements management. A high number of changed test cases relating to one requirement or many changes of a test case within a short period of time allows us to conclude that requirements are vague or ambiguously defined and that they will only gradually be specified more precisely during the course of the development phase.

Also interesting for test processes control are metrics concerning test execution, such as these, for instance:

- Number of executed test cases (already mentioned)
- Number of successfully (without failure, *passed*) executed test cases
- Number of failed (with *failure*) test cases
- Number of blocked test cases (not executable due to violated preconditions)

A high number of executed test cases is an indication of well-structured, largely independent test cases, whereas a high number of blocked test cases indicates that too many dependencies exist between test cases. If some of these tests fail, many subsequent test cases based on postconditions of previous ones cannot be executed either.

Of course, the number of successful or failed tests executed on the test object is not only interesting for test control, it is particularly interesting in the evaluation of product quality.

In maintenance testing or in case of new software versions in regression testing, these metrics are often separately collected for current, new, and changed test cases. Often the number of unplanned new test cases executed (with/without defect) is also collected separately.

The values of the test-case-based metrics, too, are often shown separately per test level and priority of the test cases (e.g., in cumulative diagrams).

In a wider sense, metrics on elements of the test environment (e.g., test bed with test drivers and stubs, test data, simulators, analyzers, etc.) are also classed with the test-case-based metrics. Here are a couple of useful examples:

Plan and control the test environment setup

- Number of planned or available test drives or stubs
- Number of planned or available lines of code per test driver or stub

Essentially, test-case-based metrics take into account all test cases specified in the test schedule. However, a hundred percent test progress in terms of test schedule does not necessarily mean that the test object has been sufficiently tested.

Consider different test coverage concepts.

Therefore, additional suitable product-oriented test coverage metrics are needed that measure test progress against the test base or the size of the test object.

The next section describes some corresponding metrics.

11.5.2   Test-Basis- and Test-Object-Based Metrics

The metrics outlined in this section are aimed at the features and coverage of the test basis and test object. Depending on test level, elements such as requirements, design elements, program code, and user manuals are measured by test metrics in relation to the test process—for instance, to measure the quality of the test case design or the progress of the test activities in relation to the size of the test object.

In code, for instance, we can measure how many lines of code or instructions were executed during testing. In case of (functional) specifications we can measure which system functions (features) were verified by the test. Based on the system architecture, we can trace which system components have been tested. Regarding the system requirements, we can trace how many requirements have been validated by tests.

Trace requirements   To do so, it is necessary to record which requirements have been specified by whom and by means of which functional and technical design documents; furthermore, we need to document which program parts were used for the implementation of which requirements and which test cases were taken for the verification of these requirements. This information is necessary to ensure that we have bidirectional traceability from the requirement's source to implementation and back, that they can be traced to corresponding test cases, and that we can measure the coverage.

Such coverage metrics are always useful if their abstraction level correlates with the test level for which they are intended.

System and acceptance test: function- or requirements- based metrics   Depending on the requirements engineering methodology used, it is possible to collect function- or requirements-oriented coverage metrics during system and acceptance testing:

- Number of tested functions/total number of functions
- Number of tested dialogue/number implemented dialogues
- Number of executed test cases/number of specified test cases per function
- Number of tested hours per function

The application of specification-based metrics requires the traceability of requirements from the requirements to their functional and technical system design and right up to their test cases. In this case, measurements like the following can be made:

- Percentage of all requirements covered by test cases
- Percentage of all use case scenarios executed

- Percentage of all functional classes or data types created/read/changed or deleted

Metrics must also be collected for tests regarding nonfunctional requirements:

- Number of platforms covered by test
- Number of localized[2] versions
- Number of performance requirements per platform covered by test

During integration testing, special focus is put on design components and particularly on interface interaction—which and how many interfaces are there in the system and which of them have been covered by test? Metrics examples are as follows:

Integration testing:
Focus on interface metrics.

- Percentage of interfaces tested
- Percentage of interface usage tested
- Percentage of interface parameters tested with test technique XYZ

After execution of the specified test cases, all software parts not covered according to the specifications in the test plan are checked to see if test cases may possibly be missing in the test design specification. If this is the case, they will be added and the test repeated with the new test cases. One useful metric in this connection is the defect-based "test design verification" metric (see section 11.5.3).

In component testing, measurement typically focuses on structure-oriented metrics based on program code ("code coverage"). Measurable are, for example, the following:

Component testing:
structure-oriented metrics

- Number of new or changed functions or operations
- Number of lines of code or executable instructions (kilo lines of code (KLOC) or kilo delivered source instructions (KDSI))
- Code complexity (cyclomatic complexity or McCabe metric)
- Number of covered paths in the control flow graph

Complexity metrics serve as product risk indicators and for risk-based control of the test effort (see chapter 9). Structure-oriented dynamic metrics such as statement coverage (C0) and branch coverage (C1) require

---

2. "Localization" is the process of adapting software to another language—for example, by translating user interfaces; adapting date formats, currencies, and measurement units; and even perhaps adapting the software to local legal requirements.

the previous instrumentation of the programs. Appropriate instrumentation tools allow us to make measurements such as these:

- Percentage of operations or procedures called
- Percentage of instructions that have been executed
- Percentage of branches in the control flow graph that were covered
- Percentage of procedure calls that have been executed

Many other test-basis- and test-object-based metrics are found in [Kaner 95] and [Zhu 97]. Test-object- and test-basis-based metrics for object-oriented software are listed in [Winter 98] or [Zuse 98].

11.5.3 Defect-Based Metrics

Besides tracking test progress with test-case-, test-basis- and test-object-based metrics, the test manager is also asked to evaluate test results, in particular detected failures and defects, and use them for controlling the test process.

For ease of reading, we shall in the following also use the terms "defect" and "fault" for "failure".

The IEEE Standard Dictionary of Measures of the Software Aspects of Dependability ([IEEE 982.1]) recommends, among others, the collection of the following defect-based metrics whose values are normally separately classified according to defect severity and test level:

- Defect density (fault density): number of defects in relation to the size of the test object—e.g., number of defects/KLOC (or KDSI)—hence also the defect distribution as the number of defects per test object or test level, etc.
- →Failure rate: the number of failures detected or expected to be detected during the execution time of a test or program
- →Fault days: number of days from defect injection into the system and proof that a resulting failure has occurred

Especially in complex or distributed development projects, we often get different defect densities in different components. This is expressed in different defect detection percentages during test execution (if test quality and efficiency are the same for all components). As long as component testing has not been fully completed, we will go on to find more defects per test in components with a higher initial defect density.

In reference to values estimated earlier by the test manager (e.g., based on data of earlier projects), these metrics can also be combined with indirect metrics to measure test effectiveness (number of found failures per test) and test efficiency (number of found failures per given period of time), for instance as the following:

Indirect defect-based test metrics allow conclusions on test effectiveness and efficiency.

- Defect detection rate: number of detected defects/number of estimated defects
- Defect correction rate: number of detected defects/number of corrected defects
- Number of defects per new or changed lines of code in case of product enhancements or changes

The test manager in the VSR project tracks the progress of the defect detection rate to control the test intensity of the different components. For better visibility, test effort was put on the x-axis and the cumulated number of detected failures was put on the y-axis. Figure 11-8 shows a stable if not slightly rising defect rate during testing (i.e., failure occurrence); in this case, it makes sense to continue or even intensify the test effort. However, figure 11-9 indicates saturation over time, which is a possible indicator to reduce the effort for this component.

Example:

Defect detection rate in VSR

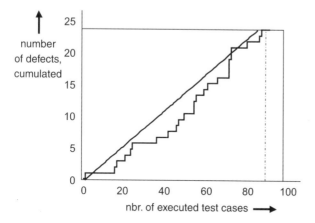

Figure 11–8

Component A: stable defect detection percentage

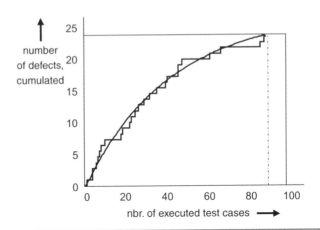

Defect-based metrics can also be used for trend analyses and predictions to make quantitative statements about defects still to be found during testing and defects that will remain after testing is completed. Such calculations, mostly based on statistical models, can be used for accompanying test control (see [Grottke 01], see also section 11.6).

Several more defect-based metrics are available:

- Number of defects relative to test intensity (defect trend)
- Number of defects relative to criticality (defect severity)
- Number of defects per status (defect correction progress)
- and so on

As time goes on, such metrics allow test management to make increasingly objective statements about the defect density expected in the system under development. Here and in many other test metrics, detected defects are classified and weighted prior to evaluation. IEEE Standard 1044 defines the defect classes and weights shown in table 11-3.

Defect class	Weight
Fatal	8
Severe	4
Medium	2
Minor	1
Nice to have	0.5

Further interesting indirect defect-based metrics can be created, for instance, by putting defect detection rates of different test levels in relation to each other.

The "defect removal leverage" (DRL), for example, is calculated as follows:

DRL = defect rate in test level X / defect rate in subsequent test level

In [Graham 00], we find a description of the "defect detection percentage" (DDP) metric, dividing all defects found at one test level by the sum of defects found at this and all subsequent test levels and in operation:

DDP metric

$$DDP = \text{defects at test level X / defects at X and subsequent test levels}$$
$$\text{(including operation)}$$

If, for example, 40 defects were found in component testing, 19 in integration test, 30 in system test, 9 in acceptance test, and another 20 in production, the component test DDP is calculated as

40 / (40 + 19 + 30 + 9 + 20) = 40 / 118 = 0,339

that is, approximately 34%.

For integration test, DDP is calculated as

19 / (19 + 30 + 9 + 20) = 19 / 78 = 0,244

that is, approximately 24%.

For system testing, the DDP is

30 / (30 + 9 + 20) = 30 / 59 = 0,508

that is, approx. 50%.

In this case, effort could be shifted from system test to component and integration test. To be able to truly justify such shifts, the DDP is to be seen in relation to the effort planned for each test level.

Although defect-based test metrics are very important, care should be taken not to evaluate product quality solely on the basis of these metrics. If at some stage, test can only detect few or no defects at all, it depends on the quality of the test cases or the test process whether we are in a position to say that we have good product quality.

Caution: Do not use only defect-based metrics!

In order to get clear about the actual status of the "test quality" regarding particular functions, the "test design verification" metric puts quality (i.e., the number of detected defects) in relation to the quantity or test intensity (i.e., the number of test cases specified for and executed on a function). In addition, information is needed about the complexity or

Test design verification" metric

functional volume of the tested functions. Metrics underlying this metric are the number of test cases for a function and the number of failures detected by them, as well as a complexity measure appropriate to the test level—e.g., at the program text (in component testing) or requirements level (in system test).

The "test design verification" metric provides some answers to the following questions:

- Which functions show a high and which show a low number of failures?
- What is the effort needed? That is, what is the number of required test cases needed to detect the defects?
- Have the "right" (i.e., efficient) test cases been specified?

The following example explains the application of this metric.

Example:
Test design verification
chart

Figure 11-10 illustrates the graphical representation of the test design verification in form of a bubble diagram. For each function, the number of associated test cases is put on the x-axis, whereas the number of found failures is put on the y-axis.

The size of the bubbles represents the complexity of the respective function. We may expect in this kind of presentation to see the bubbles align on a straight line in the order of their size, because the more complex a function is

- the more test cases are needed to test them, and
- the more failures will occur during test execution.

Figure 11–10

Test design verification

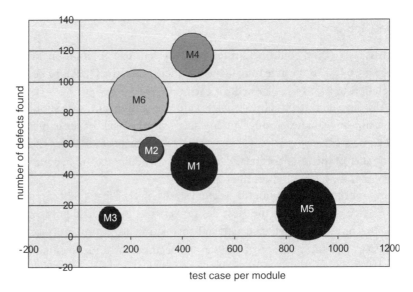

If a bubble is in the lower-right quadrant of the diagram, it means that the corresponding function has a large number of test cases assigned to it. These, however, find few failures. If the bubble is large, defect density is low and one may conclude that the function is obviously stable (see the M5 bubble in the example). If the bubble is small, it may be inferred that test design is inadequate in this area ("overengineering" of test cases).

If a bubble is in the top-left quadrant, the function has only a few test cases assigned to it; these, however, find many defects. Consequently, the defect density is high and the function is obviously unstable.

If we have a large bubble in the bottom-left quadrant (i.e., a small number of test cases and low defect detection), test cases are underengineered; i.e., test coverage of this function is low.

To track the defect rate, all detected failures must be reported during test execution. This requires an incident management system in which all reports and (status) changes are stored and historicized; i.e., they are time-stamped. Test completion, for instance, may be reached if the defect rate remains at a very low level over a certain period of time. This is an indication that test efficiency has been exhausted and that further effort spent on additional tests that will hardly find further failures may not be justified.

Keep track of progress!

The defect rate should be tracked separately for the different test levels, and ideally also for the different test techniques being used. The length of time that an actual defect rate stays below the maximum defect rate level and the required difference to the maximum defect rate are very sensitive values for the definition of test completion. A lot of experience and a sure instinct are needed for accurate targeting of theses values.

Studying the (typical) progression of the defect rate in the VSR system test, as shown in figure 11-11, the test manager notices that the defect rate bottoms out in weeks 6 to 9 only to show (as is often the case in practice) an upswing again in weeks 10 to 11. The first defect rate maximum is exceeded after most of the easily detected defects are found, whereas the renewed upturn marks the point where the more-difficult-to-find defects are uncovered. This rise, for instance, may have been caused by the test team's better orientation toward the application to be tested.

Example:
Progression of the defect
rate in the VSR system test

Figure 11–11

Typical defect rate progression in system test

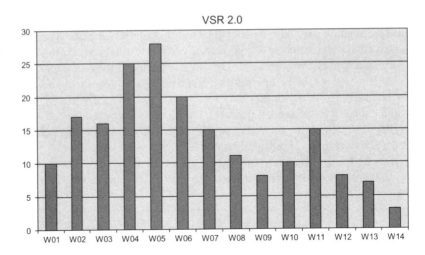

Figure 11–12

Defect report status

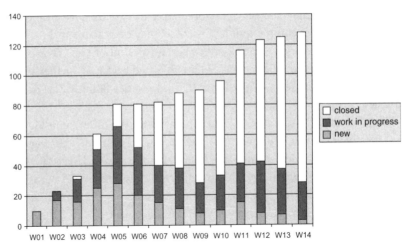

A look at the proportion of defect reports with status open (new), in progress, and closed shows that only very small software changes are to be expected as a result of further defect corrections. The test manager decides to continue testing for another week and then to break it off if the defect rate gets any lower.

 To allow statistical projections regarding defect rates and residual defect probability, the data must be historicized in the incident database.

One hundred thirty-seven incidents were reported within one month of VSR acceptance testing, with 39 of them rated as class-1 defects. Out of the total of 524 incident reports held in the incident database at that time, 30% are change requests. Hence, the proportion of "genuine" defect reports is approximately 70%. Three hundred fifty-seven of the reports were written during integration test (internally reported failures), which corresponds to about 68% of the total reports. One hundred sixty-seven incident reports (i.e., 32%) come out of system and acceptance testing (externally reported failures).

Example:
Defect rate progression in the VSR system test

Taking a code size of 100,284 new or changed lines and a number of 70% of 524 = 367 "genuine" incident reports, we get a defect density of 3.66 defects per 1,000 lines.

We may estimate the total number of defects in a newly implemented program to be at around 10 to 50 defects per 1,000 instructions; i.e., every 20th to 100th instruction is defective (see also [Hatton 97]). This rough estimate correlates with experiences made with spelling mistakes in newly written texts, and there is no reason to expect that fewer mistakes are made in coding (see also [Ebert 05]). However, at least half of all the defects injected during implementation should be found by the developers themselves during component testing.

New lines of code:
Approximately 1–5 defects per 100 instructions!

The remaining 5 to 25 defects per 1,000 instructions should be found at the higher test levels. All in all, the defect rate is below average and testing has to be intensified.

11.5.4   Cost- and Effort-Based Metrics

Effort-based metrics provide the context for financial and time-related measurements and can, once they have been collected in some projects, be used in the planning of future test projects. Here are some examples:

- Number of person days for test planning or specification
- Number of person days for the creation of test procedures
- Number of person days per detected defect
- Number of person hours per defect removal

Measurement values of that kind are to be anonymized and reported to project members in the form of feedback, including mean values.[3] Interpreting values, we must always bear in mind that besides specifying, executing, and documenting test cases, testers require additional time for the planning of their own tests as well as for setting up the test environment and checking in and out version-dependent test cases, etc.

Make metrics anonymous.

---

3.   For legal reasons, employees must be informed about the collection and intended use of measurements regarding their work or productivity (see also section 6.6).

In the end, the most important success criterion is that during the introduction of a measurement program, everybody involved or impacted fully understands the purpose of data collection.

11.5.5 Evaluating Test Effectiveness

Testing means detecting defects and providing confidence.

Software tests are effective if they find defects and increase confidence in the software. To assess test effectiveness, defect rate, test coverage, and test effort are taken into account.

In order to calculate the degree of defect detection (DDD), the weighted defect or failure ratio (see the example in table 11-3) detected during test is divided by the total number of detected defects or failures. Thus, we get

$$DDD = \text{number of weighted defects in test / total number of defects found}$$

Confidence in a system grows in proportion to the used measure (e.g., system use time, CPU time, etc.) if no failures occur. For test, system use is primarily understood to be the number of already executed test cases, and confidence in the system decreases in the same proportion as the number of detected failures increases.

The basic idea behind the following metric is that the defect rate states only the number of weighted defects per test case but does not say anything about the software part that is covered or not covered by test. Let us assume that the first test cycle has detected 0.05 weighted defects per test case and a later cycle with exactly the same test cases comes up with only 0.01 weighted defects per test case. Is this an indication that our confidence in the system can rise by 500%? Of course not, because we can have confidence only in what has truly been tested. Hence, we have to see defect rate relative to the degree of test coverage. The confidence level (CL) is calculated as

$$CL = 1 - (\text{number of weighted defects/} \\ \text{number of executed test cases}) \times \text{degree of test coverage}$$

Finally, test effectiveness (TE) is the product of the two metrics, degree of defect detection and confidence level:

$$TE = DDD \times CL$$

Tom DeMarco recommends collecting the following eight metrics for each version of a software product to obtain information about the (financial) effectiveness of the test processes ([DeMarco 86]):

DeMarco's metrics on test effectiveness

- Detected project faults: number of defects found and corrected prior to delivery of the product
- Project fault density: detected project defects/KDSI
- Project damage: defect correction costs prior to delivery in $/KDSI
- Delivered faults: Number of defects found after product delivery
- Product fault density: delivered defects/KDSI
- Product damage: defect correction costs after delivery in $/KDSI
- Total damage: project damage + product damage
- Product damage at six months: defect correction costs in the first six months after delivery in $/KDSI

In this connection, it is necessary to use the actual accrued overall diagnosis and repair costs and not merely the defect detection costs. The test process is effective if test costs do not exceed the overall cost of damage.

11.6 Residual Defect Estimations and Reliability

Based on available data about the product and the development and test processes, the techniques described in this section will enable us to use statistical means to make statements about the expected system reliability, which can be estimated based on the residual defects in the system after test completion. In particular, these statements serve as indicators for the product risk (see chapter 9). Principally, this can be done as follows:

- Experience-based estimation of the residual defect probability
- Statistical analysis of the defect data and reliability growth model

Both experience-based estimation of the residual defect probability and defect data analysis require that test cases adequately reflect the operational profile (see also [Voas 00]); i.e., the expected distribution of the use frequency of the product functions during operation. Considering the test techniques described in *Software Testing Foundations* on the specification of methodical tests, this only holds true for business-process-based tests. In order to apply the techniques for residual defect estimation described on the following pages, one usually needs to define additional test cases

Identify the operational profile for reliability analysis.

that complement the existing system tests with regard to the operational profile.

11.6.1 Residual Defect Probability

There are basically three possibilities to evaluate the test process based on the observed number of detected defects:

- Estimate the number of defects inherent in the system prior to test and estimate the number of defects to be found.
- Monitor the defect detection percentage.
- Inject artificial failures into the program code of which a certain proportion is to be found during testing.

To be able to work with estimated target defect numbers, you must estimate the total number of all system inherent failures. Since these are failures that have remained in the system after code reviews or other quality assurance measures, this process is also called →residual defect estimation.

These estimations are based on data and experience values present in a particular development unit and especially in a well-managed incident database. Subsequently, the effectiveness of future tests is estimated for each test level (as a percentage of the detected defects). Based on these estimations, the number of defects still to be found can be calculated as follows:

$$\text{target number of defects} = \text{residual number of defects} \times \text{effectiveness}$$
$$\text{(in \%)}$$

From this we can see that the effectiveness estimation in fact corresponds with the target number of failures expected to be detected by test.

Example   The following sample calculation explains the estimation of defects found by test (effectiveness estimation), which is done based on targets set in table 11-4.

Table 11–4

Test effectiveness targets

Test level	Found coding errors	Found design errors
Component testing	65%	0%
Integration testing	30%	60%
System testing	3%	35%
Sum	98%	95%

All in all, about 98% of all coding errors and 95% of design errors are supposed to be detected during test. These defects have remained in the system despite all the other quality assurance activities.

A number of 5 defects per 100 instructions is assumed as an estimation of the residual defects in a system with more than 10,000 instructions. Thus, a system with approximately 10,000 instructions has a residual defect rate of approximately 500 defects.

As a target for the number of defects still to be found, we also assume that the ratio of coding or design errors among the residual defects is 2:3; i.e., out of the approximately 500 residual defects we get 200 coding and 300 design errors.

Using the above formula, the defect targets for columns "Target coding errors" and "Target design errors" can now be calculated quite easily (table 11-5).

Test level	Defect target (total)	Target coding errors	Target design errors
Component testing	130	130	0
Integration testing	240	60	180
System testing	111	6	105
Sum	481	196	285

Table 11–5

Calculated defect targets for code and design errors

These targets can be used as a test completion criterion with regard to coding and design errors if the detected failures have been classified accordingly. The total defect target is the sum of defects to be found at the respective test level.

11.6.2 Reliability Growth Model

The statistical software reliability calculation tries to make statements about future abnormal software behavior based on existing defect data (times of detection of a failure or defect) of defects found primarily in integration and system test. This may be the number or rate of future expected failures or the supposed number of defects still resident in the software.

Infer reliability from defect data.

Here we need to consider that because statistical software reliability calculations are based on the theory of probability, the quality of prediction will rise with the amount of data that can be used for calculation and with the size of the project and organization. The larger the database, the less impact "outliers" have. Moreover, the earliest time from which we should consider defect data is the beginning of integration test, since in component testing we can not expect representative use of the software. There, only certain individual aspects of the software are tested and tests do certainly not reflect the system's operational profile.

This section describes two software reliability calculation models and provides some directions concerning the preconditions and application of such models. Basic conditions that must be adequately satisfied before using the statistical software reliability calculation models are as follows:

Statistics only work if the context is stable.

- Software development and test processes are stable; i.e., the software is developed (further) and tested by well-trained engineers following a defined development model with recognized methods and known tools.
- Test cases and test data reflect the operational conditions of software in production sufficiently well (test profile corresponds to operational profile). Some models, however, are also suitable for predictions in the area of systematic, structured testing (see [Grottke 01]).

Gross simplification

- Test cases cover all defects in a particular defect class with the same probability.
- Failures can be clearly mapped to defects.

The Jelinski-Moranda model ([Jelinski 72], see also [Lyu 96]) is described as a simple model and based on some further, simplifying preconditions in addition to the ones just mentioned:

- The defect rate is in proportion to the total number of defects residing in the software.
- The interval between the occurrence of every two defects is constant (constant test intensity).
- During fault correction no new defects are injected into the software.

The first supposition concomitantly implies the model's basic idea: The current defect rate is used to deduce the total number of defects. Take N_0 to be the total number of failures prior to testing, p a constant of proportionality, and λ_0 the defect rate at the beginning of test.

The basic idea of the model is expressed as

$$\lambda_0 = p \times N_0$$

At a later point in time i, after $N_0 - N_i$ defects have been corrected, we have

$$\lambda_i = p \times N_i$$

Here, N_i constitutes all the failures still residing in the software at the time i. The probability that the software will function without failure for a specific period of time ($\rightarrow$survival probability) is calculated as follows (see [Liggesmeyer 02]):

$$R(t) = e^{-\lambda_i \cdot t}$$

At the beginning of VSR integration testing, a new failure is detected every 1.25 hours (operational or test execution time); at the end of system test, a new failures is detected only every 20 hours. The test team detected 725 failures in these tests and removed them. The test manager calculates the following equations:

Example:
VSR system reliability

$$\lambda_0 = p \times (N_0 - 0) = 1 / 1.25\ h = 0.8 / h$$

and

$$\lambda_{End} = p \times (N_0 - 752) = 1 / 20\ h = 0.05 / h,$$

i.e.,

$$\lambda_0 / \lambda_{End} = 16$$

This equation is first solved to give

$$N_0 = 802$$

Inserting this value into the first equation gives

$$p = 0.001$$

He continues to calculate:

$$R(10h) = e^{-0.05 \times 10h} = 0.6065$$

This means that the probability that the VSR software will function for 10 hours without failure is approximately 61%.

Since this does not seem acceptable to the project team, the test phase is extended. During the extension period, 25 more failures are detected, giving the following picture:

$$\lambda_n = 0.001 \times (802 - 777) = 0.025 / h$$

This means that the test manager can expect further failures to be found only every 40 hours.

$$R(10\ h) = e^{-0.025 \times 10h} = 0.779$$

As a result of further testing, the system's probability to last 10 hours without failure has increased by approximately 17%, thus directly quantifying the benefit of further testing.

Another model worth looking at is the Musa-Okumoto model ([Musa 84]), which puts particular focus on the fact that at the beginning of the test phase we are more likely to detect the "simple" failures, as a result of which software reliability will only grow slowly. Instead of the inverse-exponential increase of the probability of survival, we get an S-shaped progression.

Figure 11-13 shows the progression of $N(t)$ for a (normalized) number of defects $N_0 = 1, \beta = 0.05 \times 1 / h$ and 100 hours of test execution time.

Figure 11–13

Reliability growth in the Musa-Okumoto model

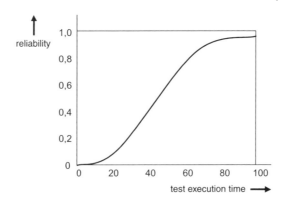

Many more reliability estimation models can be found in the literature; a general overview is given in [Liggesmeyer 02] (in German), and the standard reference regarding software reliability is still [Lyu 96].

11.7 Summary

- For each test level, suitable test metrics need to be defined and collected. Test metrics allow quantitative statements regarding product quality and the quality of the development and test processes and form the basis for transparent, reproducible, and traceable test process planning and control.
- Based on the measurement objects, we get test-case-based metrics, test-basis- and test-object-based metrics, defect-based metrics, and and cost- and effort-based metrics.
- Complexity metrics such as lines of code (LOC) and cyclomatic complexity (McCabe metric) are required for risk-based testing. Test metrics, too, serve as indicators for project and product risks.
- Historicized incident data allows for defect-based metrics as well as statements regarding residual defect probability and system reliability.

12 Selecting and Implementing Test Tools

There is often much hope and money invested in the acquisition of tools—the sad truth is that only too often they end up unused in some office cabinet. This chapter is intended to offer sound advice and guidance in the identification of possible tool application areas, the selection of appropriate tools, and their introduction in the test process.

12.1 Why Test Tools?

Test tools can be a means to increase the efficiency of individual test activities in a well-defined and effective test process. This is achieved if the tool saves time and money or if it increases the scope or quality of the results. A typical example are tools for automated test execution—they "merely" make the execution of already defined test cases cheaper, faster, and more accurate, without, however, adding any new dimension to testing. For such tools to be efficiently run, existing processes usually need to be enhanced with activities involving the identification of the test cases that are to be automated and their automated execution. The test process as such remains more or less unchanged.

Increase efficiency

Yet, by creating new or additional technological or organizational possibilities, it may be only through the deployment of test tools that new processes or new activities in an existing test process become possible.

Create new capabilities

Tools for the automated generation of test cases from abstract models of the system under test fall into this second category (e.g., [URL: AGEDIS]). The introduction of such tools has an impact on the entire test process:

- Individual test cases can no longer be planned as they are only created during testing and are no longer individually identifiable. The specification phase no longer aims at the description of test cases but provides us with generation strategies for required test cases.

- The execution of generated tests must be automated in order not to lose the advantage of automated test generation, i.e., the creation of a very large amount of test cases at little cost.
- The evaluation of test coverage and product quality must refer to the system's abstract model underlying the generation of test cases.

This shows that one ought to be quite careful when introducing a tool as one may very quickly find oneself facing the dilemma that existing processes need to be adapted to tools and not vice versa.

12.2 Evaluating and Selecting Test Tools

Systematic tool selection is done in several stages or phases:

1. Principal decision to use a tool
2. Identification of the requirements
3. Evaluation
4. Selection

Standards for tool selection   Two different standards may help in the selection of tools: [IEEE 1209] and [ISO 14102]. Both standards are suited for practical use and similar in content; however, both name and structure the individual phases of the process differently. ISO 14102 is noticeably more detailed than IEEE 1209 and more oriented toward an organization-wide selection process. IEEE 1209 is more compact and probably better suited for smaller companies or where decision making is limited to individual teams. The techniques described here are the result of years of practical experience and essentially compatible with both standards.

The following sections will deal in detail with each of the main phases mentioned above and the subphases they contain.

12.2.1   Principal Decision Whether to Use a Tool

Identifying and Quantifying the Goals

Prior to the procurement of a tool, the purpose of its deployment must be identified:

░   Which test activities are to be improved or supported?
░   What are the expected benefits or savings and/or improvements?

These objectives must be quantified and prioritized:

░   Are new processes or activities to be introduced as a result of the tool?
░   What are the consequences?

Again, objectives must be quantified.

These objectives must be understood by all the stakeholders. If goals are   *Traceable objectives*
unclear, badly communicated, or contradictory, and if a tool is acquired
without the knowledge of the person who is supposed to work with it, it is
quite likely that it will not be used but rather assigned a permanent loca-
tion in some dusty cabinet.

Considering Possible Alternative Solutions

Once the problems that need to be addressed have been accurately identified, the following question must be raised: Can all these objectives be
achieved with only one tool or are there any alternatives?

░   Are the objectives feasible and can they only be covered by a tool? Or   *Evaluate alternatives.*
    could it be possible that the root causes of the problems that we want to
    resolve are down to incomplete or out-of-date process documents,
    insufficient staff qualification, or bad communication channels? In this
    case, we ought of course to eliminate these insufficiencies directly
    rather than try to conceal them with the introduction of a tool.
░   Would it be possible to cover the objectives by extending or parameter-
    izing a tool that already exists or by providing suitable working instruc-
    tions to make its application easier? If we cannot give a clear no to this
    question, it makes sense to at least include the existing tool and addi-
    tional measures in the subsequent selection process.
░   Would the in-house or commissioned development of a tool be a possi-
    ble alternative to an existing tool on the market. This need not neces-
    sarily impede continuation of the selection process; the decision in
    favor of a new development may be the end result of our evaluation.
░   Perhaps the best thing would be to accept the status quo and to save the
    effort of introducing a new tool? To answer this question, we need to
    do a cost-benefit analysis.

Cost-Benefit Analysis

Principally, based on a quantified evaluation of the goals, the expected benefits or savings from tool deployment are set against the various direct and indirect costs, some of which are already known early, whereas others can be ascertained only during subsequent steps. Consequently, the cost-benefit analysis needs perhaps be questioned and revised several times during the selection phase.

Direct costs   To start with, the direct costs for tool acquisition and deployment are to be identified. Of course, costs need to be determined for each evaluation candidate, so in practice, this step can only be completed during the evaluation phase:

- How much does one license cost?
- What is the nature of the licensing model? Does it allow one non-transferable installation per user or workplace or is it based on the maximum number of concurrent users? What does the expected usage profile look like in the organization; i.e., what is the expected number of users and average operating life?

> **Hint** Caution: Some tool producers have started to sell licenses that are valid for only one specific project, thus limiting the use of the tool and making amortization much more difficult.

- What is the average update or upgrade cost and what is the update or upgrade frequency?
- Is a service maintenance contract offered for support, updates, and, where required, upgrades? If so, what are the costs?

> **Hint** Economically, tool leasing may make more sense than buying, particularly if maintenance is included in the leasing agreement. Has such a model been offered?

- Is there a rebate scale based on the number of purchased licenses?
- Depending on the tool's application, the number of users may vary largely between the minimal, average, and maximum number of users (for example, tools supporting test execution are only needed for test execution cycles). Is there a model for peak licenses that can be used temporarily during peak periods?

▨ Cost considerations are also necessary for the evaluation itself:
  ◦ How much staff is tied up for this task and for how long?
  ◦ What kind of hard and software environment must be set up?
  ◦ Is there a need to purchase software licenses for the evaluation period or can they be obtained from the toolmakers free of charge?

▨ Now the indirect costs need to be considered: *Indirect costs*
  ◦ Do the tool's system requirements necessitate possible hard- and software upgrading of the testers' workstations?
  ◦ How expensive is a new installation, an update or upgrade installation, and its configuration? Is there support for centralized installation management?
  ◦ What are the training costs involved to have users qualified?
  ◦ What is the effort for setting up an operational concept, i.e., the necessary adaptations/enhancements to the process documentation?
  ◦ Are customer-specific adaptations to interfaces necessary or do we need to create new ones? How much effort do we need for such customizations? Can the tool manufacturer provide this kind of support or can he find a competent partner for us?

Costs must be weighed against the expected benefit and quantified as much as possible, including, for example, the following: *Quantify the benefits.*

▨ Resource savings through more efficient task performance
▨ Possible extension of test coverage without, however, spending more resources
▨ Enhanced repetition accuracy and precision of test task execution
▨ Standardization of test documentation
▨ Economical generation of complete standards-compliant documentation
▨ More effective use of test teams less engaged in repetitive routine activities
▨ Increased test team satisfaction

Identification of Constraints

Finally, we need to localize further possible cost factors, constraints, and negative effects of introducing tools that we have not thought of before. This can be done, for example, in a brainstorming session:

▨ Could the introduction of the tool negatively affect other processes— e.g., through the loss of an interface supported by the new tool's predecessor?

▓ Which factors or persons can negatively affect tool selection? Can we guarantee that selection is made objectively? There are sometimes people in an organization who are generally biased against innovations and specifically against new tools and who would prefer developing their own tool rather than buy one off the shelf.

▓ What could happen after the tool has been chosen to turn its implementation into a failure? Does its implementation put a running project at such risk that the required quality or planned schedules cannot be kept?

Use risk management to deal with possible constraints. Such risk factors must be documented as constraints influencing the tool selection and implementation processes and must be part of a consistent risk management.

12.2.2 Identifying the Requirements

One can assume that in most cases several tool alternatives can be used to achieve a particular goal. Without detailed preparation and serious comparisons between the alternatives, we run the serious risk of wasting a lot of money on the acquisition and implementation of a tool that will be used little or, worse, not at all.

The comparison must be fair and traceable. During the preparatory stages, the set of requirements collected from the different interest groups must be as comprehensive as possible. The required functional and non-functional features such as performance and usability are derived from the tool's deployment goals:

Same requirements process as in software development

▓ Collection of the user requirements: Clear identification of the goals of all involved stakeholders; classification and prioritization of these requirements

▓ Analysis: Summary of similar and identification of contradictory requirements; conflict resolution

▓ Specification: Itemization of the user requirements into a set of selection criteria; written summary of the criteria, adopting the prioritizations already made for the user requirements

▓ Review: Presentation of the requirements to the stakeholders for review and joint release

Prioritization and traceability are very important aspects of this process; i.e., at each step it must be absolutely clear who made the requirement (in order to be able to resolve later requirements conflicts or to resolve cases of doubt) and how important it is for that particular person or for the entire, future user group. Since it is very unlikely that one product will fulfill all the requirements, the final selection of the tool must be based on the importance attributed to each of the requirements and the frequency with which they have been raised.

Functional Requirements of the Test Tool

Typical functional requirements regarding a tool could look like this:

- "The test management system requires an interface for importing requirement objects from the requirements management database; besides importing the requirement's content, all predefined and user-defined attributes must also be importable."
- "The test automation system must be able to recognize and control all the objects of the test object's graphical user interface (e.g., test objects implemented in Java Swing)."

Examples of functional requirements

Nonfunctional Requirements of the Test Tool

Principally, this class of requirements can be collected using the same techniques used for the functional features; in our experience, however, they are more difficult to collect. Typical requirements, like "the system must be user-friendly" and "the system must be fast enough for 20 parallel users" cannot be directly validated against the evaluation candidates. On the one hand, one must try to describe the required nonfunctional features in such a way as to make them clearly quantifiable (e.g., "the system must provide a user interface following the standard MS Windows style guide allowing easy induction and facilitating daily operation"). On the other hand, provision must be made for some nonfunctional tests without which some of the nonfunctional requirements (e.g., usability and performance) cannot be verified without.

Here are some examples for a useful criteria catalogue:

- "The terminology used in the test management system must be compliant with the 'ISTQB Certified Tester' glossary."
- "Test management system performance must satisfy simultaneous use by the test manager, three test designers, and five testers with typical user profiles; that is, average system response time may not exceed 3 seconds."

Examples for nonfunctional requirements

The results of the previous cost-benefit considerations are listed as special nonfunctional requirements. As mentioned before, some of them can be assessed only during the actual evaluation. Moreover, functional, nonfunctional, and financial requirements and requirements pertaining to product attendant services can be uniformly treated and managed in the criteria catalogue (more on that later) so that the evaluation result reflects both costs and benefits.

Requirements of Product Attendant Services

Today's software development tools have acquired a complexity that often necessitates the manufacturer's support during their implementation phase and operational lifetime. A vendor providing no after-sales service could be considered less attractive than, for example, a solution vendor providing a broad spectrum of products and services. The following questions may help in the assessment of product attendant services:

Examples:
Product attendant services

- What kind of product support may we expect—an outsourced call center or a vendor's own in-house competence center? This may perhaps give us important hints pertaining to staff competency; further statements about competency can only be made during the evaluation period and after direct contact with support.
- At what times and by which means (e-mail, telephone, on-site) is support available? Are maximum response times guaranteed? What are they?
- In the case of international organizations, is on-site support available in different countries? Are multiple language telephone and e-mail support available? Are different time zones supported?
- Does the tool manufacturer offer training, introductory packages, coaching, and consulting by competent staff during operational use?
- How reliable is the manufacturer? That is, how long has he been on the market and how stable is he? For example, does his portfolio consist of several or only one product?
- How good is the quality of the products? That is, how many defects are detected in the product, documentation, etc. during the evaluation period?

 Hint   The DIN/ISO 9126 standard provides help in identifying functional and nonfunctional requirements; see chapter 5 and [Spillner 07, section 2.1.3]. The [ISO

14102] standard, too, contains a catalogue of generic requirements for different classes of tools for the software development process.

Creating the Criteria Catalogue

Once all requirements have been collected, the criteria catalogue is created. Typically, the catalogue is structured in the form of a so-called benefit value analysis using a spreadsheet so that the evaluation results can automatically be condensed to partial and total evaluations of the individual tools.

Create a criteria table.

The objective is to grade each tool in such a way as to show its usability with respect to its required operational profile.

Criteria catalogues can be set up using very diverse techniques. Here is some advice regarding structure:

1. **Group Forming**
    Individual requirements can be sorted into groups so that later on strengths and weakness profiles of individual tools can be worked out in relation to these groups. Ideally, these groups correspond to the usage objectives drafted during the target definition phase. It may make sense to give each of the groups its own group weighting, which then finds its way into the identification of the overall result. This weighting reflects the prioritization of the original objectives.
2. **Classification of the Selection Criteria**
    Each criterion is now classed into one of the groups where it is weighted again to represent its local importance with respect to the other requirements in the same group.
3. **Definition of Metrics for the Criteria**
    During the evaluation, each criterion is to be valued by a number (a mark) based on a suitable value range valid for the whole catalogue (i.e., 0 = not suitable to 5 = ideal). Each criterion must be accompanied by concrete classification notes explaining the circumstances by which the tool is classified in relation to the criterion.

12.2.3   Evaluation

The evaluation constitutes a well-ordered procedure for the neutral, complete, and reproducibly documented evaluation of the worked-out criteria.

Selection of Evaluation Candidates

Depending on available budget, an evaluation may comprise one or several tools. A suitable entry point for the localization of suitable candidates is an Internet search, looking, for example, for suitable key words such as "Test Automation Tool". To further simplify the search, already available tool lists on the Internet are useful:

WWW links related to test tools

- [URL: TESTINGFAQ]
- [URL: SQATEST]
- [URL: APTEST]
- [URL: OSTEST]

Market studies

Market studies and evaluation reports are also possible sources. These, too, are to a large degree accessible via the Internet; however, in most cases you will be charged money for them. On the other hand, they will save you part of your evaluation effort.

Here are some representative sites:

- The OVUM Report on Software Testing Tools [URL: OVUM]
- The Software Test Tools Evaluation Center [URL: STTEC]

Other selection criteria

It is highly likely that such a search results in a larger number of candidates than can be evaluated within the available scope. In order to be able to draw up a final list, you can take the following steps:

- Individual selection criteria as KO criteria; i.e., if a particular tool cannot meet this criterion, it is struck off the list of candidates. An in-depth study of the tool documentation must make it possible to evaluate the criteria.
- Interviewing current reference customers.
- Interviewing users of the tool at conferences and tool exhibitions.
- Reviewing test reports from projects already using the tool.

Planning and Setup

Evaluation project planning

Prior to actual execution, typical project management activities must be performed:

- Agree on **staffing** for the evaluation and selection team. In addition to the project leader, who in a larger company may come from the IT department, team members are required from each department and role that is going to work with the tool.

- **Individualization** of the criteria catalogue. "Non-controversial", objectively evaluatable criteria need not be dealt with by each team member separately. To avoid redundant effort, it can be covered by one person (for example, installability on different platforms). Evaluation criteria that for subjective or individual reasons—or depending on department or role of the team members—may be differently evaluated, need to be considered by the whole team (for example usability issues). You must keep in mind that experience and training of team members must be documented together with the evaluation results.
- Definition of the **evaluation scenarios**. The closer team members keep to the predefined procedure, the more goal oriented the evaluation process will be. Providing a scenario or sample exercises (as is common in usability testing, too) has this effect but may result in team members adopting a "tunnel vision" that prevents them from noticing incidental irregularities.
- **Time and resource planning**.
- **Documentation planning**. What is to be issued by the project in addition to the completed criteria catalogue (sample data and sample projects in the tool, etc.)?
- Provision of **resources**. For instance, of the necessary hardware needed for installing the tool. In principle, it needs to be decided whether each tool will be installed on a separate workstation and whether members of the evaluation team change workstations for evaluation or if all tools are installed on each of the workstations. A side effect of the latter is that during evaluation, several tools can be run in parallel, thus making comparisons easier—with the risk that the software tools may adversely affect and destabilize each other.
- Organization of the **installation media** and, if necessary, of evaluation licenses.
- **Preparation** of the workstations through installation of the tools, provision of the criteria catalogue for online completion, etc.
- **Briefing** of the team members.

Tool Evaluation Based on Criteria

To prepare for the evaluation, it may be a good idea to organize, together with the team members, a presentation of the tool by the manufacturer. This will provide a first impression of how the tool works and an opportunity to ask the manufacturer some concrete questions. It also provides the opportunity to validate some evaluation criteria without much effort.

It makes sense to ask for the presentation to be run based on a small self-developed test task, since the manufacturer's ready-made "video-clip-like" demos naturally have some one-sided bias toward the strengths of its respective tool. The tool manufacturer's preparedness to provide such individualized presentations will of course grow in proportion to the customer's preparedness to pay some sort of consultancy fee for this kind of service.

Individual, criteria-based evaluation

This expenditure quite often pays off by bringing to light tool usage problems and pitfalls at this early stage rather than later in a project and under time pressure.

Subsequently, in accordance with resource and time planning, each team member is to evaluate the tool individually and independently through studying and evaluating the documentation, working with given scenarios, and completing the criteria catalog. The latter can be done either in parallel to the other activities or very soon afterward. Any observed irregularities or precarious findings and any subjective impressions are to be documented.

Report Creation

After completion of the evaluation, the evaluation team leader consolidates the results and checks on completeness and consistency. Results are compiled in form of an evaluation report that typically contains the following information:

Detailed evaluation report

- Name, manufacturer, and version identifier of the evaluated tool, as well as a brief tool profile in form of a "management abstract"
- Evaluation base; i.e., the used hard- and software configuration
- Background; for example, process and process phase in which the tool is to be deployed
- Short description of the evaluation process providing, for example, a reference to one of the norms mentioned above (or to this section of the book)
- Detailed evaluation results per criterion
- A list containing subjective observations, together with the observers' profiles

12.2.4   Selecting the Tool to Be Procured

Consolidating Evaluations and Preparing for Decision

If possible, the evaluation results must be consolidated to one individual figure, an "overall score" for each tool. This is done by multiplying the group and criteria weightings with the values assigned during the evaluation and subsequent summation of the results. Provision of a graphical illustration may help in the evaluation of the results.

Consolidating the evaluation results

ISO 14102 describes further evaluation and decision techniques in appendix B.

When consolidating individual evaluation results, it is possible to work with simple multiplication and addition. However, in order to work out tool differences more clearly, one may, for instance, also work with square weighting factors. Moreover, a principal decision has to be made whether an absolute evaluation of the tool is to be achieved in relation to the ideal objectives (i.e., an evaluation of practically all tools with considerably less than 100%) or whether the tools are to be evaluated relative to each other (i.e., one tool will achieve 100%).

The former focuses on the question whether, within a relevant scope, the set objectives can be achieved at all by one or several of the tools, whereas the latter emphasizes the differentiation of the individual features among the tools themselves.

Figure 12-1 illustrates a spreadsheet-based Microsoft Excel evaluation catalogue. It shows the structure of a rating group used to evaluate the tools in absolute and relative terms to each other or, in other words, calculating one value with respect to the maximum obtainable number of scores and one standard value relative to the highest score of a tool in the group. Subsequently, the normalized score is weighted with the importance of the group. In addition, the KO criteria mentioned in section 12.2.3 are used to obtain a consistent representation of the decision basis in one document.

Example for a criteria catalogue and evaluation

Weighting	Requirement	Weighting	Tool 1	Tool 2	Tool 3	Tool 4	KO criterion
	Hardware platforms						
	Support of Windows 95	3	0	3	0	0	
	Support of Windows NT	3	0	3	0	0	
	Support of Windows 2000	3	5	5	5	0	1
	Support of Windows XP	3	5	5	3	3	
	Support of Solaris	3	0	2	0	0	
	Support of HP-UX	3	0	2	0	0	
	Support of Linux	3	0	4	3	5	
	Support of SCO Unix	3	0	4	0	0	
	Documents/tests interchangeable between platforms	3	5	3	4	3	
	Hardware platforms – percentage of max. score		33.3%	73.3%	46.7%	0%	
	percentage normalized		45.5%	100.0%	63.6%	0%	
3	percentage normalized and weighted		136.4%	300.0%	190.9%	0%	

Figure 12-1

Rating of a criteria catalogue

The example shows the evaluation of the tools' usability on different platforms, with the value ranges shown in table 12-1.

Table 12-1

Classification of tool criteria

Value	Classification of tool usability on operating system X
0	Not supported
1	Installable, but no manufacturer support
2	Usable but unstable
3	Usable, requires increased effort; for example, loading patches into the operating system
4	Usable with some restrictions; for example, GUI inconsistent with the rest of the operating systems, no comprehensive drag&drop or similar
5	Unconditionally usable

With the evaluation of all criteria completed, the ratings are graphically shown as in figure 12-2.

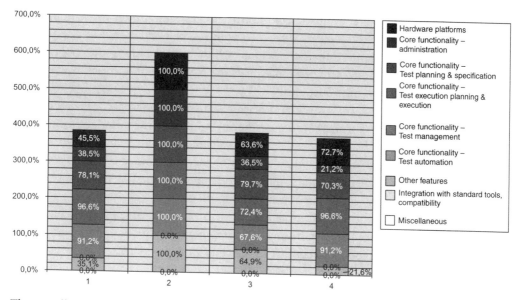

The overall evaluation shows tool 2 as number 1, whereas tool 4 is a dead loss because it cannot meet one KO criterion relating to platform compatibility (see figure 12-3):

Figure 12–2

Rating according to area

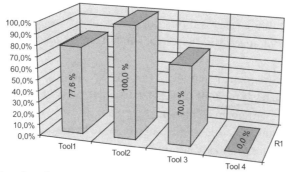

Figure 12–3

Score in % of maximum point

[URL: Tooleval-imbus] offers a simple, readily implemented criteria catalogue for downloading. For practical use, names, group numbers, and descriptions of the individual criteria need to be adapted. Partial group results, overall results per tool, and a graphical evaluation are automatically calculated.

Evaluation catalogue for downloading

Decision Making

Typically, the final decision on which tool to use is made by management based on the technical data and sometimes further, nontechnical criteria.

Winner by points

Ideally, after evaluation of the criteria catalogue and the evaluation report, we will have a clear "winner by points". The evaluation may also possibly result in more than one winner whose overall ratings are very close, or none of the evaluated tools meets the requirements sufficiently enough to justify its introduction.

In case of a neck-and-neck result, further decision criteria may be needed. This may be done either by modifying the criteria prioritization, adding criteria for an ex-post evaluation, or—in many cases the most practical way—by piloting some of the tools under consideration. This way particularly, the evaluation of some nonfunctional features such as usability will be put on a broader footing.

If none of the selected tools turns out to be suitable, the conclusion may be to invest in in-house development, modify or enhance an already existing tool, or reconsider tool acquisition altogether.

12.3 Introduction of Tools

Once the decision is made, it needs to be finally validated by comparing the original objectives and requirements with the evaluation results in a formal review.

The best tool is useless if it is not prudently introduced. The basis for long-term tool success is the establishment of an adequate test process framework.

The process maturity model TPI (see section 7.3.2) comprehensibly identifies the basis for tool success—particular parts of the test processes must show a certain minimum maturity before the use of a tool makes sense. For example, it does not make any sense to introduce a test automation tool without prior establishment of formal test specification methods. TPI, therefore, forms a good basis for identifying test process improvement actions that might be necessary prior to the introduction of a tool and for obtaining concrete implementation assistance. Conversely, test tools will positively affect the maturity grade of particular activities in the test process or at least facilitate the improvement of these activities.

The following are examples of important tasks to perform prior to the introduction of the tools:

- Ensure the necessary maturity of the basic processes to identify the necessary improvement actions.

Create a basis for the broad implementation of the improvement potentials or for the achievement of the original objectives regarding tool usage (see section 12.2.1).

As with the selection procedure, standards exist for the introduction of tools. [IEEE 1348] and [ISO 14471] serve as orientation guides for the correct procedure and again contain brief descriptions of the target finding and selection processes. They also add essential concepts to aid in the introduction of the tool: pilot project and distribution.

Standards regarding tool implementation

12.3.1   Pilot Project

A pilot project serves to validate the usability of the tools. Ideally, its duration is manageable but not too short (3–6 months) and is of a size and criticality representative of the organization. Management must grant the pilot project sufficient support—for instance, by providing additional resources.

Keep the pilot project manageable.

The pilot project evaluates whether the (quantified) objectives for tool deployment can actually be achieved. For this reason, it is important to provide timely definitions of suitable metrics and necessary measurement techniques.

A further goal is the validation of the diverse assumptions of the initial cost-benefit estimation, for example, of the estimated cost for tool introduction and training. Staff training, tool installation, tool configuration, etc. must also be accompanied by corresponding effort measurements.

These measurements and other observations during the pilot project are the basis for essential data that contributes to the later creation of the distribution plan.

Another important outcome of a pilot project is a concept of operations that should, for instance, contain the following information:

Concept of operations as a result of a pilot project

- Architectural changes to current testware (if, for example, previous specification documents are to be created with a test design tool or if the design method for test automation changes)
- Role distribution and responsibilities, necessary staff training
- New or redefined procedures involving the tool
- Naming conventions and rules for configuration management
- Necessary interfaces to the existing work environment
- Changes in technical infrastructure, such as hardware or software requirements, backup concept, setup of databases and other back office components

In the pilot project, some introduction-specific roles must be assigned that are typically adopted by members of the project teams themselves (next to the project-specific roles such as test manager or tester, which they may also adopt). The choice of the right pilot project depends also on the assignment of several roles: coach (or initiator), change manager (or integrator), tool master, and sponsor.

The Coach (or Initiator)

He is convinced of the tool and often it is he who initiates or strongly recommends the tool's acquisition. He quickly recognizes potential problems and positive aspects of the tool's operational use.

   This, together with his enthusiasm, pushes the introduction of the tool. He is the team's catalyst and likes to cooperate with it.

The Change Manager (or Integrator)

Compared to the initiator, his method is more methodical and deliberate; consequently, he can plan, organize, and document the tool's introduction better than the initiator. Often he is the main author of the resulting concept of operations.

The Tool Master

He has cutting-edge expertise regarding tool usage and provides internal support. He often acts as the main contact for external product support, channeling internal queries and communicating support information.

The Sponsor

To assure proper recognition of these roles in addition to the project roles already described, a management sponsor is needed, also to gain management awareness of the additional risks that the introduction of the tool may imply for the pilot project. The sponsor officially supports the introduction of the tool and keeps team members free for the additional task.

After completion of the pilot project, an assessment is made whether or not the introduction objectives can be reached and whether the operational concept allows the tool to fit seamlessly into the existing processes.

   Piloting outcomes, for example, can be facts that restrict the application of the tool:

   ▪ The tool does not address all objectives except for the most important ones.

- The tool can only be economically used for a particular type of project or corporate division.
- In order to use the tool successfully, tool modifications, further training, or consulting services by the manufacturer are necessary.
- Piloting was successful, but problems were discovered during piloting concerning the tool selection and/or tool introduction process, necessitating future changes to the process.

12.3.2   Distribution

If piloting results in a positive decision, the test tool and the concept of operations will be rolled out into the organization via the process improvement scheme.

Ideally, during the rollout phase, participants of the pilot projects serve as multipliers and are used as internal consultants in the next projects to accompany the tool's further introduction.

Here are some typical questions for rollout planning and execution:

Keep rollout flexible.

- Is distribution supposed to be done in one step in the form of a "big bang" throughout the entire organization or will there be a step-by-step changeover in the individual projects or organizational units? The former carries a higher risk of far-reaching productivity setbacks in case the introduction fails totally or partially; the latter requires more detailed planning and carries the risk of temporary incompatibilities or inconsistencies regarding internal cooperation during the conversion period.
- What are the total conversion costs based on the original cost-benefit considerations and the observations made during the pilot projects?
- What is done about the resistance of individual team members or groups that may, for example, "have grown to love" the previous tool?
- What is done to ensure the necessary staff training?

12.4 Summary

- Tools, by nature, cannot solve process-related problems.
- Prior to the introduction of a test tool, the goals/objectives for using it, a cost-benefit analysis, and an evaluation of alternative solutions must be performed. This way, unnecessary tool acquisition is avoided and it is ensured that a tool will actually be used.

- Objectives are primarily related to increased efficiency of existing test activities or to the development of completely new possibilities through the introduction of new technologies provided by the tool. In both cases, it is necessary to try to quantify the intended benefit of these improvements in advance.
- When finally comparing costs with benefit, it is important to consider not only the acquisition and licensing costs but also the evaluation, introduction, and operational costs.
- If a decision is made to purchase a tool, in most cases one candidate must be chosen from among several products on the market. First, these candidates must be chosen by reviewing the market. Different tool lists are helpful and available via the Internet.
- A criteria catalogue is used whereby the criteria are derived from the requirements. These may comprise functional as well as nonfunctional features of the actual tools but also requirements related to accompanying services and the tool manufacturer itself.
- The evaluation catalogue is best structured in such a way that a weighting factor and a measure for evaluation is assigned to each criterion. A "rating" is then calculated for each tool during the evaluation.
- The evaluation itself must be well planned and carried out in the form of a project, and it must be staffed with sufficient resources. If the first evaluation does not yield a clear result, the evaluation may be extended using additional criteria or transferred to a follow-up pilot where candidates are compared in parallel.
- The subsequent introduction of the selected tools must again be conducted in form of a project, following an orderly, step-by-step approach:
  - Initially, the pilot project is used to draw up the concept of operations for the tool. This concept supplements or modifies existing process definitions.
  - During the pilot project, some staff members adopt important roles that speed up the introduction process: the initiator, the integrator, and the tool master.
  - Once the pilot project has been successfully completed, the tool and the concept of operations are rolled out. Former members of the pilot project may now act as multipliers. The majority of the decisions regarding tool distribution again require proper project planning and execution.

13 Standards

Standards define generally recognized rules reflecting the "state of the art" of technology. As such, they constitute the frame of reference within which projects operate, promoting consistency of products and processes and providing, at least from a legal point of view, the minimum requirements for professional work.

In this chapter, standards relevant to test management are listed, characterized, and put in relation to each other.

13.1 Objectives and Positioning

In software development, it is increasingly important—not the least for legal reasons—to observe generally recognized engineering rules that have been tried and tested in industry practice and are valid according to the prevailing majority of practitioners. These rules are often described in national and international standards developed and published worldwide.

Standards are developed and maintained by national and international organizations

The following organizations and committees are responsible for standardization, that is for creation, publication and maintenance of respective documents:

- At the international level, the "International Organization for Standardization" (ISO, [URL: ISO]) and the "International Electrotechnical Commission" (IEC [URL: IEC])
- At the European level, the "European Committee for Standardization" (CEN [URL: CEN]) and the "European Committee for Electrotechnical Standardization" (CENELEC [URL: CENELEC])
- In Germany, the "German Institute for Standardization" (DIN [URL: DIN]) and in Austria the "Austrian Standard Institute" (ON [URL: ON])
- In the United States, the "American National Standards Institute" (ANSI [URL: ANSI])
- In the United Kingdom, the "British Standards Institution" (BSI [URL: BSI])

Domain-specific organizations cooperate with standardization organizations.

These standardization bodies governed by public law work in cooperation with many domain-specific organizations such as these:

- The "Electronic Industries Alliance" (EIA [URL: EIA])
- The "International Telecommunication Union" (ITU [URL: ITU])
- The "European Telecommunications Standards Institute" (ETSI [URL: ETSI])
- The "Institute of Electrical and Electronics Engineers" (IEEE [URL: IEEE])
- The "Association of German Engineers" (VDI [URL: VDI])
- The "Gesellschaft für Informatik" (GI, [URL: GI])

ISTQB defined training contents for the professional software tester

In the area of software testing, the "International Software Testing Qualifications Board" (ISTQB [URL: ISTQB]) and its national boards, such as, for instance, the "American Software Testing Qualifications Board" (ASTQB [URL: ASTQB]) and the "German Testing Board" (GTB [URL: GTB]), define the training contents for professional software testers, thereby contributing to further standardization and international harmonization of technical terminology.

Domain-specific specifications reflecting the state of the art in technology are, for example, published by the following:

- The "Object Management Group" (OMG [URL: OMG])
- The "World Wide Web Consortium" (W3C [URL: W3C])
- The "Motor Industry Software Reliability Association" (MISRA [URL: MISRA])
- The "European Computer Manufacturers Association" (ECMA [URL: ECMA])

Often, these publications enjoy the status of preliminary or draft standards that after consolidation will be incorporated into the international standards catalogue. Valid national and international patents, too, are to be considered part of the state of technology.

In addition, some international alliances or bodies corporate, such as the "North Atlantic Treaty Organization" (NATO [URL: NATO]), the "American Department of Defense" (DoD [URL: DOD]), and the "European Organization for Civil Aviation Equipment" (EUROCAE [URL: EUROCAE]), maintain their own "domain-specific" rules and standards.

It is one of the tasks of quality or test managers to determine which norms, standards, and perhaps statutory regulations are applicable either for the product under test (product standards) or the project (process standards) and to ensure their compliance.

Audits assess product and process adherence to norms and standards.

Adherence of software products or of development processes to applicable standards, guidelines, and specifications is assessed in audits (see [IEEE 1028]).

This chapter considers different types of standards, structured by their increasing applicability:

- Corporate standards
- Best practices and technical specifications
- Domain-specific standards
- Generally valid standards

13.2 Corporate Standards

Particularly in large, international corporations and organizations with a large number of products and projects, corporate internal directives and process instructions (possibly also specified by the customer) are applied to ensure that processes run smoothly locally and beyond national borders.

Corporate internal guidelines and process instructions

To these belong, for example, the following:

- Specifically tailored process models
- Quality management manuals to be applied across an entire organization
- Product-area-specific test manuals
- Document templates
- Coding and design conventions

Standardized coding conventions, in particular, are important to foster exchange and reusability of developed software and hence the establishment of product lines. Since developers are known to resist having their freedom to design code curtailed, code conventions must be mutually defined and agreed upon by quality assurance and development and regularly checked for their usefulness and applicability.

Keep coding conventions lean and practicable!

Moreover, standard templates are necessary for the entire documentation. Test managers create and use such templates, e.g., for test plans (see chapter 5), deviation reports (see chapter 8), and metric definitions (see chapter 11).

> ▪ Support members of staff by providing electronic templates and appropriate tooling (macros, scripts, etc.) for document creation.
> ▪ Do not provide any code conventions that cannot be verified through static analyzers.

13.3 Best Practices and Technical Specifications

Best practices represent the state of the art in particular fields of application.

So-called "best practices" are not yet standardized but widely accepted methods and procedures representing the state of the art in their field of application.

In many areas, technical specifications are developed as a preliminary step toward standardization, and products are then manufactured, marketed, and used according to them. The line between these kinds of technical specifications and corporate standards is blurred, especially if such companies have a sufficiently large market share ("de facto standards").

Project-oriented consortiums establish technical specifications that also reflect the current state of the art.

For this reason, companies and organizations often combine their efforts to create larger market opportunities for their specifications, evolving, for instance, into consortiums such as W3C [URL: W3C], OMG W3C [URL: OMG], ECMA [URL: ECMA], MISRA [URL: MISRA], HIS [URL: HIS], AUTOSAR [URL: AUTOSAR], and others. All of them develop specifications and publish them as soon as possible. However, this can lead to certain premature, ad hoc publications that are then revised several times and available in as many versions, forming the basis of concrete products that, regrettably, may in some cases be quite incompatible.

Body of knowledge lists best practices of an area of application.

Best practices are listed together with corresponding references in so-called "bodies of knowledge". The standard [ISO 19759], "Guide to the Software Engineering Body of Knowledge" (SWEBOK [URL: SWEBOK]), for instance, categorizes relevant methods regarding all sections of software engineering, dedicating a chapter each to the description and listing of test techniques and software quality methods. In its regularly revised syllabus, the "International Software Test Qualifications Board" refers to important practices in the area of testing [URL: ISTQB].

Part of the best practices in software development are practices listed in process models such as the life cycle model of the Federal German republic (V-model XT) and the Rational Unified Process (RUP) (see chapter 3).

Many technical specifications are freely available and may be used free of charge. The OMG specifications, for instance, are available for free (see also [URL: OMG]).

13.4 Domain-Specific Standards

In many areas of life, software has replaced man as a controlling and regulating body. Defects often had, and have, catastrophic consequences in industries such as the aerospace and medical industries, whereas in the consumer sector defects have at most been considered a nuisance to users or as having an image-damaging effect on the manufacturers. But even here the consequences of defects are becoming more and more noticeable. One example is the automotive sector where many electronics failures are traced back to software defects.

Software (and its defects) are omnipresent!

Many fields of application pose very specific requirements on the systems being deployed or the software used in them. National and international organizations, partly governed by public law, have been established to create standards for product development, quality assurance, and deployment, ranging from informal guidelines up to international standards.

Most of the domain-specific standards relate to software development for safety-critical applications in sectors such as the aerospace industry, the military, railroad engineering, medical technology, pharmaceutics, and power plant engineering. Some corresponding standardization bodies and related domain-specific standards are summarized in table 13-1. Documents marked (*) are considered in some more detail in the course of this chapter.

Domain-specific standards, especially for safety critical software

Table 13–1

Domain-specific standards

Sector	Body	Norm/Standard
Aviation	RTCA (USA) EUROCAE (Europe) ECSS (Europe)	DO 178 B/ED-12B (*) EN 14160
Space industry	NASA (USA) ECSS (Europe)	NASA-STD-8719.13B NASA-STD-8739.8 ECSS–Q–80A EN 14160
Military	DoD (USA) NATO (International)	MIL-STD-498 (replaced by IEEE/EIA Std 12207:1998) AQUAP-150, AQUAP-160
Medical technology	FDA (USA) CENELEC TC 62	FDA-535, FDA-938 EN 62304
Pharmaceutics	FDA (USA) GAMP	FDA-21 CFR Part 11 GAMP 4
Railroad engineering	CENELEC SC 9XA	EN 50128 (*)
Nuclear technology	DOE (USA) IAEA IEC TC 45A	DOE G 414.1-4 IAEA TR-384, IAEA NS-G-1.1 IEC 60880
Telecommunications	ITU T-SG17 ETSI	ITU X.290-X.296 (ISO/IEC 9646-x) ETSI ES 201 873-x (TTCN-3)

DO 178 B applies to "flying" software

In the aviation industry, the "Software Considerations in Airborne Systems and Equipment Certification" (DO 178 B/ED12B, [DO 178 B]) standard developed in cooperation between RTCA and EUROCAE contains guidelines for the development of software for equipment deployed in avionic systems. DO 178 B distinguishes five different categories depending on defect severity (table 13-2).

Table 13–2

DO 178B failure categories

Software level	Potential failure condition	Potential consequences
A	Catastrophic	Continued safe flight and landing impossible
B	Hazardous/severe-major	Severe failure condition for the aircraft (e.g., flight characteristics or controls severely restricted, safety at great risk, serious injuries possible)
C	Major	Major failure condition for the aircraft (e.g., flight management system could be down, safety at risk, minor injuries possible)
D	Minor	Minor failure condition for the aircraft (e.g., safety could be at risk, some inconvenience possible)
E	No effect	No effect on safety or aircraft operation

Based on these categories, software is divided into (safety) levels A through E depending on the consequences of a potential software failure.

The DO 178 B demands on software development and testing increase with the software level.

DO 178 B also contains technical guidelines, such as, for example, the application of test techniques "Modified Decision/Condition Coverage" (MC/DC) (see [Spillner 07, section 5.2.3]) for level A software. The standard also requires the measurement of code coverage at source code level for levels B through E. Moreover, for level A object code, instrumented instructions that cannot be directly traced back to source code (for instance, compiler-inserted array bounds checks).

DO 178 B requires MC/DC coverage for level A software.

It is up to the test manager to ensure that the methods and techniques required by the standard are implemented, although he does not have much leeway left for the organization of the test activities. It's important that evidence can be provided of the methods and techniques applied and that required coverage has been achieved.

For railroad control and monitoring applications within the scope of the European railroad authorities, standard EN 50128 is to be complied with in all software development activities. This applies to completely new software development as well as to small or large software changes, independent from whether the regulatory authority is involved or not.

EN 50128 applies to software in railroad control and monitoring applications.

However, in the case of existing software, it only applies to the modifications made to the software.

Similar to the DO 178 B safety levels, EN 50128 contains so-called safety integrity levels (SILs) and distinguishes between safety-relevant (SIL > 0) and non-safety-relevant software (SIL=0). Categorization into SIL = 0 or SIL > 0 is proposed by the software manufacturer and certified either by the railroad authority itself or by a recognized expert. In this context, the integration of the software into the complete automotive or railroad system in terms of absence of feedback or error propagation to the basic system (e.g., the bus system) should be considered, taking into account the currently applicable guidelines of the railroad authority. This happens before the software is developed.

EN 50128 contains detailed work instructions.

EN 50128 contains detailed working instructions for all software development and quality assurance activities. With regard to test management, for example, it states that for component testing, a component test specification must exist that checks its intended function. This test specification must also define the necessary degree of test coverage. Tests must be repeatable and, if practicable, should be automated.

An auditable component test report is to be drawn up comprising the following points:

1. Test results and statement whether each component does meet the requirements of its design specification

EN 50128 requires C0 coverage for component testing.

2. Test coverage to prove that each source code line has been executed at least once (complete instruction coverage)
3. Test cases and their results, which are to be recorded in machine-readable form for subsequent analysis

Such guidelines facilitate the work of the test manager because he does not need to think about which basic tasks are to be performed. In most cases, however, the exact methods and techniques that are to be employed to complete the required activities need to be defined. Above all, all activities and their achieved results must be documented in detail.

Another central issue of EN 50128 and DO 178 B is the traceability of all documents across the entire development process. Here test managers are particularly asked to prove requirements and code coverage through corresponding test cases.

To a large extent, the other standards listed in table 13-1 also provide domain-specific working instructions; some of them even contain concrete descriptions of applicable methods and techniques. Since these have been developed by boards whose members come mostly from their respective subject areas, they are in most cases more directly applicable and therefore appear to be more practicable than those general standards presented in the next section.

 Often the standard documents are expensive and/or difficult to obtain. Provide for sufficient number of printed copies or licenses for electronic versions so that the norms or standards are actually available for use to each member in the project.

13.5 Generally Applicable Standards

ISO/IEC JTC 1/SC 7 and IEEE S2ESC develop important standards for software development.

In addition to domain-specific standards, there are, in the area of information technology, currently more than 280 generally applicable standards registered at ISO (see [URL: ISO]), starting from basic definitions of terminology to detailed working instructions and reference software source code for multimedia applications. Limiting the scope to norms or standards relevant to software development, we still have almost 90 standards, to which we need to add the IEEE Software Engineering Standards collection with its over 40 standards.

In the following sections, we shall list and briefly characterize only those standards that due to their content and technical relevance are important to test management. Many of these standards were developed by the following bodies or organizations:

- "ISO/IEC Joint Technical Committee 1/Subcommittee 7: Software & System Engineering" (ISO/IEC JTC 1/SC 7, [URL: JTC1SC7])
- "ISO/IEC Joint Technical Committee 1/Subcommittee 27: IT Security Techniques" (ISO/IEC JTC 1/SC 27, [URL: ISO])
- "IEEE Software and Systems Engineering Standards Committee (S2ESC, [URL: S2ESC]) of the Institute of Electrical and Electronics Engineers" (IEEE, [URL: IEEE])

To keep track in view of such a large number, the simple categorization into process and product standards provided in *Software Testing Foundations* is no longer sufficient. We therefore use additional categories for classification of these standards, for instance, with respect to their normative objectives:

Categorization into process and product standards is not granular enough.

- Terminology, vocabulary: standards defining the terminology of a specific area of application
- Principle standards: standards explaining the underlying principles of an area of application
- Element standards: standards containing detailed conformity requirements for products and processes
- Application guides and supplements: documents containing application guidelines and documentation standards
- Toolbox of techniques: descriptions of methods and techniques applied to support adherence to standards

On the other hand, standards are often categorized based on their applicability to the process models, shown in figure 13-1.

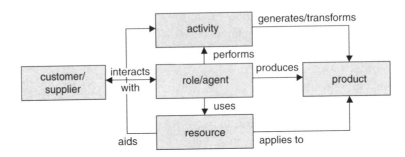

- Customer relationships: standards that help with the definition of customer or contractor responsibilities
- Processes: standards that describe the activities to be performed during the software life cycle in generic terms
- Products: standards that contain concrete particulars relating to the characteristics, specifications, metrics, and evaluation techniques of the artifacts to be developed
- Resources: standards that deal with the documentation and methods, models, and tools for the development of software products and associated processes

Ultimately, standards can also be classified according to the field of application's granularity (left of figure 13-2).

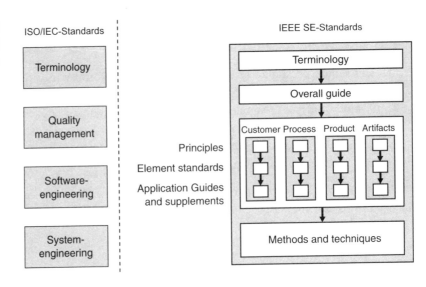

The subsequent deliberations regarding generally applicable standards are based on the following list, simplifying the above categories in a pragmatic way:

- Terminology and contractual standards
- Process standards
- Product and documentation standards
- Methods and engineering standards

13.5.1 Terminology and Contractual Standards

The standards listed in this section form the basis for all other standards, since their content and statements can be written down and understood only in a consistent and unambiguous way using standardized terminology. The most important terminology standards are among the following:

Terminology standards define the terminology of a particular area of application.

- ISO/IEC 2382 part 1-33 [ISO 2382] and IEEE 610.12-1990, which is the standard glossary of software engineering terminology [IEEE 610.12].
- ISO 9000 [ISO 9000]is important for test management and explains the basis for quality management systems and the terminology used in the ISO 9000 and ISO 900x series of standards.
- The British standard BS 7952-1 defines terms used in software testing [BS 7952-1] and is currently revised to harmonize it with the ISTQB Certified Tester glossary [URL: ISTQB].

It is particularly important for the development, procurement, and use of software to unambiguously define the responsibilities of customer (buyer, client, user) and contractor (vendor, developer, broker) for all parties concerned. There is a whole range of corresponding contractual standards, among them the following:

Contractual standards deal with customer/buyer and contractor/developer relationships.

- "IEEE Recommended Practice for Software Acquisition" (IEEE Std 1062-1998, [IEEE 1062]), helping the test manager in the acquisition of test tools.
- The "Software Engineering – Product Evaluation" series of standards (ISO/IEC 14598, [ISO 14598-4]), which provides the test manager with advice on how to design acceptance testing while supporting him in the evaluation of test tools. The underlying quality model is described in the ISO/IEC 9126 series of standards, which belongs to the product standards.

In addition, relevant for test management are also standards for the design of requirements specifications (IEEE 1233, "System Requirements Specifications" [IEEE 1233]) and general requirements for system safety (e.g., the ISO/IEC 15408 series of standards, "Information technology – security techniques; evaluation criteria for IT security").

13.5.2 Process Standards

Processes are correlative activities that, using resources, turn inputs into results (see figure 13-1). Process standards subsume all across-the-board standards that specify minimum requirements for processes or process evaluation and improvement, in some cases without stating concrete requirements regarding implementation.

The ISO 9000 family belongs to the important process standards.

The best-known example for process standards is the ISO 9000 family, whose standards help organizations of all shapes and sizes in the realization of effective quality management systems.

- **ISO 9000** [ISO 9000] comprises the fundamentals as well as the terminology of quality management systems. It may therefore also be considered a terminology standard.
- **ISO 9001** [ISO 9001] contains requirements on quality management systems by means of which organizations can prove their capability to meet customer and official requirements with their products and to enhance customer satisfaction.
- **ISO 90003** [ISO 90003] forms a guideline for the application of ISO 9001 on the development, release, installation, and maintenance of computer software. Amplifications of ISO 9001 specific to test management are, for instance, sections on quality planning, risk management, validation, and test as well as software quality criteria. For example, ISO 90003 requires the planning of suitable (intermediate) checks during the manufacturing process (also applicable to the special case of a software development process) without, however, specifying when and how these are to be performed. ISO 90003 can be used to build a bridge from ISO 9001 to process improvement models such as ISO 15504 (SPICE, [ISO 15504]) and CMMI ([URL: CMMI], see chapter 7) since they are all based on the ISO/IEC/IEEE Standard 12207 (see below).
- **ISO 9004** is a guideline that considers the effectiveness and efficiency of the quality management system. The objective of this standard lies in

organizational performance improvement and in enhancing the satisfaction of customers or other interested parties.

- **ISO 19011** is a guideline for quality and environmental management
systems audits.

In combination, these standards facilitate mutual understanding of quality
management in national and international trade relations.

Standard [ISO 12207.0] describes in detail issues to be considered in
designing software development processes without, however, providing
concrete methods and techniques. Relevant implementation guidelines are
provided by [ISO 12207.2]. Interesting for test management is the early
integration of testing in the overall development process.

ISO/IEC 12207 – the generic "standard software development process."

The process described in chapter 12 concerning tool selection follows
ISO/IEC 14102:1995, "Evaluation and Selection of CASE Tools", the procedure for the introduction of test tools is based on ISO/IEC TR
14471:1999, "Guidelines for the Adoption of CASE Tools".

Part 3 of IEC 61508-3 describes functional software safety requirements in safety-related systems and represents a hybrid between process
and product standard.

As defined in the domain-specific standards DO 178 B and EN 50128,
IEC 61508-3 defines safety integrity levels (SILs) 1 to 4, which describe
the assumed hazard potential. The higher the level, the higher the hazard
potential, accompanied by stricter requirements on system reliability [IEC
61508-3].

Using such standards for guidance makes sense even where compliance with
them is not mandatory.

Finally, when it comes to litigation, "state of the art" development must be
proved, including compliance with standards. Naturally, this also applies to all
other standards whose application is not mandatory.

Hint

13.5.3   Product and Documentation Standards

Standards relating to quality requirements and the concrete design of
material and immaterial products fall under the category "product and
documentation standards", providing document and product specifications together with quality attributes and appropriate means of verification. These standards can be further divided into those relating to intermediate software development products such as requirements, design, and

test specifications and those relating to the end product software together with maintenance and user documentation.

- With respect to quality goals, the ISO 9126 series [ISO 9126] contains a quality model as well as concrete specifications including metrics for evaluation of the quality in use and product quality. Consequently, it supports the test manager in his test planning; i.e., the definition of test objectives for individual quality features as well as measurement and test procedures (see chapters 5 and 11).
- The ISO/IEC 12119:1994, "Software Packages: Quality Requirements and Testing" [ISO 12119], defines a quality model for application software and supports the test manager in the design of system and acceptance testing.
- The [ISO 9241] series describes in 17 parts ergonomic requirements for office work with visual display terminals and, with regard to test management, serves as a basis for the specification of usability tests.

Concrete specifications concerning the creation of documents are provided by standard [IEEE 730] for the test plan and by standard [IEEE 829] for the entire test documentation. Both were already discussed in *Software Testing Foundations*. IEEE 829 prescribes the documents referenced in figure 13-3.

Figure 13–3

Test document reference structure according to IEEE 829

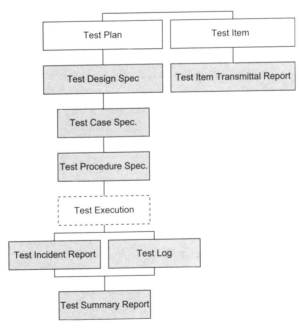

IEEE Standard 1044-1993, "IEEE Standard Classification for Software Anomalies" [IEEE 1044], is also important for the test manager and provides a detailed classification for the management of incident reports. IEEE 1044 has already been explained at length in section 8.4.

IEEE 1044:
Incident management

Additional standards relevant for documentation are the IEEE Standard 1063-2001, "IEEE Standard for Software User Documentation" [IEEE 1063], and the ISO/IEC standard 15910:1999, "Information Technology – Software User Documentation Process" [ISO 15910]. They can assist test management in drawing up checklists for corresponding reviews.

Last but not least there are standards that define specific data formats regarding the interoperability of systems. EN 9735, for instance, defines syntactic rules for the preparation of messages for electronic data interchange between partners in the fields of administration, commerce, and transport (EDIFACT, [ISO 9735]). The ISO/IEC 13818-x family describes MPEG formats for encryption of multimedia data. Such standards are invaluable to test management when specifying concrete test cases such as syntax tests.

13.5.4 Methods and Engineering Standards

This category comprises concrete working instructions for the constructive, testing, and supporting activities in software development. Several software test standards are of central importance to test management and, independent from concrete products, define how software tests are professionally planned, specified, and performed.

- Based on the IEEE Standard 730, "IEEE Standard for Software Quality Assurance Plans" [IEEE 730], the ANSI/IEEE Standard 730.1-1995, "IEEE Guide for Software Quality Assurance Planning", supports test managers in the creation, evaluation, and maintenance of test schedules.

- The IEEE Standard 1044.1-1995, "IEEE Guide to Classification for Software Anomalies" [IEEE 1044.1], provides assistance for deviation management according to the IEEE 1044-1993 standard, "IEEE Standard Classification for Software Anomalies" [IEEE 1044].

- IEEE 1059-1993, "IEEE Guide for Software Verification and Validation Plans" [IEEE 1059], provides guidelines and practical advice on validation/verification planning and documentation in all software development phases.

▦ The ISO/IEC standard 16085:2004, "Information Technology – Software Life Cycle Processes – Risk Management" [ISO 16085], gives test managers concrete instructions for risk management (see chapter 9).

The following standards are already cited in *Software Testing Foundations* [Spillner 07]:

▦ The British Standard 7925-2, "Software Testing, Part 2: Software Component Testing" [BS 7925-2], describing component testing methods and techniques.

▦ The IEEE Standard 1028-1997, "IEEE Standard for Software Reviews" [IEEE 1028], which deals in detail with the planning, performing, and documentation of reviews.

In addition there exist a series of standards relating to methods and techniques that test managers should know. To these belong, for instance, [IEC 60812] for Failure Mode and Effects Analysis (FMEA, see section 9.8.1), [IEC 61025] for Fault Tree Analysis, and [ISO 5806] for decision table practices.

13.5.5 Application of Standards

For the application of standards, we recommend the following approach (see [Schmidt 00]):

1. First, examine your own approach regarding gaps and inconsistencies in applied process and quality management standards and align the terms used for performed activities and artifacts with the standard terminology.
2. Second, align and complete your own artifacts such as documents, specifications, and guidelines with respect to product and documentation standards
3. Building on this, complete your own activities in reference to the methods and engineering norms.
4. Observe your own processes over time using productivity and quality measurements. Optimize them applying standards for process improvement and adapt them to suit organizational and technological changes.

At the end of this chapter, table 13-3 lists all generally valid test management standards, grouped according to the different phases of the test process and the type of standard. Standards applicable to several areas are listed in each area. Documents vital to the test manager are listed in bold.

Type of standard / Test phase	Terminology and contracts	Processes	Products	Documentation	Methods and techniques
Test planning **Test control**	**BS 7925-1** ISO 2382 **ISO 9000** ISO 12207-0 **IEEE 610.12**	ISO 12207-0 **ISO 9000-3** **IEEE 730** **IEEE 1008** **IEEE 1012** IEEE 1061	**ISO 9126-x** ISO 12119 ISO 12207-1 ISO 15026 IEEE 982.1 IEEE 1228	**IEEE 730** **IEEE 829** IEEE 1012 IEEE 1228	ISO 12207-2 ISO 16085 IEEE 730.1 IEEE 982.2 **IEEE 1059**
Test analysis **Test design**	[ISO 14598-4] ISO 15408 IEEE 1062 IEEE 1228	IEEE 1008 IEEE 1012 ISO 15939	**ISO 9241** ISO 12119 IEEE 1044 IEEE 982.2	**IEEE 829** IEEE1063	**BS 7925-2** IEEE 1028 ISO 60812 EN 61508-3 EN 50128 IEC 61025 ISO 5806
Test realization and test execution		IEEE 1008	ISO 9241 IEEE 828 IEEE 1209 IEEE 1348	**IEEE 829** IEEE 1209 IEEE 1348	IEEE 1028 ETSI 201-873 IEEE 1042 IEEE 1209 IEEE 1348
Test evaluation and reporting		IEEE 1008	IEEE 982.2 **IEEE 1044**	**IEEE 829**	IEEE 1044.1 ISO 12119

Table 13–3

Standards in the phases of the test process

- Always involve developers in the selection of standards, distinguishing between those that have to be applied at all times and those whose application is only recommended.
- Consider standards as an opportunity to improve professional practices; do not use them as surrogates.
- Standards to be applied are to be reviewed regularly with respect to changed methods, approaches, and technology. If necessary, a new selection must be made.
- If possible, use templates and tools for easier application of standards.

13.6 Summary

- Test managers must know which standards are relevant for the product under test or for the (test) process and need to ensure compliance, if necessary through audits.

- Categorized by increasing general validity and applicability, there are corporate standards, best practices, technical specifications, domain-specific standards, and generally applicable standards.
- Domain-specific standards and generally applicable standards define generally recognized codes of practice and form the framework within which projects are performed. They promote consistency of products and processes and constitute the minimal requirements for professional work.
- We can distinguish between terminology and contractual standards, process standards, product and documentation standards, and methods and engineering standards.
- In defining the test strategy and the test techniques to be applied, general and domain-specific standards such as [IEC 61508-3], [DO 178 B], [EN 50128], nuclear industry standards, pharmaceutical standards, and the MISRA Guidelines for Vehicle Based Software are to be applied.
- IEEE Standard 829–1998, "IEEE Standard for Software Test Documentation" [IEEE 829], is a recognized standard for the form and content of the test documentation. Test plans and test level plans, in particular, are developed in compliance with this standard.
- The four standards of the ISO/IEC 9126 series, "Software Engineering – Product Quality" [ISO 9126-x], contain a model and measurements for the evaluation of the quality of software products.
- The IEEE Standard 1028-1997, "IEEE Standard for Software Reviews" [IEEE 1028], describes in detail the planning, execution, and documentation of reviews.
- The IEEE Standards 1044-1993, "IEEE Standard Classification for Software Anomalies" [IEEE 1044], and 1044.1-1995, "IEEE Guide to Classification for Software Anomalies" [IEEE 1044.1], provide a process and detailed classification for the management of incident reports.
- The two standards BS 7925-2, "Software Testing – Part 2: Software Component Testing" [BS 7925-2], and IEEE Std 1008, "IEEE Standard for Software Unit Testing" [IEEE 1008], describe methods, practices, and processes for the test level "component testing".

Glossary

This glossary contains terminology specifically related to the areas of software testing and test management, and other terms that are related to the topic of this book.

The first occurrence of a term in the book which is defined in the glossary is preceded by an arrow "→". Terminology that has already been defined in »Software Testing Foundations« [Spillner 07] will not be repeated here. Refer to [URL: ISTQB Glossary] for an up-to-date version of the ISTQB glossary.[1]

acceptance criteria: The exit criteria that a component or system must satisfy in order to be accepted by a user, customer, or other authorized entity. [IEEE 610.12]

acceptance testing: Formal testing with respect to user needs, requirements, and business processes conducted to determine whether or not a system satisfies the acceptance criteria and to enable the user, customers or other authorized entity to determine whether or not to accept the system. [After IEEE 610.12]

anomaly: Any condition that deviates from expectation based on requirements specifications, design documents, user documents, standards, etc. or from someone's perception or experience. Anomalies may be found during, but not limited to, reviewing, testing, analysis, compilation, or use of software products or applicable documentation. [IEEE 1044].

application expert: expert who, as a result of training, or because of his professional function, has comprehesive expertise in the application domain of the system under test assessment: see audit.

---

1. Terms flagged with an asterisk are included in the [Spillner 07] glossary; the definitions can also be found on [URL: ISTQB Glossary].

audit: An independent evaluation of software products or processes to ascertain compliance to standards, guidelines, specifications, and/or procedures based on objective criteria, including documents that specify:

(1) the form or content of the products to be produced

(2) the process by which the products shall be produced

(3) how compliance to standards or guidelines shall be measured. [IEEE 1028]

baseline: A specification or software product that has been formally reviewed or agreed upon, that thereafter serves as the basis for further development, and that can be changed only through a formal change control process. [After IEEE 610.12]

build: An operational version of a system or component that incorporates a specified subset of the capabilities that the final product will provide. [After IEEE 610.12]

CAST: Acronym for Computer Aided Software Testing. See also test automation.

configuration: The composition of a component or system as defined by the number, nature, and interconnections of its constituent parts.

coverage: The degree, expressed as a percentage, to which a specified coverage item has been exercised by a test suite.

coverage item: An entity or property used as a basis for test coverage, e.g., equivalence partitions or code statements.

defect analysis: part of debugging; tracing a failure back to its causal defect and perhaps even to the original error.

defect classification: practice used to define the defect class.*

defect density: The number of defects identified in a component or system divided by the size of the component or system (expressed in standard measurement terms, e.g., lines-of-code, number of classes or function points).

Defect Detection Percentage (DDP): The number of defects found by a test phase, divided by the number found by that test phase and any other means afterwards.

defect distribution: percentage share of incident reports of a particular nature in relation to the total number of all recorded reports (e.g., defects in a particular component).

defect management: The process of recognizing, investigating, taking action and disposing of defects. It involves recording defects, classifying them and identifying the impact. [After IEEE 1044]

defect management tool: A tool that facilitates the recording and status tracking of defects and changes. They often have workflow-oriented facilities to track and control the allocation, correction and re-testing of defects and provide reporting facilities. See also incident management tool.

defect management system: see defect management tool.

defect report: A document reporting on any flaw in a component or system that can cause the component or system to fail to perform its required function. [After IEEE 829]

defect trend: progression of the number of incident reports or defects discovered by testing (e.g., number of newly created incident reports, number of corrected defects).

domain expert: see application expert.

equivalence class: See equivalence partition.

equivalence partition: A portion of an input or output domain for which the behavior of a component or system is assumed to be the same, based on the specification.

failure: Deviation of the component or system from its expected delivery, service or result. [After Fenton]

Failure Mode and Effect Analysis (FMEA): A systematic approach to risk identification and analysis of identifying possible modes of failure and attempting to prevent their occurrence.

failure rate: The ratio of the number of failures of a given category to a given unit of measure, e.g., failures per unit of time, failures per number of transactions, failures per number of computer runs. [IEEE 610.12]

fault days: number of days from defect injection into the system and proof that a resulting failure has occurred.

feature: An attribute of a component or system specified or implied by requirements documentation (for example reliability, usability or design constraints). [After IEEE 1008]

Function Point Analysis (FPA): Method aiming to measure the size of the functionality of an information system. The measurement is independent of the technology. This measurement may be used as a basis for the measurement of productivity, the estimation of the needed resources, and project control.

handover test: A subset of all the tests of a test level that either serves as an acceptance test of the receiving test level (or from development) or as a -> release test to the next test level (or release).

horizontal traceability: The tracing of requirements for a test level through the layers of test documentation (e.g., test plan, test design specification, test case specification, and test procedure specification or test script).

image: byte-identical image of the content of a hard drive for data backup purposes, for saving a particular system state or a particular system configuration.

imaging: creating a hard drive image (see image).

IT expert: expert who, as a result of training, or because of his professional function, has comprehesive expertise in the area of computer sciences, information technology, telecommunication etc.

measure: The number or category assigned to an attribute of an entity by making a measurement. [ISO 14598]

measurement: The process of assigning a number or category to an entity to describe an attribute of that entity. [ISO 14598]

measurement scale: A scale that constrains the type of data analysis that can be performed on it. [ISO 14598]

metric: A measurement scale and the method used for measurement. [ISO 14598]

migration testing: See conversion testing.

operational profile: expected distribution of the frequency with which product functions are used during operation.

PREview: early, up-stream review in which testers participate in order to check documents with regard to their applicability to testing, specifically for the creation of test cases.

priority: The level of (business) importance assigned to an item, e.g., defect.

product risk: A risk directly related to the test object.

project: A project is a unique set of coordinated and controlled activities with start and finish dates undertaken to achieve an objective conforming to specific requirements, including the constraints of time, cost and resources. [ISO 9000]

project risk: A risk related to management and control of the (test) project, e.g., lack of staffing, strict deadlines, changing requirements, etc.

quality: The degree to which a component, system or process meets specified requirements and/or user/customer needs and expectations. [After IEEE 610.12]

quality gate: milestone* focusing on quality control.

quality management: Coordinated activities to direct and control an organization with regard to quality. Direction and control with regard to quality generally includes the establishment of the quality policy and quality objectives, quality planning, quality control, quality assurance and quality improvement. [ISO 9000]

quality policy: overall intentions and directions of an organization as regards quality.

release candidate: Build considered sufficiently stable and mature to be a candidate for (external) release. If this evaluation is supported by test, the release candidate becomes a "real" release.*

release plan: schedule (issued by product management) indicating at what time and in what frequency development is going to deliver builds and releases (either for testing or for external release).

release test: test subset of a test level; used to either pass the test object on to the next test level or to release it.

requirement: A condition or capability needed by a user to solve a problem or achieve an objective that must be met or possessed by a system or system component to satisfy a contract, standard, specification, or other formally imposed document. [After IEEE 610.12]

requirements coverage: percentage share of all (system) requirements which were validated by at least one test case. See also coverage.*

requirements tracing: see traceability.

residual defect estimation: estimation of the total number of defects remaining in the system after code reviews, testing, and other quality assurance activities.

risk analysis: The process of assessing identified risks to estimate their impact and probability of occurrence (likelihood).

risk-based testing: Testing oriented towards exploring and providing information about product risks.*

risk control: The process through which decisions are reached and protective measures are implemented for reducing risks to, or maintaining risks within, specified levels.

risk identification: The process of identifying risks using techniques such as brainstorming, checklists and failure history.

risk inventory: A project's current and historical risk-related information including the risk management context, along with the chronological record of risks, priority ordering, risk-related measures, treatment status, contingency plans, and risk action requests.

risk management: Systematic application of procedures and practices to the tasks of identifying, analyzing, prioritizing, and controlling risk.

risk mitigation: See risk control.

risk priority number (RPN): used in the FMEA to quantify defect opportunities by calculating the product of probability of occurence, expected damage, and probability of detection.

risk profile: see risk inventory.

severity: The degree of impact that a defect has on the development or operation of a component or system. [After IEEE 610.12]

stakeholder: the objective of system development is to satisfy the needs and requirements of several people, groups, institutions, or documents (e.g., legal documents). These needs and requirements can be very different and may even be contradictory and opposing to each other. All involved persons, groups, institutions, and documents are stakeholders.

standards: Mandatory requirement employed and enforced to prescribe a disciplined uniform approach to software development, that is, mandatory conventions and practices are in fact standards. [After IEEE 610.12]

Survival probability: The probability that no failure will occur within a specified time interval.

system configuration: See configuration.

system failure: See failure.

test activity: activity or part of an activity performed as part of the test process.*

test approach: The implementation of the test strategy for a specific project. It typically includes the decisions made that follow based on the (test) project's goal and the risk assessment carried out, starting points regarding the test process, the test design techniques to be applied, exit criteria and test types to be performed.

test center: institution, or organizational unit, which provides testing as an external or internal service for development projects.

test control: A test management task that deals with developing and applying a set of corrective actions to get a test project on track when monitoring shows a deviation from what was planned. See also test management.

test coverage: See coverage.

test design: See test design specification.

test design specification: A document specifying the test conditions (coverage items) for a test item, the detailed test approach and identifying the associated high level test cases. [After IEEE 829]

test design technique: Procedure used to derive and/or select test cases.

test framework: See test harness.

test handbook: See test policy.

test harness: A test environment comprised of stubs and drivers needed to execute a test.

test intensity: intensity with which a particular quality attribute is checked by a number of test cases. This may be determined quantitatively by coverage measurements or purely qualitatively by comparing different testing techniques (a business process based test with synchronous application of a thorough equivalence analysis has a significantly higher test intensity than one without it).

test management: The planning, estimating, monitoring and control of test activities, typically carried out by a test manager.

test management tool: A tool that provides support to the test management and control part of a test process. It often has several capabilities, such as testware management, scheduling of tests, the logging of results, progress tracking, incident management and test reporting.

test manager: The person responsible for project management of testing activities and resources, and evaluation of a test object. The individual who directs, controls, administers, plans and regulates the evaluation of a test object.

test metric: A quantitative measure of a test case, test run or test cycle including measurement instructions.

test monitoring: A test management task that deals with the activities related to periodically checking the status of a test project. Reports are prepared that compare the actuals to that which was planned.

test object scope: size of the test object, which can be measured by means of different metrics*, e.g., lines of code, function points, and others.

test plan: A document describing the scope, approach, resources and schedule of intended test activities. It identifies amongst others test items, the features to be tested, the testing tasks, who will do each task, degree of tester independence, the test environment, the test design techniques and entry and exit criteria to be used, and the rationale for their choice, and any risks requiring contingency planning. It is a record of the test planning process. [After IEEE 829]

test planning: The activity of establishing or updating a test plan.

test policy: A high level document describing the principles, approach and major objectives of the organization regarding testing.

Test Process Improvement (TPI): A continuous framework for test process improvement that describes the key elements of an effective test process, especially targeted at system testing and acceptance testing.

test progress: metric for the status of a test project. See also test monitoring.

test progress report: See test monitoring and test summary report.

test project: basically a temporary endeavor to achieve specified test goals within a defined period of time. Usually, a test project is part of a software or system development project.

test report: See test summary report.

test schedule: A schedule that identifies all tasks required for a successful testing effort, a schedule of all test activities, and their corresponding resource requirements.

test specification technique: See test design technique.

test summary report: A document summarizing testing activities and results. It also contains an evaluation of the corresponding test items against exit criteria. [After IEEE 829]

test technique: See test design technique.

test tool: A software product that supports one or more test activities, such as planning and control, specification, building initial files and data, test execution and test analysis. [TMap] See also CAST.

test topic: a group of test cases that are collectively executed and / or managed because they test related aspects of the test object or share the same test objectives.

test type: A group of test activities aimed at testing a component or system focused on a specific test objective, i.e. functional test, usability test, regression test etc. A test type may take place on one or more test levels or test phases. [After TMap]

traceability: The ability to identify related items in documentation and software, such as requirements with associated tests. See also horizontal traceability, vertical traceability.

TTCN-3: (Testing and Test Control Notation, Version 3) A flexible and powerful language applicable to the specification of all types of reactive system tests over a variety of communication interfaces.

usability testing: Testing to determine the extent to which the software product is understood, easy to learn, easy to operate and attractive to the users under specified conditions. [After ISO 9126]

use case: A sequence of transactions in a dialogue between a user and the system with a tangible result.

vertical traceability: The tracing of requirements through the layers of development documentation to components.

Literature

[Amland 99]

Amland, S.: Risk Based Testing and Metrics. 5th International Conference EuroSTAR '99, Barcelona, 1999.

[Basili 84]

Basili, V. R.; Weiss, D. M.: A Methodology for Collecting Valid Software Engineering Data. IEEE Transaction on Software Engineering, SE-10, No.6, 1984, pp. 728-738.

[Beck 00]

Beck, K.; Fowler, M.: Planning Extreme Programming. Addison-Wesley, 2000.

[Belbin 93]

Belbin, R. M.: Team Roles at Work. Butterworth-Heinemann Ltd., 1993.

[Boehm 79]

Boehm, B. W.: Guidelines for Verifying and Validating Software Requirements and Design Specification. EURO IFIP 79, P. A. Samet (eds.). North-Holland, IFIP 1979, pp. 711-719.

[Burnstein 96]

Burnstein, I.; Suwanassart, T.; Carlson, C. R.: The Development of a Testing Maturity Model. Proceedings of the Ninth International Quality Week Conference, San Francisco, USA, May 21-24, 1996.

[Burnstein 03]

Burnstein, I.: Practical Software Testing. Springer, New York, 2003.

[Charette 89]

Charette, R. N.: Software Engineering Risk Analysis and Management. McGraw-Hill, New York, 1989.

[CMMI 01]

CMMISM for Systems Engineering and Software Engineering (CMMISE/SW). Version 1.1, Carnegie Mellon University, Software Engineering Institute, CMU/SEI-2002-TR-002, 2001.

[Crispin 02]

Crispin, L.; House, T.: Testing Extreme Programming. Addison-Wesley, 2002.

[Chrissis 06]

Chrissis, M. B.; Konrad, M.; Shrum, S.: CMMI. Guidelines for Process Integration and Product Improvement (Sei Series in Software Engineering), 2nd Edition, Addison-Wesley, 2006.

[DeMarco 86]

DeMarco, T.: Controlling Software Projects. Prentice Hall, Englewood Cliffs, 1986.

[DeMarco 95]

DeMarco, T.: Why Does Software Cost So Much? Dorset House Publishing, New York, 1995.

[DeMarco 97]

DeMarco, T.: The Deadline, A Novel about Project Management. Dorset House Publishing, New York, 1997.

[DeMarco 03]

DeMarco, T.; Lister, T.: Waltzing with Bears: Managing Risk on Software Projects. Dorset House Publishing, New York, 2003.

[Ebert 05]

Ebert, C.; Dumke, R.; Bundschuh, M.; Schmietendorf, A.: Best Practices in Software-Measurement – How to Use Metrics to Improve Project and Process Performance. Springer, New York, 2005.

[Fenton]

Fenton, N.: Software Metrics: a Rigorous Approach. Chapman & Hall, 1991.

[Garmus 00]

Garmus, D.; Herron, D.: Function Point Analysis: Measurement Practices for Successful Software Projects. Addison-Wesley, 2000.

[Gilb 96]

Gilb, T.; Graham, D.: Software Inspections. Addison-Wesley, 1996 (Reprint 1993).

[Goetsch 02]

Goetsch, D. L.; Davis, S. D.: Quality Management: Introduction to Total Quality Management for Production, Processing, and Services. 4th Edition, Prentice Hall, 2002.

[Graham 00]

Graham, D.; Fewster, M.; Roden, L.: Practical Guide to Software Test Management – Task & People Issues. Tutorial, 8th European Conference on Software Testing Analysis and Review, EuroStar'00, Kopenhagen, 2000.

[Grottke 01]

Grottke, M.; Dussa-Zieger, K.: Prediction of Software Failures Based on Systematic Testing. Proc. 9th European Conference on Software Testing Analysis and Review, EuroSTAR'01, 2001.

[Gutjahr 95]

Gutjahr, W. J.: Optimal Test Distributions for Software Failure Cost Estimation. IEEE Transactions on Software Engineering, Vol. 21, No. 3. March 1995, pp. 219-228.

[Hatton 97]

Hatton, L.: Reexamining the Fault Density-Component Size Connection. IEEE Software, March 1997, pp. 89-97.

[Imai 86]

Imai, M.: Kaizen – The Key To Japan's Competitive Success. McGraw-Hill/Irwin, 1986.

[Jelinski 72]

Jelinski, Z.; Moranda, P.: Software Reliability Research. In: W. Freiberger (ed.): Statistical Computer Performance Evaluation. Academic Press, 1972.

[John 06]

John, A.; Meran, R.; Roenpage, O.; Staudter, C.: Lunau, S. (eds.): Six Sigma + Lean Toolset. Springer, New York, 2006.

[Jones 98]

Jones, C.: Estimating Software Costs. McGraw-Hill, New York, 1998.

[Juran 88]

Juran, J. M.: Juran's Quality Control Handbook. McGraw-Hill, New York, 1988.

[Kaner 95]

Kaner, C.: Software Negligence & Testing Coverage. Software Quality Assurance Quarterly, Vol. 2, No. 2, 1995. Online: [URL: Kaner].

[Kneuper 06]

Kneuper, R.: CMMI – Verbesserung von Softwareprozessen mit Capability Maturity Model Integration. 2nd Edition, dpunkt.verlag, Heidelberg, 2006.

[Koomen 99]

Koomen, T.; Pol, M.: Test Process Improvement: a Practical Step-by-Step Guide to Structured Testing. Addison-Wesley, 1999.

[Kruchten 04]

Kruchten, P.: The Rational Unified Process. An Introduction. Addison-Wesley, 3rd Edition, 2004.

[Kuhrmann 06]

Kuhrmann, M; Niebuhr, D.; Rausch, A.: Application of the V-Modell XT – Report from a Pilot Project. In: Li, M.; Boehm, B.; Osterweil L. J. (eds.): Unifying the Software Process Spectrum: International Software Process Workshop, SPW 2005, Beijing, China, May 25-27, 2005 Revised Selected Papers (Lecture Notes in Computer Science), Springer, 2006, pp. 463-473.

[Liggesmeyer 02]

Liggesmeyer, P.: Software-Qualität – Testen, Analysieren und Verifizieren von Software. Spektrum Akademischer Verlag, Heidelberg, 2002.

[Lyu 96]

Lyu, M. R. (ed.): Handbook of Software Reliability Engineering. IEEE Press, Los Alamitos/McGraw-Hill, New York, 1996.

[Martin 91]

Martin, J.: Rapid Application Development. Macmillan, USA, 1991.

[Musa 84]

Musa, J. D.; Okumoto, K.: A Logarithmic Poisson Execution Time Model for Software Reliability Measurement. Proc. 7th International Conference on Software Engineering (ICSE'84), 1984, pp. 230-238.

[Neumann 95]

Neumann, P. G.: Computer Related Risks. ACM Press/Addison-Wesley, 1995.

[Ould 99]

Ould, M.: Managing Software Quality and Business Risk. John Wiley & Sons, Chichester, 1999.

[PMBOK 04]

A guide to the Project Management Body of Knowledge (PMBOK® Guide), 3rd Edition, © 2004 Project Management Institute.

[Pol 02]

Pol, M.; Teunissen, R.; Van Veenendaal, E.: Software Testing – A Guide to the TMAP® Approach. Addison-Wesley, 2002.

[Rashka 01]

Rashka, J.: Test Effort Sizing. The Journal of Software Testing Professionals, March 2001.

[Schaefer 96]

Schaefer, H.: Surviving under Time and Budget Pressure. Proc. EuroSTAR'96, Amsterdam, 1996.

[Schettler 06]

Schettler, H.: Precision Testing: Benefit-Cost-Balancing by Test Planning. SQAM Conference 2006, Warsaw, Poland, 2006.

[Schmidt 00]

Schmidt, M. E. C.: Implementing the IEEE Software Engineering Standards. SAMS Publishing, Indianapolis, 2000.

[Sherer 91]

Sherer, S. A.: A Cost-Effective Approach to Testing. IEEE Software, March 1991, pp. 34-40.

[Spillner 02]

Spillner, A.: The W-Modell – Strengthening the Bond Between Development and Test. STAReast´2002, Orlando, Florida, USA, 15.-17. May 2002. On the Internet: www.stickyminds.com -> search "spillner"

[Spillner 07]

Spillner, A.; Linz, T.; Schaefer, H.: Software Testing Foundations – A Study Guide for the Certified Tester Exam, Foundation Level, ISTQB Compliant. 2nd edition, Rocky Nook Inc., Santa Barbara, 2007.

[Standish 04]

Standish Group: 2004 Third Quarter Research Report; CHAOS Demografics. West Yarmouth, 2004.

[TMap]

Pol M.; Teunissen R.; van Veenendaal, E.: Software Testing, A guide to the TMap Approach. Addison Wesley, 2002.

[van Veenendaal 02]

van Veenendaal, E.; Swinkels, R.: Guidelines for testing maturity: Part 1: The TMM model. Professional Tester. Vol. 3, No. 1, March 2002, pp. 8-10.

[Voas 00]

Voas, J.: Will the Real Operational Profile Please Stand Up? IEEE Software, Vol. 17, No. 2, Mar/Apr, 2000, pp. 87-89.

[Winter 98]

Winter, M.: Managing Object-Oriented Integration Testing. Proc. EuroSTAR'98. Munich, 1998.

[Zhu 97]

Zhu, H.; Hall, P. A.V.; May, J .H .R.: Software Unit Test Coverage and Adequacy. ACMACM Computing Surveys, Vol. 29, No. 4, December 1997, pp. 366-427.

[Zuse 98]

Zuse, H.: A Framework of Software Measurement. Walter de Gruyter, Berlin, 1998.

Standards

[BS 7925-1]

British Standard 7925-1: Software Testing, Part 1: Vocabulary, 1998.

[BS 7925-2]

British Standard 7925-2: Software Testing, Part 2: Software Component Testing, 1998.

[DO 178 B]

DO 178 B/ED-12B: Software Considerations in Airborne Systems and Equipment Certification, RTCA/EUROCAE, 1992.

[ECSS Q–80A]

ECSS Q–80A: Space Product Assurance – Software Product Assurance. European Cooperation For Space Standardization (ECSS), 1996.

[EN 50128]

EN 50128: Railway Applications – Communications, Signalling and Processing Systems – Software for Railway Control and Protection Systems. CENELEC, Bruxelles, 2001.

[FDA 21]

21 CFR Part 11: Title 21 – Food and Drugs Chapter I –, Department Of Health And Human Services Part 11 – Electronic Records; Electronic Signatures. U.S. Food and Drug Administration, March 20, 1997.

[FDA 535]

FDA 535: Guidance for Industry, FDA Reviewers and Compliance on Off-The-Shelf Software Use in Medical Devices. U.S. Food and Drug Administration, September 9, 1999.

[FDA 938]

FDA 938: General Principles of Software Validation; Final Guidance for Industry and FDA Staff. U.S. Food and Drug Administration, January 11, 2002.

[IAEA NS-G-1.1]
IAEA Safety Standards Series Safety Guide No. Ns-G-1.1: Software for Computer Based Systems Important to Safety in Nuclear Power Plants. International Atomic Energy Agency, Vienna, 2000.

[IAEA TR 384]
IAEA Technical Reports Series No. 384: Verification and Validation of Software Related to Nuclear Power Plant Instrumentation and Control. International Atomic Energy Agency, Vienna, 1999.

[IEC 60812]
IEC 60812:2006: Analysis techniques for system reliability – Procedure for failure mode and effects analysis (FMEA). IEC, Geneva, 2006.

[IEC 61025]
IEC 61025: Fault tree analysis (FTA). ISO, Geneva, 2006.

[IEC 61508-3]
IEC 61508-3: Functional safety of electrical/electronic/programmable electronic safety-related systems - Part 3: Software requirements. IEC, Geneva, 1998.

[IEC 62198]
IEC 62198: Project risk management – Application guidelines. IEC, Geneva, 2001.

[IEEE 610.12]
IEEE 610.12-1990: IEEE Standard Glossary of Software Engineering Terminology. Institute of Electrical and Electronics Engineers, May 1990.

[IEEE 730]
IEEE Std 730-2002: IEEE Standard for Software Quality Assurance Plans. IEEE, New York, 2002.

[IEEE 730.1]
IEEE Std 730.1-1995 IEEE Guide for Software Quality Assurance Planning. IEEE, New York, 1995.

[IEEE 828]
IEEE Std 828-1998: IEEE Standard for Software Configuration Management Plans. IEEE, New York, 1998.

[IEEE 829]

IEEE Std 829-1998: IEEE Standard for Software Test Documentation. IEEE, New York, 1998.

[IEEE 982.1]

IEEE Std 982.1-2005: IEEE Standard Dictionary of Measures of the Software Aspects of Dependability. IEEE, New York, 2005.

[IEEE 982.2]

IEEE Std 982.2-1988 IEEE Guide for the Use of IEEE Standard Dictionary of Measures to Produce Reliable Software. IEEE, New York, 1988

[IEEE 1008]

IEEE Std 1008-1987: IEEE Standard for Software Unit Testing. IEEE, New York, 1987.

[IEEE 1012]

IEEE Std 1012-1998: IEEE Standard for Software Verification and Validation. IEEE, New York, 1998.

[IEEE 1028]

IEEE Std 1028-1997: IEEE Standard for Software Reviews. IEEE, New York, 1997.

[IEEE 1042]

ANSI/IEEE Std 1042-1987: IEEE Guide to Software Configuration Management. IEEE, New York, 1987.

[IEEE 1044]

IEEE Std 1044-1993: IEEE Standard Classification for Software Anomalies. IEEE, New York, 1993.

[IEEE 1044.1]

IEEE Std 1044.1-1995: IEEE Guide to Classification for Software Anomalies. IEEE, New York, 1995.

[IEEE 1059]

IEEE Std 1059-1993: IEEE Guide for Software Verification and Validation Plans. IEEE, New York, 1993.

[IEEE 1061]

IEEE Std 1061-1998: IEEE standard for a software quality metrics methodology. IEEE, New York, 1998.

[IEEE 1062]

IEEE Std 1062-1998: IEEE Recommended Practice for Software Acquisition. IEEE, New York, 1998.

[IEEE 1063]

IEEE Std 1063-2001: IEEE Standard for Software User Documentation. IEEE, New York, 2001.

[IEEE 1209]

IEEE Std 1209-1992: IEEE recommended practice for the Evaluation and Selection of Computer-Aided Software Engineering (CASE) tools. IEEE, New York, 1992.

[IEEE 1228]

IEEE Std 1228-1994: IEEE Standard for Software Safety Plans. IEEE, New York, 1994.

[IEEE 1233]

IEEE 1233-1998: IEEE Guide for Developing System Requirements Specifications. IEEE, May, 1998

[IEEE 1348]

IEEE Std 1348-1995: IEEE Recommended Practice for the Adoption of Computer-Aided Software Engineering (CASE) Tools. IEEE, New York, 1995.

[ISO 2382]

ISO/IEC 2382-x: Information Technology – Vocabulary – Part 1-33. ISO, Bern, 2002.

[ISO 5806]

ISO 5806: Information processing – Specification of single-hit decision tables. ISO, Geneva, 1984.

[ISO 9000]

DIN EN ISO 9000:2005: Qualitätsmanagementsysteme – Grundlagen und Begriffe. ISO, Bern, 2005.

[ISO 9001]

DIN EN ISO 9001:2000: Qualitätsmanagementsysteme – Anforderungen. ISO, Bern, 2000.

[ISO 9126]

ISO/IEC 9126-1:2001: Software Engineering – Product quality – Part 1: Quality model, Quality characteristics and sub-characteristics.

[ISO 9241]

ISO 9241-1:1997: Ergonomic requirements for office work with visual display terminals (VDTs) – Part 1: General Introduction. ISO, Bern, 1997.

[ISO 9735]

ISO 9735-1: Electronic data interchange for administration, commerce and transport (EDIFACT) – Application level syntax rules – Part 1: Syntax rules common to all parts. ISO, Geneva, 2002.

[ISO 12119]

ISO/IEC 12119:1994: Information Technology – Software Packages – Quality Requirements and Testing. ISO, Bern, 1994.

[ISO 12207.0]

IEEE/EIA12207.0-1996: IEEE/EIA Standard Industry Implementation of International Standard ISO/IEC 12207: 1995 (ISO/IEC 12207) Standard for Information Technology Software Life Cycle Processes. ISO, Bern, 1996.

[ISO 12207.1]

IEEE/EIA12207.1-1997: Industry implementation of International Standard ISO/IEC 12207: 1995. (ISO/IEC 12207) Standard for Information Technology – Software Life Cycle Processes – Life Cycle Data. ISO, Bern, 1997.

[ISO 12207.2]

IEEE/EIA12207.2-1997: Industry implementation of International Standard ISO/IEC 12207: 1995. (ISO/IEC 12207) Standard for Information Technology – Software Life Cycle Processes – Implementation Considerations. ISO, Bern, 1997.

[ISO 14102]

ISO/IEC 14102: Information Technology – Guideline for the Evaluation and Selection of CASE Tools. ISO, Bern, 1995.

[ISO 14143]

ISO 14143: Information technology – Software measurement – Functional size measurement

Part 1: Definition of concepts. ISO, Bern, 1998.

Part 2: Conformity evaluation of software size measurement methods to ISO/IEC 14143-1:1998. ISO, Bern, 2002.

Part 3: Verification of Functional Size Measurement Methods. ISO TR 14143-3:2003, ISO, Bern, 2003.

Part 4: Reference Model. ISO, Bern, 2002.

Part 5: Determination of Functional Domains for use with Functional Size Measurement. ISO, Bern, 2004.

[ISO 14471]

ISO/IEC TR 14471: Information Technology – Guideline for the Adoption of CASE Tools, ISO, Bern, 1999.

[ISO 14598]

ISO/IEC 14598-1:1999

Information technology – Software product evaluation – Part 1: General overview

ISO/IEC 14598-2:2000

Software engineering – Product evaluation – Part 2: Planning and management

ISO/IEC 14598-3:2000

Software engineering – Product evaluation – Part 3: Process for developers

ISO/IEC 14598-4:1999

Software engineering – Product evaluation – Part 4: Process for acquirers

ISO/IEC 14598-5:1998

Information technology – Software product evaluation – Part 5: Process for evaluators

ISO/IEC 14598-6:2001

Software engineering – Product evaluation – Part 6: Documentation of evaluation modules

[ISO 14598-4]

ISO/IEC 14598-4: Software Engineering – Product Evaluation – Part 4: Process for Acquirers. ISO, Bern, 1999.

[ISO 15026]

   ISO/IEC 15026: Information Technology – System and Software
   Integrity Levels. ISO, Bern, 1998.

[ISO 15504]

   ISO/IEC 15504: Information Technology – Process Assessment
   (SPICE) – Part 1-5. ISO, Bern, 2004.
   Part 1:   Concepts and Vocabulary.
   Part 2:   Performing an Assessment.
   Part 3:   Guidance on Performing an Assessment.
   Part 4:   Guidance on Use for Process Improvement and Process
              Capability Determination.
   Part 5:   An Assessment Model and Indicator Guidance.

[ISO 15910]

   ISO/IEC 15910: Information Technology – Software User
   Documentation Process. ISO, Bern, 1999.

[ISO 15939]

   ISO/IEC/IEEE 15939: Information Technology – Software
   Measurement Process. ISO, Bern, 2002 and IEEE, New York, 2002.

[ISO 16085]

   ISO/IEC 16085: Information Technology – Software Life Cycle
   Processes – Risk Management. ISO, Bern, 2004.

[ISO 19759]

   ISO/IEC TR 19759: Software Engineering – Guide to the Software
   Engineering Body of Knowledge (SWEBOK). ISO, Bern, 2005.
   Online: [URL: SWEBOK].

[ISO 90003]

   ISO/IEC 90003: Software- und Systemtechnik – Richtlinien für die
   Anwendung der ISO 9001:2000 auf Computersoftware. Beuth-Verlag,
   Berlin, 2004.

[ISO 9126-x]

   ISO/IEC 9126-1:2001, Software Engineering "Product quality"
   Part 1:   Quality model, Quality characteristics and sub-
              characteristics.   ISO, Geneva, 2001.
              ISO/IEC TR 9126-2:2003, Software engineering "Product
              quality"

Part 2:   External metrics. ISO, Geneva, 2003.
          ISO/IEC TR 9126-3:2003, Software engineering "Product quality"
Part 3:   Internal metrics. ISO, Geneva, 2003.
          ISO/IEC TR 9126-4:2004 , Software engineering "Product quality"
Part 4:   Quality in use metrics. ISO, Geneva, 2004.

WWW pages

[URL: AGEDIS]

http://www.agedis.de/documents/AGEDIS_Methodology.pdf
Agedis Testing Methodology, Agedis – Automated Generation and
Execution of Test Suites for Distributed Component-Based Software

[URL: ANSI]

http://www.ansi.org
American National Standards Institute (ANSI)

[URL: APTEST]

http://www.aptest.com/resources.html

[URL: ARM]

http://www.arm.com/aboutarm/quality.html

[URL: ASTQB]

http://www.astqb.org/
American Software Testing Qualifications Board, Inc.

[URL: AUTOSAR]

http://www.autosar.org/
Automotive Open System Architecture (AUTOSAR)

[URL: BSI]

http://www.bsi-global.com/
British Standards Institution (BSI)

[URL: CEN]

http://www.cenorm.be/
European Committee for Standardization (CEN)

[URL: CENELEC]

http://www.cenelec.org/
European Committee for Electrotechnical Standardization
(CENELEC)

[URL: CMMI]

http://www.sei.cmu.edu/cmmi/
Carnegie Mellon Software Engineering Institute – Capability Maturity Model Integration (CMMI)

[URL: CMMI-Models]

http://www.sei.cmu.edu/cmmi/models/models.html
CMMI Models and Modules

[URL: CMMI-TR]

http://www.sei.cmu.edu/publications/documents/02.reports/
02tr002.html or 02tr001.html
CMMI for Systems Engineering and Software Engineering (CMMISE/
SW, V1.1) Staged Representation: CMU/SEI-2002-TR-002, ESCTR-
2002-002. Continuous Representation: CMU/SEI-2002-TR-001,
ESC-TR-2002-001.

[URL: CMMI V1.2 Model]

http://www.sei.cmu.edu/cmmi/models/model-v12-components-
word.html
Word Version of CMMI V1.2 Model

[URL: CPPUnit]

http://sourceforge.net/projects/cppunit
CppUnit – C++ port of JUnit

[URL: DIN]

http://www2.din.de/
Deutsches Institut für Normung (DIN)

[URL: DISG]

http://en.wikipedia.org/wiki/DISC_assessment

[URL: DOD]

http://www.dod.mil/
Department of Defense (DoD)

[URL: ECMA]

http://www.ecma-international.org/
European Computer Manufacturers Association (ECMA)

[URL: EIA]

http://www.eia.org/
Electronics Industries Alliance (EIA)

[URL: EP]

http://www.extremeprogramming.org/
Extreme Programming: A gentle introduction, by Don Wells.

[URL: ETSI]

http://www.etsi.org/
European Telecommunications Standards Institute (ETSI)

[URL: EUROCAE]

http://www.eurocae.org/
European Organisation for Civil Aviation Equipment (EUROCAE)

[URL: GI]

http://www.gi-ev.de/
Gesellschaft für Informatik (GI)

[URL: GTB]

http://www.german-testing-board.info/
German Testing Board (GTB)

[URL: HIS]

http://www.automotive-his.de/
Herstellerinitiative Software
(vehicle manufacturers software initiative)

URL: IEC]

http://www.iec.ch/
International Electrotechnical Commission (IEC)

[URL: IEEE]

http://www.ieee.org/
Institute of Electrical and Electronics Engineers (IEEE)

[URL: Imaging]

http://en.wikipedia.org/wiki/Disk_image

[URL: INTACS]

http://www.int-acs.org/web/assessorcertification.html
International Assessor Certification

[URL: ISO]

http://www.iso.org/
International Organization for Standardization (ISO)

[**URL: iSQI**]

http://www.isqi.org/
International Software Quality Institute

[**URL: ISTQB**]

http://www.istqb.org/
International Software Testing Qualifications Board (ISTQB)

[**URL: ISTQB Glossary**]

http://www.istqb.org/download.htm
ISTQB Glossary of Testing Terms

[**URL: ITU**]

http://www.itu.int/
International Telecommunication Union (ITU)

[**URL: JTC1SC7**]

http://www.jtc1-sc7.org/
ISO/IEC Joint Technical Comittee 1/Subcomittee 7: Software & System
Engineering

[**URL: JUnit**]

http://www.junit.org/
JUnit-Homepage

[**URL: Kaner**]

http://www.kaner.com/coverage.htm

[**URL: Longstreet**]

http://www.ifpug.com/Articles/using.htm
David Longstreet: Using Function Points

[**URL: MBTI**]

http://en.wikipedia.org/wiki/Myers-Briggs_Type_Indicator

[**URL: MISRA**]

http://www.misra.org.uk/
Motor Industry Software Reliability Association (MISRA)

[**URL: NATO**]

http://www.nato.int/
North Atlantic Treaty Organisation (NATO)

[URL: OMG]

http://www.omg.org/
Object Management Group (OMG)

[URL: ON]

http://www.on-norm.at/
Österreichisches Normungsinstitut (ON)

[URL: OSTEST]

http://opensourcetesting.org/functional.php

[URL: OVUM]

http://www.ovum.com

[URL: RAD]

http://sysdev.ucdavis.edu/webadm/document/radpeople-intro.htm
RAD Website of the University of California

[URL: Rothman]

http://www.jrothman.com/Papers/ItDepends.html
Johanna Rothman: It Depends: Deciding on the Correct Ratio of
Developers to Testers

[URL: S2ESC]

http://standards.computer.org/sesc/
IEEE Software and Systems Engineering Standards Committee
(S2ESC)

[URL: SCAMPI]

http://www.sei.cmu.edu/collaborating/partners/lead-assessor.html
Lead Appraiser Authorization for SCAMPI Appraisal Services

[URL: Schaefer]

http://home.c2i.net/schaefer/testing/
Homepage of Hans Schaefer

[URL: Scrum]

http://www.controlchaos.com/

[URL: Sogeti]

http://www.sogeti.com
Homepage of Sogeti

[URL: SPICE]

http://www.sqi.gu.edu.au/spice/

SPICE Homepage, and http://www.isospice.com/

[URL: SPICE doc]

http://www.sqi.gu.edu.au/spice/

-> Document Suite -> Download -> Part 2 – A model for process management

[URL: SQATEST]

http://www.sqa-test.com/toolpage.html

[URL: Standish Group]

http://www.standishgroup.com/

Homepage of Standish Group

[URL: STTEC]

http://test-tools.technologyevaluation.com

[URL: SWEBOK]

http://www.swebok.org

IEEE Guide to the Software Engineering Body of Knowledge (SWEBOK)

[URL: Templates]

http://www.imbus.de/download/index.shtml

[URL: Tessy]

http://www.razorcat.com/frame_main/produkte/unterpunkte/tessy_e.html

Tessy – Automated testing for embedded systems

[URL: TestBench]

http://www.imbus.de/engl/produkte/testbench/index.shtml

[URL: TESTINGFAQ]

http://testingfaqs.org/

[URL: Tooleval-imbus]

http://www.imbus.de/download/papers/tool.zip

[URL: Tool-List]

http://www.imbus.de/engl/tool-list.shtml

List of test tools

[URL: TPI]

http://www.sogeti.nl/tpi
-> Survey

[URL: TTCN-3]

http://www.ttcn-3.org
Testing & Test Control Notation

[URL: VDI]

http://www.vdi.de/
Verein Deutscher Ingenieure (VDI)

[URL: Virtualization]

http://www.virtualization.info/ and http://en.wikipedia.org/wiki/
Virtualization

[URL: V-Modell XT]

http://www.v-modell-xt.de/

[URL: V-Modell XT Browser]

http://ftp.uni-kl.de/pub/v-modell-xt/Release-1.2/Dokumentation/
html/
V-Modell XT online documentation of the University of Kaiserslautern

[URL: W3C]

http://www.w3.org/
World Wide Web Consortium (W3C)

[URL: XUnit]

http://www.junit.org or
http://sourceforge.net/projects/junit
http://sourceforge.net/projects/cppunit
http://sourceforge.net/projects/nunit

Index